HELMAND

HELMAND

The Diaries of Front-Line Soldiers

Foreword by **Simon Weston**

First published in Great Britain in 2013 by Osprey Publishing,
Midland House, West Way, Botley, Oxford, OX2 0PH, UK
43-01 21st Street, Suite 220B, Long Island City, NY 11101

E-mail: info@ospreypublishing.com

Osprey Publishing is part of the Osprey Group

A CIP catalogue record for this book is available from the British Library

ISBN: 978 1 78096 906 0
E-pub ISBN: 978 1 78200 911 5
PDF ISBN: 978 1 78096 907 7

Index by Sharon Redmayne
Typeset in Sabon and Univers
Originated by PDQ Media, Bungay, UK
Printed and bound by CPI Group (UK) Ltd, Croydon, CR0 4YY

13 14 15 16 17 18 10 9 8 7 6 5 4 3

Osprey Publishing is supporting the Woodland Trust, the UK's leading woodland
conservation charity, by funding the dedication of trees.

www.ospreypublishing.com

Front cover: A Royal Marine foot patrol in Helmand Province. (Photo Si Ethell © Crown
Copyright)
Back cover (left to right): Getty Images; Sean Clee © Crown Copyright; Cpl Barry Lloyd
© Crown Copyright

EDITOR'S NOTE:
Brief explanations for the abbreviations and slang terms are provided at the first instance
of use; please see the glossary for a full list of abbreviations and explanations used
throughout the diaries.

CONTENTS

All royalties from the sale of this book will go to the John Thornton Young Achievers Foundation and the Royal Marines Charitable Trust Fund.

The John Thornton Young Achievers Foundation (JTYAF) was established in 2008 to honour the memory of John Thornton, a young Royal Marines Officer who was tragically killed at the age of 22, whilst serving in Afghanistan.

The JTYAF supports young people from a wide range of youth organisations, providing them with scholarships and bursaries to support their personal development and the pursuit of their ambitions.

Since its formation in 2008 the JTYAF has made awards to over 250 young people, which total nearly £170,000.

John touched the lives of many people and now his legacy lives on, making a real difference to the lives of young people.

The Royal Marines Charitable Trust Fund is the overarching Royal Marine charity and money raised can be used for very wide purposes, probably the widest of any service charity.

The RMCTF is run by Royal Marines for Royal Marines, and is governed by a group of serving and retired Trustees who have a very wide view of need and a determination to ensure that any money donated is used to best effect.

The RMCTF runs its own fund-raising activities and donates regularly to other service charities providing direct benefit to Royal Marines – SSAFA; St Dunstan's; Combat Stress; BLESMA; RN/RM Children's Fund; etc.

'Climb as high as you can dream.'

www.jtyaf.org

http://www.rmctf.org.uk/

FOREWORD

I have been asked many times to write a contribution for a new book, but this is the only time that I have felt it an honour, a privilege and something I really wanted to do with all my soul.

I never met John and knew nothing of him until this moment. But I feel I know him. His words are more than simply moments on a page. They are full of feeling; emotional moments that take me back to my own memories.

The fact that we are being permitted a glimpse into John's world, a look at his thoughts and fears, highs and lows, makes this journey poignant, moving and so powerful.

To read in print the heartbreak of writing one's 'death letters' in such a thought-provoking way, makes us reflect on our own tenuous hold on life.

The diary entries are so crisp and well written; you can almost hear John speak the words on the paper. His concerns for his brother, his parents and his comrades reveal the innermost struggles of life in a combat zone.

In being asked to undertake this foreword, I am awestruck by the number of people who have come together to support this most worthy of charities in John's name. I feel sure that he would have been so proud that his innermost thoughts were to be put in print for this cause.

Although over the years there have been memoirs, books and articles produced to commemorate many different conflicts, I truly believe this diary is a 'one of a kind' piece of work.

If, as they say, we are to pull out of Afghanistan in two years, then it is all the more powerful and remarkable. It is a historical document; truthful, honest and at times painful.

I am sure that John would be delighted to know that his writings are to be used to inspire charity, to go on despite hardship and to motivate those to achieve greater heights.

Go on my son!

Simon Weston
April 2012

INTRODUCTION: 'THE ROAD TO HELMAND'

40 Commando Royal Marines in Afghanistan 2007–08

From September 2007 through to April 2008, 40 Commando Royal Marines, known simply as 40 Commando, deployed to Helmand Province in Afghanistan as the core Battle Group in the UK's contribution to the international military operation in that country. Following the devastating terrorist attack on the Twin Towers in New York in September 2001, the international community became involved in military activity in Afghanistan and by the time 40 Commando came to deploy, over 40 nations had committed military forces to the UN-mandated, International Security Assistance Force (ISAF) to bring peace and security to Afghanistan. The seven month deployment was to be one of the most complex, and challenging, in the unit's recent history; indeed, such was the human cost to the unit the only comparable recent military operation, in terms of casualties sustained, was over a sustained period during the Malaya Campaign in the 1950s. The unit was being deployed to bring security and military support to a region of southern Afghanistan, with a clear focus on enabling activity to be undertaken by the institutions of Afghanistan's government. But to achieve this it would be necessary to face an intractable, determined and utterly ruthless enemy. As a result, all constituent parts of the unit would see action, and one or other element would be in action on 188 out of the 194 days during which 40 Commando was deployed as Battle Group North in the UK sector.

This extreme level of enemy engagement across Helmand was, however, by no means atypical for ISAF forces deployed at that time. The insurgency was well established and the Government of the Islamic Republic of Afghanistan (GIROA) had little, or no, control over vast swathes of territory. From 2006, when UK forces first deployed to Helmand in significant numbers, the situation had been exceptionally dangerous and when 40 Commando deployed as part of Operation *Herrick 7* (*Herrick* being the official codename for UK military operations in Afghanistan), the situation remained complex and highly fluid. But progress was being made, albeit slowly, and footholds were being established across the UK's area of responsibility. 40 Commando were determined to maintain the forward momentum that previous UK forces had generated. The operational experience of the men in the unit was varied. For the vast majority of the men in the unit this would be their first major operational deployment since completing commando training with the Royal Marines. For a few it would be a return to familiar ground, having deployed with 45 Commando Royal Marines some years earlier during the initial military response to the 9/11 attacks. Others had experience of military operations such as Iraq and Northern Ireland. Regardless of their starting point, it rapidly became clear that the nature of military operations in Afghanistan throughout the 2007–08 deployment would be a unique experience that would test their resolve, determination and courage to the maximum.

A Royal Marines Commando unit is manned, equipped and trained to undertake amphibious operations, recognised as one of the most complex and challenging types of military operation that modern forces undertake. With this pedigree they are well suited to highly fluid, dynamic environments such as Afghanistan, but as with any military operation, they would need to train and prepare for the specifics of the terrain and enemy they would face. In the 12 months preceding 40 Commando's deployment, the unit was providing a rapid response component of the Naval Service, known as the Lead

Commando Group, which would spearhead any UK engagement in contingency operation, anywhere in the world. From its base in Taunton, Somerset the unit was held at extremely high readiness and on a very short notice to deploy globally, and undertook training exercises in Europe and West Africa to continuously hone both its amphibious and general military skills. Fortuitously this proved to be an outstanding period of preparation for Afghanistan. Split into four generic companies (each of approximately 125 men) equipped with a variety of weapon and vehicle types, with a headquarters company providing command and control and a logistics element to provide the essential life-support both in barracks and on deployment, the unit bonded in the jungles of Sierra Leone, on the beaches of Poland and Denmark, and across the military training areas of Great Britain. And when it was time to switch focus and concentrate wholly on the challenges of Afghanistan, the core of the unit was already a well-drilled and exceptionally capable military force.

There was however still a considerable road that the unit had to travel before it would be ready to deploy to Helmand. Numerous issues had to be overcome and the unit headquarters developed a plan of action to address these. Manpower was the immediate concern. As the Lead Commando Group, 40 Commando was optimised for conventional force-on-force military operations; in order to get the unit to the fighting strength it would require for a counter-insurgency operation in Afghanistan, 40 Commando would require some additional manpower and this came primarily from members of the Royal Marines Reserve. Some 87 part-time commandos volunteered to deploy with the unit to Afghanistan, representing 10 per cent of the unit's manpower. It would be a significant undertaking to prepare such a large contingent of reservists, both physically and mentally, for the forthcoming operation but such was their motivation and determination that, by the time the unit deployed, it was almost impossible to tell reservist from his regular counterpart. They were subsequently to play a part, and do so with distinction, in every event or action that the unit undertook in Afghanistan.

The Commando unit deployed to Afghanistan as part of 52 Infantry Brigade, a British Army Infantry Brigade, the headquarters of which was located within the spectacular setting of Edinburgh Castle. 40 Commando was transferred from its parent formation, 3 Commando Brigade Royal Marines based in Plymouth, to provide the principle fighting and ground holding force of the nascent Task Force. They would be joined by 2nd Battalion the Yorkshire Regiment, an infantry battalion who would deploy to mentor officers and soldiers from the Afghanistan National Army; two squadrons and the headquarters from the Household Cavalry Regiment, an armoured infantry regiment equipped with tracked reconnaissance vehicles; elements of the Coldstream Guards, another infantry battalion; and a wide assortment of other army units who would provide essential combat and logistical support. The Task Force headquarters rapidly expanded and as they worked to get to know one another, the command elements of the various units and smaller sub-units developed a programme of activity and joint training which would develop operating procedures and processes between them, prior to committal into the operational theatre. This proved to be a busy time for the unit. As well as developing the wide range of new skills that would be needed to operate in Afghanistan (such as explosive search training, driver training, language training and numerous other such courses), the unit needed to train and exercise alongside a variety of units and organisations who would deploy at the same time, and who would shortly be required to fight alongside them. This was to prove a very demanding task but the daily reports received from the units already deployed in Afghanistan, detailing the nature of the fight and the casualties they were sustaining, undoubtedly helped focus minds and ensure that enthusiasm for the pre-deployment training never waned.

The training progression, concentrating initially on individual skills through to small team tactics and then whole unit training with other elements of the Task Force either attached or in support, was a major undertaking and required considerable flexibility and improvisation to make it work. In early 2007, as the unit got into its stride, access to Afghanistan-specific equipment that was being developed was limited. However, pragmatic as ever, the Marines pushed forward with their UK preparations, with the knowledge that a period of acclimatisation and further training would follow at

Camp Bastion, the main UK base in Helmand Province. By the time 40 Commando, now operating in its Afghanistan configuration as Battle Group North, conducted its final Mission Rehearsal Exercise in late summer 2007 the unit was ready, indeed was eager, to deploy. And given the steady flow of situation reports emanating from Helmand throughout its preparation period, there was no doubt in anyone's mind, from the most junior Marine to the experienced officers and warrant officers, that the unit would be war-fighting. To a man, they were keen to get on with it but the rapidly evolving situation in Afghanistan, and the mission that the unit would be undertaking, required very careful consideration before the troops were committed to action. When deployed in a conventional war-fighting role, a commando unit will fight as a cohesive entity with sub-units positioned on the battlefield in such a manner as to be able to provide direct support to one another; in Helmand it would be different. The unit was not being deployed to conduct large-scale Battle Group attacks (although it would subsequently undertake a major Task Force operation in exactly this role around the Taliban sanctuary of Musa Qala), rather it was to deploy to provide security and stability across an exceptionally wide region in order that development and progress could be made on governance and population-focussed projects. As such the unit would be widely dispersed, with the individual sub-units required to operate as small, largely self-reliant enclaves of military capability. Selecting the right individual for the right area of Helmand would be the key to unit's success or otherwise.

In constructing the overarching operational design for the deployment there was a significant complicating factor; each of the areas into which the sub-units were to be deployed were quite different (economically, geographically, tribally) and each would place different demands and challenges on the men and officers deployed. It was clear that one size would not fit all. It was essential to match the correct commanders and their sub-units with the correct area. The decision as to which sub-unit deploys to which location rests with the Commanding Officer and, whilst the unit personnel continued their Helmand-specific preparation (such as weapon training, explosive search training, fitness and medical training), during the first six months of 2007 a number of exploratory deployments were made by 40 Commando's command group to determine exactly what was required at each site. The Battle Group North area of Helmand was extremely large and contained a number of population centres of various sizes and tribal disposition. As gaining the trust and support of the population would be the key to success, for both sides in the conflict, these small towns and villages naturally became the focus for much of 40 Commando's effort. The population centres were, however, widely dispersed across the unit's area of responsibility but the majority tended to be close to, or in, the Green Zone, the highly cultivated area immediately adjacent to the Helmand River. A criss-cross of irrigation ditches and man-made canals, the Green Zone would prove to be a dangerous and deadly environment. It provided perfect cover, camouflage and concealment for the insurgent, and would be a heavily contested region for the duration of the unit's deployment. Also within the Battle Group's area of responsibility lay Kajaki Dam with its attendant hydroelectric sub-station, a hugely emblematic construction which, although not functioning at the time of the unit's deployment, had the potential to deliver much needed electrical power for the Helmand Valley and beyond. Both the Taliban and ISAF/GIROA forces understood the potential significance of the dam to the population of Helmand and recognised that it provided an opportunity to positively influence ordinary Afghans. Like the Green Zone, this would also be a heavily contested area for the duration of 40 Commando's deployment.

The initial force laydown for 40 Commando's tour was confirmed in mid-summer 2007, enabling the officers and men of each sub-unit to focus upon the unique challenges they would face in their particular area, and to prepare both mentally and physically for this. The Battle Group headquarters would be based at Camp Bastion, a large tented facility that was rapidly expanding across an isolated region on the Helmand desert plain. It would be co-located with many of the assets that would provide direct support to the unit, such as helicopters (both heavy lift Chinook support helicopters, which were critical for casualty evacuation and logistic resupply, and the outstanding Apache attack helicopter) and the first class medical facility, which provided trauma and intensive care services of the very highest order. At Camp

Bastion, the headquarters staff would direct and support operations in accordance with the overarching plan, and would co-ordinate the logistics activity necessary to provide essential support for an organisation that rapidly expanded to over 1,000 personnel (at its peak 40 Commando, as Battle Group North, numbered over 1,500 men and women from some 15 different sub-units). Bravo Company would deploy to the major population centre in the Battle Group's area, Sangin, and would be predominately focussed on the civilian population and the challenges of patrolling in an urban environment; Sangin was the designated Main Effort for the Battle Group and all other activity across the region was shaped and developed to provide support to activities such as education programmes, governance meeting and police training being undertaken there. Delta Company would deploy north-west of Sangin to another population centre called Nowzad, at that time an abandoned settlement which the Taliban routinely transited through en-route to their safe-haven in Musa Qala (which itself was situated only 20km directly north of Sangin). Alpha Company would deploy north-east of Sangin, following the run of the Helmand River towards the Kajaki Dam feature. They would occupy an extremely basic location, little more than a square of protective sandbags when they arrived, which would become known as Forward Operating Base (FOB) Inkerman. Situated right on the edge of the Green Zone, their task would be to intercept and disrupt enemy movement towards Sangin and effectively soak up the pressure that the enemy would apply in an attempt to counter the activity which Bravo Company would attempt to initiate. Charlie Company was given the task of defending and maintaining security at the Kajaki Dam, the furthest manned outpost in the Battle Group's area. Accessible only by helicopter, this was a particularly exposed location where leadership of the highest order would be required. Finally, Echo Company, with personnel drawn from the unit's headquarters and logistic personnel, was formed to operate from FOB Robinson due south of Sangin. From here they would perform the same function as Alpha Company at FOB Inkerman, effectively acting as a block to prevent enemy infiltration into Sangin.

The confirmed laydown was briefed to the sub-unit commanders along with Confirmatory Orders detailing their missions and tasks prior to the unit taking summer leave through August 2007. This was the last time the whole unit would be together until the deployment was completed. Immediately after summer leave, the Battle Group deployed over a five-week window of frenetic activity. The Main Effort was developing the security situation in Sangin. Supported by activity to disrupt the enemy in and around FOBs Inkerman and Robinson, Bravo Company would set about this task alongside the Afghan Army and newly established Afghan Police units. Delta Company would be attempting to expand the area of Afghan government influence by seeking ways to entice the local population back into Nowzad, whilst concurrently interfering with Taliban movement in the north of the area, and Charlie Company would hold the Kajaki complex, maintaining a buffer zone between the dam and the Taliban controlled territory a mere 2km away. All sub-units would be on the ground and interacting with civilians daily. They would, however, operate with significant constraints on their actions as they operated within clearly defined Rules of Engagement and legal constraints through adherence to the Laws of Armed Conflict, both areas covered in detail during the pre-deployment training. The enemy had no such constraints upon them. The insurgent moved amongst the people, looked like the local population, and both through intimidation and tribal ties and family allegiances, was permitted to live amongst them. This would demand the most amazing restraint from commanders, Marines and soldiers alike and, if the Battle Group was to succeed in its mission, the very highest standards to command and control would be necessary.

From the outset, Battle Group North reached out to the civilian population across its area, and sought to work alongside the indigenous security forces. Working in conjunction with military forces from a range of ISAF countries (particularly Estonia, Denmark and the US), activity was shaped in order to develop an environment of trust with the people. But gaining trust from a population that had known little but conflict for over 30 years was an immense challenge, and it was clear from the outset that success in Helmand would be measured in inches gained rather than the hard miles run. The anticipation of the Marines in the days leading up to deployment was palpable, but so too was the trepidation and nervousness of the friends and families that would be left behind. As the unit headed to Helmand it was clear about what it needed to do, and was equipped with the skills necessary to do it. This was, after all, what each man had chosen to be a part of. Each had reconciled himself to the risks and prepared himself, and his family, as best he could. And each, regardless of role or task, would work selflessly for the men and women around him. The actions of those who deployed as part of Battle Group North, 40 Commando's 2007–08 deployment to Helmand Province, demonstrated the very highest standards of honour and integrity, of service and sacrifice throughout. The unit played its part with conviction, determination and the utmost professionalism, and when it was time to return to the UK at the end of the deployment, it left behind a situation markedly improved for the people of the region.

With this context for the deployment laid out, it is now for the diaries of those intimately involved with the activity on the ground, both officers and men, to provide substance to the story of 40 Commando's participation in Operation *Herrick 7*.

LIEUTENANT JOHN THORNTON'S DEPLOYMENT DIARY

30th September 2007: Deployment Day

Spirits are high and the anticipation of the coming six months is clear to see on the faces of the young and those who consider themselves hardened warriors (the truth is they probably are). Excitement builds as we 'clock watch' our lives towards 0100hrs sat in our grots [accommodation] at Norton Manor Camp. However before the adrenalin can build for the job we all must go through our goodbyes with family and friends. My friends are very understanding and although we will miss one another's company, we still have our own focus on life and so it is in no way emotional. Grandparents are waved goodbye a week or so before and therefore too long before deployment for it to be seen to matter. My brother is second to last and as he has recently joined the Royal Marines Officer training it will be harder for me thinking I can't support him, than for him busy getting thrashed and concerned with his own survival foremost. Then the last of the goodbyes, face to face with my Mum and Dad; this is always what makes me upset with guilt. All of Saturday (29th) I tried to act like any normal Saturday, getting up in time to watch *Soccer AM*, then the early kick off between Man City and Newcastle, followed by *Soccer Saturday* intermingled with *Final Score*. After a good morning of football a second half of rugby and watching Wales disappointingly getting knocked out of the World Cup. This gives the impression that I spend every Saturday indoors glued to the TV. Of course this is not the case but this day I felt I should spend all day at home for at 1810hrs, after watching polar bears catching whales in the Arctic (Gen! [genuine]), I said goodbye and as I watched my Mum cry and my Dad comfort [her] I got into my car and drove to Taunton whilst fighting back my own tears.

Once we had all loaded our baggage onto a lorry we had a further 4 hours before departure. This is the time that I put my worries and fears to bed: something I did before Iraq in 2006 and this deployment to Afghanistan in 2007. My 'death letters' are obviously full of feeling and emotion, therefore as I write to my parents and brothers imagining that I was dead, I have to allow my tears to shed. This is the only time I expect to and the only time I feel I need to. Once it is done I feel content that if I die I can rest in peace and my family and friends can live feeling someway comforted with my words.

Eventually we reach our terminal where our lives are at the mercy of the RAF 'movers'. An epic situation as always occurred in which our aircraft was delayed nearly 24 hours and having to use a different aircraft meant that only around 90 of the 120 or so individuals could fly. Those from my Company (C Coy) were forced to travel home and would have the say their goodbyes one more time on the 5 October.

I was one of the chosen men who boarded around 1930hrs and after some fairly standard technical difficulties eventually got airborne at 2100hrs and left the green fields of England as a fond and distant memory.

1st October

A very smooth 6 hours flying had us descending into Kandahar Airfield in Afghanistan. We donned body armour and helmet during a smooth landing and my initial impression was surprise to see some small civilian aircraft waiting in the taxiways for their spot to go flying around the local scenery I suppose. A fairly quick turnaround and we were on a Hercules en route to Camp Bastion in the Helmand Province. I had been led to believe that this flight would be an epic take off almost straight up, a bit of level flying for around 10 minutes then the final 10 minutes descent dodging RPGs [rocket propelled grenade] and bullets until bracing for a heavy impact. None of this happened and despite the nervous faces we landed at Bastion with a polite bump. We were bussed to some temporary accommodation to begin our RSOI [Reception, Staging, Onward Movement and Integration], which started later that evening with some legal briefs and ROE [rules of engagement]. The officers and seniors then attended a series of briefings at the JOC [Joint Operations Centre]. They seemed to go on forever as although they were interesting we had not slept properly for around 48 hours and therefore delight filled my body as I slept for the first time in ganners [slang for Afghanistan]. I was particularly impressed with one of my recent purchases back in the UK, [a] travel pillow. HOOFING!

2nd October

The beginning of this day was the hardest yet though you can bet it will not remain in that position. We started lectures at 0730hrs and after enjoying sleep so much this is all I wanted to do throughout the lessons. That was until about 0900hrs when the wets [slang for hot drink] arrived. Smashed a coffee down and then worked on the basis of 2 cups of tea for every 30 minutes of lesson. It worked the proof being that my eyes remained open even during the Chief Driver's brief!! Every lecture was preceded with a chad [slang for cheesy] montage of photos set to music but these were far from inspiring or worrying and instead featured convoy moves and Sangars. As a result, most of the group moved from sitting down just as the music began to having just one more wet and getting called in after it had finished. Bootnecks [slang for Royal Marines] learn very quickly. After the lectures, a bite of lunch and then a walk just outside the camp to zero [slang for zeroing rifle sights]. Very warm weather outside but certainly bearable and with no heavy kit on you might even say pleasant. During the day I also discovered how good it was not being an officer. Of course I am a Royal Marine lieutenant but when wearing the new UBACS [Under Body Armour Combat Shirt] you have no rank and so people who don't know you will chat to you in a way in which they wouldn't speak to an officer they didn't know. It was on a level that I appreciated. It is different with your own lads because they know you and it is easier for you and them to speak on a level, which I enjoy, yet as the 'Boss' they (more than I) will never allow it to be the same as it is with friends back home, yet I look forward to the next 6 months with them.

3rd October

A Good Day! Pleasant lie in until just before breakfast ended, which was morale in itself, then a bit of kit filling. Last night we were issued with ammo, morphine, osprey body armour and my favourite; pistols for selected individuals. It's beginning to sink in now, as we get closer to the LD [Line of Departure] and excitement and apprehension build.

The flight to Kajaki was a nervous one. First the buck of the Chinook was rammed beyond the space overhauls with blokes and kit. Then when you thought it must be over, they rammed some more kit and blokes onto the tailgate. The aircraft struggled off the ground and I never believed it would make it, but somehow, against my odds it did and before long we were high above the threat. Our descent was rapid as we dove down so we were almost skimming the water, which with its golden sand banks looked like an idyllic holiday destination. The surrounding mountains only add to the areas beauty as we touched down on HLS [helicopter landing site] Broadsword in COB [contingency operating base] Zeebrugge which we would call home for our foreseeable future. After the standard briefings I got to speak to Sgt Maj 'Snowy' who I will be taking over from as FSG [Fire Support Group] Command. He seems like a very switched on bloke who briefed Daz and I in a relaxed and calm manner. The brief was for the fighting patrol that we will be conducting tomorrow morning. A certain contact from enemy fire! We leave at 0400hrs. Until tomorrow I bid thee farewell.

4th October

First action on the ground began with a wakeup at 0310hrs. A quick change and I was kitted up and sat in the commanders of a WMIK [Weapons Mount Installation Kit] with Uncle Buck behind me on the GMG [grenade machine gun]. It was a fresh start but nothing too cold and the moon was bright, which negated the need for night vision equipment. We led off towards the south of our location around our mountain OPs [observation posts] and into PVCP [permanent vehicle checkpoint] manned by ANP [Afghan National Police]. To protect ourselves against mines we gave the area a once over with a metal detector and pushed forward to allow the remainder of the Company to get ferried into this FUP [forming up point] at PVCP. Once into the FUP we ... pushed forward in our 3 WMIKs to our predetermined FS [fire support] position. In the meantime the remainder of the dismounts began to push through a series of compounds down what is known as 'Talley Alley' towards the Southern forward line of enemy troops (FLET). Before we were in position our mountain Ops [operations] ID'd [identified] targets in a compound and so we began to bombard that location with 8mm mortars. We identified further firing points and engaged [the] HMG [heavy machine gun] position with a Javelin – the first missed because it was locked onto another bunker but the second smashed into the position killing two Taliban and [we] observed another two moving away injured...

(STOP!! Just as I'm writing I hear a whistle and a mighty bang. Clearly from a rocket fired into our location. Now outside I'm hearing a large amount of HMG fire, which I presume is engaging the firing point.)

I continue ... the bunker explodes around them. After this we began engaging the location with .5 [type of heavy machine gun] until the dismounts had pushed forward to their LOE [Limit of Exploitation]. Once there two sorties from FI5s were called in and they shafted the target to allow the extraction of the Coy back to Zeebrugge. We were last off the ground and maintained overwatch until all the Company had extracted before returning ourselves for the debrief at 1100hr.

After a bit of brunch we took an epic yomp to the tops of the mountains for a ground brief. Always surrounded by mines, we arrived at the top with most blowing out of their arses trying hard not to show it. A ground brief and tour followed, which consisted of another two high features spread around 3km and a walk off the peaks past the dam and back into camp. A quick shower later and I'm informed that I will be returning to Bastion tomorrow on a 1000hr flight to brief the Company and go through the training and firing with them. I'm disappointed particularly because I will be missing a massive fire-fight planned for the 8th. Threaders. However will be good to see the rest of my lads and give them the reality they should expect.

Tonight we received incoming of 4 x 107m rockets, which caused no damage/casualties but a few raised heart rates. Now every 15 minutes I expect to be awoken with our mortars firing illums. Hoofing!

5th October

I was supposed to be flying out of Kajaki at 100hrs but the flight was delayed and so I managed to jump onto a famil [familiarisation] patrol of the local area. This was mega useful to orientate me to the ground and we also had an interesting look at the dam to see what the fuss was all about. On my return I jumped in to see the orders for the fighting patrol going out tomorrow. It looks like it will be awesome but also the FSG will receive some large amounts on incoming. I don't know whether as a result of that, I want to be there more or less?

After orders I waited for a helo [helicopter] that was delayed by another 3 hours before eventually flying back to Camp Bastion with Buck. After sorting out a few G$ points I had a few wets with Leon and Chunk (who is leading a convoy to Inkerman tomorrow) before getting my head down. Foolishly however I have volunteered to assist in freight arrival in the morning. 3 o'clock in the morning. MEGA!

6th October

Today was a lazy day. Up at 0300hrs to pick up freight but before it arrived the first flight from the main body arrived. I then spent the rest of the morning spinning dits to the lads when [they] arrived. The rest of the day was a bit of a blur of G4 admin tasks. I ended up falling asleep at about 2100hrs and didn't wake up until the next morning at 1000hr. Essence!

7th October

After a nice lie in I met up with my FSG lads and spun a few more dits before getting the whole Coy moved into their new accommodation. I managed to get my lads into one 20-man tent just around the corner from me, which will be useful. Then the Coy were rounded up and I briefed them all on the points that I had and [that] the OC [officer commanding] and other troop commanders gave me before I left Kajaki for Camp Bastion. I was happy with the attention paid by the lads despite having a whole morning trying to stay awake in lectures.

Following the Coy brief I spoke to my FSG in a bit more detail and also gave them the new ORBAT [order of battle], which I had completed in discussion with my cpls a little earlier. Most were happy but I know that Dave and Hodgey were a little threaders [slang for fed up or annoyed] at being nominated drivers. Unfortunately there is no way round it.

After my evening meal I managed to get a phone call to my big bro. He's just finished his first RMYO [Royal Marine Young Officer] exercise and has his next one next week. Even though I will be on a two way range, I'm happier to be here facing incoming than there facing the joys of the bottom field and 'the flank'.

I have a day on the ranges tomorrow, which I'm not entirely looking forward to as after fighting for real last week it seems a bit of a step back for me as an individual, but it will be useful for us to shake out in our new ORBAT particularly if we get vehicles – I bet we won't! Brilliant! Gen!

8th October

This is my first day that I have fully burnt my nose. I am threaders and am having to cool with a combination of water and air conditioning before applying moisturiser. I had planned to get involved in my troops training today, however I ended having another G4/plans day. Firstly organised some WMIK training, which was a bit of a fast ball but we managed to get a good number of blokes onto the training. Afterwards I found myself spending another afternoon on the flight line. This is beginning to frustrate me a little now and therefore I am determined to get involved with my lads on the WMIK tomorrow. My hope is also that the OC flies in tomorrow as if he doesn't then I will be running as Coy Commd [company commander] during the CALFEY the day after, which would be awesome, but I'd prefer to remain in role with my boys in FSG. Legends!

9th October

An early start to drive down on WMIK to the ranges. It was an excellent morning just giving the gunners the opportunity to gain their eye. One of the guns blew up again because the barrel extension gave up, which is becoming increasingly frustrating as it happened to two guns back in the UK. The afternoon was even better with the first opportunity for us to fire and move in vehicles. I got a good run out in the commander's seat behind the GPMG [general purpose machine gun]. Finished beaming.

The biggest shock today was the local Afghans who snaked around the range. At the end of a shoot, as soon as they were allowed, they would swarm into the vehicles and around the point. The brass was gone within seconds after only a bit of in-fighting amongst the Afghans, something that would take us about 2 hours at the end of a range day. I genuinely felt sorry for the poor fellows but at the same time it was very frustrating and dangerous when we were moving and firing because they would often find themselves in front of .5s and GPMGs that are firing. Nutters!

10th October

Today we went through our final rehearsal before deploying to Kajaki. It all ran very smoothly excepting of course the Afghans who appeared determined to get shot.

11th October

A day I spent organising my flight for tomorrow. The majority of the Coy flew today but I and 33 others stayed and got some maps fabloned [covered in clear plastic] for our flight tomorrow.

A surreal end to my time in Bastion with a fresh coffee, a Pizza Hut and then a film night in my grot for one night. We watched the first *Austin Powers*, which was good light humour before getting my end down.

12th October

We have control of Kajaki. I boarded my CH-47 at around 1045hrs and after we finished loading more blokes than we had initially expected, we took off en route to the dam. Because of the numbers onboard I ended up sitting on a Bergan [type of backpack] on the tailgate, which gave me an awesome view out of the back as we came down safely to land in Kajaki.

On arrival I moved into my new grot, which I'm quite chuffed with. Although dusty it has a carpet and a bed with a mattress, which is always a bonus. It is just so fulfilling to finally arrive in our final destination for good, well for as long as we end up staying here.

Tomorrow we will be providing a QRF [quick-reaction force] for the CCTs [close combat troops] training in a deserted village just to the north of us called Tangye. Then hopefully we will push north to go through some manoeuvre training and get some ground orientation.

15th October

You will notice, I am sure, that I have missed two days out and we find ourselves at the 15th. This is because the last three days have been non-stop. On 13th October we did indeed go to the north onto a feature called 'Shrine Hill', where I led my first mine (IED [improvised explosive device]) clearance with a metal detector. A nerve racking experience to say the least. We had a brief from the JTAC [Joint

Tactical Air Controller], which after I studied the ground myself discovered that it was incorrect. Nevertheless a worthwhile patrol. Following on I went straight into orders for the patrol the next day. Me and my troops battle prep was disrupted by a rehearsal stand to and a demonstration of fire power to the north before I could even begin orders at 2215. We were to get up the next morning at 0300.

The patrol planned for the <u>14th October</u> was designed to be a feint and ground famil. It turned into an epic of physical endurance with my lads providing overwatch as the CCTs cleared slowly through compounds well outside the area of enemy influence. It was always supposed to be more kinetic but it seemed bizarre to clear so many compounds for so long (we didn't return for 10 hours), with no scran [slang for food] and for the best part of the day with no escape from the sun. To add insult to injury we returned to receive orders for the patrol the next day and were delighted to discover that reveille for the patrol would be at 0100. Early!

A cold start on the <u>15th October</u> and a few difficulties with transport including Bobby John managing to roll a Pinz [Pinzgauer, a large Land Rover-type vehicle]; fortunately he was the only one in the wagon and jumped clear. We eventually got into our fire support position and observed likely firing points whilst the CCT pushed south towards the FLET. This lasted a couple of hours until the Apache arrived on station. They were there for an hour and during this time the Taliban laid down their weapons and effectively became civilians. Once the Apache left our area location and we began to extract, the interest levels raised. 5 minutes later the Taliban fired 3 RPGs into the compounds that had been recently departed from by our lads. The firing points were highlighted and therefore I brought Coop up in his WMIK for him to engage. He fired on suppressive weight to prevent any further attempts to engage us from the same positions. Later I pulled the GMG WMIK onto the high ground but I was not convinced of its effectiveness and so to reduce the risk of casualty I sent it back into cover. Mikey P ID'd an enemy in Compound 165 and engaged with a Javelin. He struck a direct hit on the compound. Once the CCT had withdrawn through us and out into a safe area we withdrew with cover from 81mm HE [high explosive] and Bernie and his crew a km to our north. Then a simple move back into camp with 2 further contacts onto us, which we knew nothing about as the firers were out of range only to be told by the peaks who provided overwatch throughout.

We finished at a reasonable time and this has been the first full afternoon off I've had since arriving in theatre. Me and my boys take over Ops [operations] on the mountains tomorrow, which for them will be a break but for me, I am led to believe, will be an epic.

16th October

Today was a quiet day for me. After spending 3 hours on watch last night and getting some time on the welfare phones (though speaking to no-one but 6x answer phones) I was ready for a good sleep, which I succeeded in getting.

The lads changed over first thing on the mountains and it was good to see the rest of my lads that had been up the mountain since I arrived in Kajaki. They were all in good spirits yet quick to tell the story of their very near miss from an accidental firing point and a good few bursts of 7.62 winging in and around the location.

My half of the troop had taken over the peaks by late morning and I spent the rest of the afternoon squaring away their re-supply requests. I drove up to the top of the worst track known to mankind, surrounded by mines and arrived at Athens (the lowest and furthest east peak) and dropped off the re-supply ready to be yomped to Sparrowhawk East and West. East is a km away and west another 500m beyond that, and the only way to them is to yomp with kit.

The rest of the evening Sim and I spent cleaning and organising our rooms, [and] by about 2200hrs we were both satisfied in our work and so the chance for a few pages of Cornwell's *Sharpe* and some good quality zeds.

17th October

Tonight I got dropped at Athens and then yomped across to west in preparation for a patrol to the Northern FLET. No sooner had I arrived with the MFC(B) [mortar fire controller], Luke Francis, than we observed two impacts to the north of the COB from enemy mortars. We identified the firing point to north of Kajaki and began engaging with .5. The MFC(B) brought mortars down but they were off target and by the time he was hitting the enemy, [the] firers were long gone. However they fired at last light and obviously planned to use the darkness as cover to retrieve their firing equipment, unfortunately for them we called a repeat on the last fire mission into the enemy firing points. The rounds were spot on target and one pax [person] was observed taking cover behind a wall and a 8mm HE from our boys landed close enough [for] him not to stand up again. After all the excitement we provided overwatch for a night patrol where nothing happened. By the end of the patrol down the bottom I had 30 minutes to wait until first light and then the MFC(B) and I yomped down the goat track, which should be renamed 'leg breaker' for the amount of times I nearly broke mine and finished back in the COB for a quick zed before having to go back up and re-supply.

20th October

Last night and this morning we deployed on a Coy sniper ambush, which nearly went to plan. As with the other patrols over the last few days I spent the night on West providing situational awareness and target identification. Before the patrol began we were hit with three 107m rockets but despite efforts to ID the firing point we were unable to react with our own mortars like two days ago.

The CCTs moved forward to cover the snipers flanks while Daz with his half of my troop pushed up onto Essex Ridge to provide fire support if it all kicked off. Once in place Wilf and his team moved towards a compound only a few hundred metres south of their target, which was a specific compound (7) on the south-west tip of Risaji. They waited in position until the sentries in and around the area exposed themselves. The snipers fired 5 shots before they extracted but didn't hit.

On the extraction a claymore was blown on the snipers firing point to prevent the enemy following them up. Once the snipers were clear the OC decided not to waste a good opportunity and therefore ordered two GMLRs into the compounds in Risaji that we had ID'd sentries in during the build up to the shot. The impact was filmed by the Ops room with TI cameras and the BDA [Battle Damage Assessment] confirmed as 2 x TB [Taliban] KIA [killed in action]. Result!

21st October

As the sun set behind the mountains to the east I sat and watched as the Coy moved down two wadis (M4 & MB) together and into the assault into Mercie and Cpds [compounds] 18, 19, 20 to the north-east of Mercie. It all started smoothly with 7 Troop clearing through Mercie and there they identified enemy in Compound 18 and therefore engaged pre-emptively onto that area. Sim and 8 Troop then pushed out of this wadi and into what he thought was Compound 20. I had ID'd it as Cpd 21 and therefore steered him south on to the correct one. He began his clearance through to his LOE in 18 with no incident and then began his extraction.

It was during the extraction that FSG A with Doc were engaged firstly inaccurately; then Doc put a Javelin into the first firing point and they were engaged by further firing points to their west, which were effective onto their location. Mortars engaged along with Doc and his boys plus the Recce Troop snipers co-located with him.

OC then decided to use CAS [close air support] and dropped 2,000lbs bomb onto Cpd 10. It looked awesome and I'm sure as hell that I wouldn't like to be underneath it.

Wilf got a confirmed with his sniper at about 450m range, which he was obviously happy with.

I then cleared through the OC to engage the 4km distance targets and facilitate Daz's withdrawal Essex Ridge. We aimed off at first because it was night and Bernie gradually brought them onto target. Then enemy fire stopped engaging Doc and we checked fire to watch and shoot.

The extraction happened without incident and I settled down to watch *300* for the first time before going on sentry for a couple of hours. After a good chat with Bernie and a pipe on watch I got my head down for a few hours before yomping back down the goat track for orders for the next patrol.

22nd October

Tonight was good and simply I was relieved to hand the peaks over to Daz and his lads and therefore I was itching to get back onto the ground. A short run out for 2 of the WMIKs down to PVCP north and the provision of overwatch for Russ and his troop to do some paddling in the River Helmand. They were of course conducting a recce [reconnaissance] for a new 'wet' crossing point to vary our routes out to the Northern FLET.

23rd October

Spent the morning doing Iain's (2IC [second in command]) job and filling in paperwork like it's going out of fashion. Fortunately got that done rapidly and went to relieve Bernie and Bungy with their wagons who had been providing overwatch for the Gurkha Engineers to do some repair works on Unknown Left [ANP/ANA base] and Right for the ANP. I was up there for about 3 hours and what seemed to be quite a boring detail turned out to be quite painless due to a pipe and some quality banter with Pete and Fletch. It wasn't long before I was back in the FOB [forward operating base] eating a curry and looking forward to a day off tomorrow. Oh sorry, not a day off but a 'no patrols day'. A bit of tinkering with the wagons and a swim in the lake I feel is in order.

24th October

Today has been a good day. The morning was spent reorganising the vehicles, which has turned out to be a success. I was very keen to add a dismounted .5 to our vehicles on top of the 3x.5s mounted, 1GMG, 4 GPMGs, 2 GPMG(SF) [general purpose machine gun (sustained fire)], 5 Javelin missiles and 4 AT4's [anti-tank weapon]. My VM [vehicle mechanic] Will Patten got a little touchy about me overloading the WMIKs even more than they already are and so I had to work around for a solution. I decided to reduce weight in the wagons by getting as much stripped out as possible and removing items that I decided to take risks in not taking. I was delighted with the result and have now increased the fire power within FSG whilst reducing the weight the vehicles have to carry – still too much but not as much as they were. Both the VM and I are now happy. I now look forward to see them on the ground and the effect we have with them.

After a morning of work I called an afternoon of rest and the troop took a drive down to the lake. We had a hoofing [slang for brilliant] couple of hours in the cool, deep turquoise blue water. Some good fizz [exercise] in the bag with an epic swim to a tower for some crazy bootneck naked jumping and a few rope swings, followed by the epic swim back. Think I will try and build up my swimming while I'm down here. Well why not.

Orders have been given to me for tomorrow and all briefings are complete so all that is left is to finish off this paragraph, read a little of my new book *The Kite Runner* by Khaled Hosseini and maybe DVD before zeds. It's only 1850 – Very civilised.

25th October

I am tired and so I will be brief. Today we conducted a clearance and feint withdrawal on the South FLET. For us it was a dull affair despite a large burst of enemy fire in 8 Troop's position. Nothing else significant occurred and the snipers failed to have an effect. The one benefit for is that Bernie has ID'd a better mounted FSG position closer to the FLET which will reduce our range to the enemy from 2200m to 1500m.

26th October–27th October

A sniper ambush on MK and BK which unsurprisingly was uneventful. We sat on top of Shrine Hill urging the TB to engage but despite intel that suggested they were very close and going to 'ambush', nothing happened.

During the Op we had intel that the TB were going to shoot down one of our helos and so when the re-supply came in we drove back out the Shrine Hill with Benes on Crater Hill and Wilf on [Unknown Left] to prevent them firing. To our surprise Gen! No SAM was seen or fired and we returned without incident ready to receive orders for tomorrow's push down the South FLET. Hopefully a good scrap on the Corps' birthday.

28th October

Not the greatest scrap on the Corps' birthday but a scrap nonetheless. South FLET assault with the concentration on the Western Flank down Talley Alley whilst me and the FSG provide fire support onto known firing points on the west.

It was a slow bypass down to Report Line (RL) Silver but then the compounds started getting eaten up by the CCT's and whilst clearing they were engaged by Compound 261 at close range. We couldn't assist with fire onto that enemy position but did PID [positively identify] one pax moving with what we believed was an RPG in Big Top [Taliban stronghold] and therefore we engaged with 2 x .5s and two GPMG(SF). There was little fire returned in our direction initially but then the pax thinned out into cover. We stopped firing but after some time they moved back into their firing point and we reengaged with .5 at a suppressive rate just firing single shots to fix them in position. After around 20–30 minutes we stopped and observed. The enemy obviously took advantage of this and fired an RPG towards us although it struck a high feature around 500–600m to our south. Obviously at that stage we fired a very heavy rate of fire into location for around 2 minutes until going back down to single fixing rate of fire from .5. During this time Bungy PID'd [the enemy] in the Big Top [and] 2 strafing runs from FI5s went into the position.

The CCT push didn't go as far as hoped due to low light levels and difficulties, therefore an extraction was called and we stayed firm and covered the Coy's extraction. On return we had the citation spoken, well read to us by the youngest member of the Coy before toasting the 'Royal Marines' with some port as a Coy.

After we sat down for a debrief and were engaged with 107mm rockets. 2 close strikes and then a couple of minutes later another salvo of 3 rockets hitting even closer. The debrief finished a little earlier than expected and we all bombburst to our accommodation, whilst the peaks engaged with .5 and mortars.

Soon after arriving in my room I was called back to the Ops room for what I presumed was a brief to go out onto the ground and react to incoming. My excitement rose. It took a dramatic down turn when I was informed that one of my lad's grandmother had been killed in an RTA [road traffic accident]. His parents split up when he was young and therefore his Nan pretty much brought him up. He was still on the peaks and because of the dark we couldn't bring him down to inform him and so made the decision to wait until morning.

29th October

The Marine (whose grandmother had died) made his way down in the morning and was informed by the CSM [company sergeant major] of his bad news. I spoke to him later and he was very upset but a strong character who will be ok. We hope to get him home but at the moment the policy is that he is not entitled. We will see how this develops.

I gave orders for a night time sniper ambush which took some convincing the lads onside due to the previous attempts that have failed.

30th October

The first successful night ambush and the first night I really felt the cold.

We moved out into the darkness and found a good track along the side of the M3 Wadi before breaking out the Blue Pipe Compound on some high ground to the east. We set up quickly and due to the nature of the operation kept our vehicles concealed against a compound wall in the shadow of the moon.

Everything went smoothly as I was sat next to the man with the CLU [command launcher unit] who reported to me what he was seeing and then I [relayed this] onto the boss – call-sign A. Then all my comms [communications] decided to drop out on me and I had a few minutes – probably around 20 – before I was back on the net. Just after I came back I heard that the snipers had identified a target.

It took around 40 minutes for them to take the shot which was one confirmed sentry dead. Simple yet effective. We then extracted back to the FOB, which again happened seamlessly. By the time I arrived back the cold had bitten my hands through my gloves for the first time and the normal cold shower didn't seem as cold as it usually did and getting in my bag is probably the greatest moment of the day.

Still the 30th
I've spent the rest of the day thawing out and even managed to watch a bit of the news before lunch which is a treat. In the afternoon I went for my first run in over a month and despite it only being 16 minutes long (though up a significant incline and back) my lungs were burning and the three of us were wheezing like asthmatics. We had a good workout in the gym after but I was still coughing whilst watching *Transformers* during another Kajaki film night. The chick in that is essence [slang for beautiful] and really made me think how much I miss women while being away.

31st October–3rd November

A quiet period for me as I took over control of the peaks again and despite the constant nause [nuisance] of having to re-supply the lads there has been a very slow tempo of Ops and in fact no fighting patrols at all during this period. A nice break from what was previously a very busy time leading to the end of October however it really does make the time drag.

4th November

What a day! I am yet to decide whether it has been a good day or bad day and therefore I will try and be unbiased and as factual as is possible.

It began normally enough with me sitting on the summit of Sparrowhawk West drinking a wet and smoking a pipe. The only unusual thing about this picture is that we are smoking Bernie's pipe, which he received in a parcel I brought up to him on the re-supply yesterday. We observed the CCTs as they cleared new ground through Chinah and Khevalabad before reaching their LOE just after the sun had risen. It was at this stage that we had identified movement east of Compound 41 in Bibinak and got mortars to drop smoke and creep it into the suspected enemy location. Within a few minutes of this the CCTs were engaged by multiple firing points. They had accurate fire coming from 3 sides and at least 1, but more likely 4, enemy had infiltrated in between the ANA [Afghan National

Army] and 7 Troop. This was extremely confusing and by the time Russ had cleared through the enemy position they were nowhere to be seen. This leads me to believe that they have some kind of tunnel system that prevents them from being seen by us on their entry and exit from firing points.

There are always some, but in this case many, that don't get away. I was sat next to Bernie and asked him to engage two separate targets with Javelins; one at Compound 1 in Risaji, which was a direct hit and an unconfirmed BDA of 2-3; the second was 3.2km into Compound 412 in Chinah and [was] once again a hit direct with one confirmed kill and possibly up to 3 others. Cash was on the ground and engaged with a Javelin onto Compound 28, which hit its target (matching 42 Commando's previous record) and killed or wounded up to 7 Taliban. In addition, Cash's lads killed one with GPMG(SF) and Buck, who was on an outing behind the .5, got another two confirmed kills. Wilf dropped two with his sniper rifle, whilst the recce sniper scored a couple of kills also, one of which Wilf also confirmed.

Unfortunately it was not a completely one-way battle and we took the first 40 Commando casualties of Op *Herrick* 7. Sim was with his troop (8 Troop) at the point of the Company and had a fire team of his blokes on the roof of a compound with arcs to the north and north-west. A burst of machine-gun fire came from the south-west and one of the rounds passed through two of the lads' ankles. Then as the Section 2IC stepped up to try and identify the firing point another burst was fired and took out his ankles also. I heard over the net that there was one T2 [Triage Category 2 – cannot self-help] and 2 x T3 [Triage Category 3 – walking wounded] casualties and knew immediately that a helicopter would be on its way from Bastion to get the casualties evacuated. Only a couple of minutes after the first 3 casualties came the fourth, which was one of the AE [Assault Engineer] corporals who got caught out in the open and took a round in through his arse and an exit wound out of his upper thigh.

It was at this stage things became difficult due to the amount of incoming, and from so many different locations it made the movement of the casualties south a dangerous challenge to face.

After some time, 700-odd rounds of mortars, a 2,000lb bomb onto Compound 1 in Risaji, 2 x Apaches strafing and firing Hellfires into firing points, let alone the amount of small arms being fired in response and mine and Daz's .5 and GPMG(SF) engaging, Sim managed to extract his casualties back to the CSM safely and they then moved to the emergency HLS to be lifted out. The pilot made a ballsy move to fly into a contact and lift them out and it was good to see the two stretchers and two lads hobble to the tailgate and finally lifted away at low level and back into the cover of the mountains.

We continued to engage and provide target indication and warnings for the remainder of the Company as they extracted back to the FOB, exhausted, and emotionally drained.

A long debrief with tired men was frustrating, and I was then rushed to get the peaks re-supplied with the ammo they had expended before last light as a result.

The final tally for the day was 15 separate identified firing points and 15 enemy forces estimated KIA with a good number of those confirmed. The injured lads were all downgraded to T3s and will be back in the UK by tomorrow. They are said to be in high spirits yet a little threaders that they are the first people to get shot.

5th November

A big contrast from yesterday to today saw me crack a peaks re-supply in the morning before spending the whole afternoon in the Ops room as the duty watch keeper. Russ and Sims troops shared two halves of a standing patrol on Crater Hill which other than prematurely engaging a group setting up a heavy weapon was uneventful.

In the evening the boss called all C Coy officers aside and gave us all a chuck up for the contact yesterday. It was gratefully received and good to feel appreciated.

A bizarre feeling today as I look back to the massive contact that was occurring 24 hours ago and yet today it is in the past as just one of so many memories.

6th November

I am relieved to have handed over the peaks back to Daz and am returning to where I am most comfortable; orders preparation and patrolling. Tomorrow early doors will see the beginning of a big push down the 611 to Report Line Platinum for sure and maybe as far south as Titanium. It is very likely to kick off and I can foresee the CCTs being engaged heavily from their western flank. It is our job to protect that flank. We shall see what tomorrow brings.

7th November

Today was a good fight with Terry down on the South FLET and was reassuringly more one way than our last contact on North FLET.

We moved out using the cover of darkness to our FS position just south of Compound 146. West identified a dicker to our west in the sand dunes. He went to ground and we didn't see him again.

As the CCTs pushed down the 611 they encountered little resistance until they started putting a bit of pressure onto the TB main stronghold – Big Top. At this stage we were engaged with sporadic small-arms fire and an RPG which smashed into a hill only 15km away from the ANA and OMLT [Operational Mentoring and Liaison Team]. The ANA fired back with their own RPGs, which were even less accurate than the enemy's.

As our extraction began OC absolutely smashed Big Top with a significant amount of mortars and GMLRS, and a 1,000lb bomb from a French Mirage. .5 continued to engage and we confirmed a kill on Big Top, which Mikey described through the CLU T1 [Triage Category 1 – very seriously injured/needs immediate treatment] as 'hot bits flying everywhere!' The CCTs were then engaged with GPMG(SF), I laid the guns on target and as soon as I got comms with the OC to confirm it as an enemy target I called to engage.

After the Coy had dismounted my FSG began extracting. During the extraction we were engaged by inaccurate small arms and then they fired a 107mm rocket, which whizzed over our heads, over the peaks where Daz sat, and landed into Tangye.

Got home, cleaned my weapon so it was sparkling and got my head down. All of it.

8th November

Got my hair cut this morning by Sully who did a pretty fine job to be honest. Then took my weapon to Jim the armourer as I had broken a piece when putting it back together after cleaning last night. I was threaders because the bit I broke couldn't be fixed and so I got another main body, which hadn't been cleaned for some time and I spent some time cleaning my weapon all over again.

From about 1500hrs I waited around to brief the CO [commanding officer] of 2 Para and a couple of Coy Commanders. I didn't end up giving my brief until about 2230hrs by which time they were hanging out after solid briefings for about 7 hours. Got my points across however and then got my head down again though lighter due to less hair.

9th November

This morning I drove up to Athens on the peaks to give a ground brief to the 2 Para Recce. They seemed happy enough although the CO wasn't too fussed about where the sentry positions in Risaji were (fair one I think he has bigger fish to fry). I showed them the hydroelectric power station, which is the reason we are here. We returned to the FOB and I passed on responsibility for Airborne back to the OC.

Received orders for a clearance patrol of Essex Ridge with EOD [Explosive Ordnance Disposal] and REST [Royal Engineer Search Team] leading the way. Let's see if they find anything. Odds suggest that they will.

10th November

Not [wanting] to disappoint the BBC who were attached to 7 Troop, the EOD did find something and thank fuck they did as it was designed to hit our lead vehicle (me or Dave) on our approach to the fire support position on Essex Ridge. It was an artillery shell on top of an anti-tank mine. The controlled explosion was massive and I was thankful not to be sat on top of it when it went off.

During this clearance it once again kicked off big style. Rounds [came] from most directions, and even whilst I was in dead ground with the rest of the Coy ... we received accurate small arms incoming with rounds landing around our feet.

Bernie had a field day from his position firing almost all his ammo into firing points in Gasimor. Second attempt from Bungy saw a Javelin direct hit into a compound and confirmed two enemy dead.

Stacks of rounds [came] down which would have made some good footage for Alistair Leafhead, the BBC reporter, who is fairly sure it will be on the news tonight.

11th November

A day of remembrance. We held a really sombre service on HLS Lancaster looking west down the Helmand valley. It was short and pithy with an excellent address by Stu the Padre and all being broadcast live back to the UK on BBC 2 breakfast show. The only slight disappointment was Foetus and his horrendous left turn after laying a wreath and very nearly creaming into the deck. Only broadcast to millions of people back home so no real dramas. Gen!

FSG stayed behind at the end of the service and provided a backdrop for one of Alistair's live broadcasts back to London. It was incredible to see all the hangers-on come out of the woodwork and attach themselves to the wagons most likely to be in shot.

Got back down the bottom, watched the remembrance service at the Cenotaph, which was preceded by a 20 second clip of us at Kajaki and then cracked a bit of battle prep for our clearance of the PPIEDs [pressure-plate improvised explosive devices] at Cpd 105 tomorrow and now as I lie in my pit [slang for bed or bunk] – maybe some head down.

12th November

I spent the majority of the patrol working in the ICP [incident control post] with Iain the ATO [Ammunition Technical Officer] (aka Gay TO), ensuring that his team were not tactically compromised whilst he cleared 3 locations thought to contain PPIEDs.

It really is the biggest worry for us at the moment and we must work hard and be cunning in order to avoid being victims of these cowardly devices.

13th November

A restful 24 hours for me, which have allowed me to get about 3 days of washing done and still left me some time to have a pipe, read my book and phone my Mum. I had to tell a little white lie suggesting that we had taken no casualties and fortunately she bought it. It's good that they were not publicised and I hope we have no more that are newsworthy.

I'm on watch tonight which will give me some good time to catch up on paperwork before heading up the peaks for a few hours after first light tomorrow whilst we make use of ATO for one last time in the clearance of a possible enemy minefield in the M3 wadi.

14th November

A very enjoyable day, yet a very long day. It began with 4 hours on watch keeper until 0300hrs then a couple of hours sleep before climbing up the goat track at first light to my position of overwatch on Sparrowhawk West.

ATO cleared a route finding one IED, which would have been initiated by an anti-personnel mine, and the remnants of a mine strike that killed an Anglian earlier this year. They received a bit of incoming and we aided things by finding the enemy in BK and Kaji whilst the remaining Coy extracted.

I had to make my way back down the mountain for a debrief and so after a quick wet I started my descent. Just as I had begun, a 107mm rocket came and hit about 500m to the north-east of camp. I cracked on.

Debrief and then straight into the re-supply up top which I've just remembered how much I hate doing it.

The afternoon I got some of my own admin done before smashing Risk with the OC, CSM, Iain, Sim and Russ. It was an epic battle which ended in 2 victors – the OC during the first and CSM during the second. Their experience shone through.

15th November

Apparently I am still smashing the fantasy football league despite having no internet access. Matt got his green lid [green beret] a few days ago, which I've heard from everyone but him. Jonny Lasker is joining 40 Commando in theatre when he passes out in December, and Ian is getting shiters [drunk] in Dartmouth as a RMYO.

It's good to know that life is going well for friends and family back home whilst I enjoy life out in Afghanistan too. However more recently, due to the numerous IED finds in the AO [Area of Operations], it has dawned on me just how high the threat is from an IED strike within our area and worrying to think that it targets FSG (us) predominantly and the lead wagon (me) specifically. It's all just a numbers game and let's just hope we all come out on top.

18th November

It's been a quiet few days, which is the reason for me not writing for a while. All that's happened is an Amphibious Recce, a standing patrol and Duke put his chit in to leave the Corps and then took it out again a day later.

Today is another quiet day, but the reason I write is to set the scene for tomorrow, which I bet, will not be very quiet at all. I will probably be knackered tomorrow and so I will explain the plan now so all I have to do is put some meat on the bones tomorrow.

At 0330hrs the Coy moves off with Daz moving up to Essex Ridge and Cash onto Shrine Hill in order to provide the Coy overwatch for their move into assault positions. Colin will lead the ANA into Barikjo and clear, whilst the remainder of the Coy will smash into Mazdurak. The extraction will be conducted using smoke cover from FSG and the peaks, and the end state is planned as being back in the FOB with several dead Taliban still on the ground.

No plan, however, survives contact with the enemy and the area of Mazdurak is known as a contact hot spot. The Coy will be engaged on at least 3 sides and they will find the Taliban popping up in unexpected places... As I said, I don't anticipate it being another quiet day.

19th November

This day will stick in the minds of some more than others but for all who do remember it will probably be for the bad things that happened during what was a successful clearance of Mazdurak and Barikjo.

It began with us identifying 2 enemy stood on top of a roof and me just letting the OC know that 'we can engage, but I know it may be a bit early?' He rightly declined my offer as expected but from then on (0400hrs) I was just waiting for the opportunity to fire.

That opportunity came when Daz had identified pax in Compound 7 Risaji and the boss dropped a GMLRS onto the target. 'Missile away' followed about 30 seconds later by me calling 'Javelin direct hit – confirmed 2 enemy dead'. From this moment everything seemed to be going in our favour with our control of the contact being obvious to us and to the enemy. But after around 25 minutes it seemed to even out in odds with the enemy.

In all the Coy were engaged from 22 separate firing points in all from the standard – 3 different directions. These engagements included 20 RPGs, which included 6 fired onto FSG (A) on Essex Ridge; 2 of which were within 10 metres of the lads. The closest was yet to come and was either a very skilled shot or pure fluke. It was fired towards a compound with 8 Troop HQ in. There were three casualties including Sim, OC 8 Tp.

John [one of the injured] had already used out his luck earlier in the morning when he stepped on a PPIED, which initiated and threw him back 4ft onto his arse, however the main charge did not initiate. He described it as being punched square in the face but a lucky bloke whose luck unfortunately ran out with that RPG.

Clearly the main effort then became the main effort – the casualties. In order to get the lads out we fired a further 2 Javelins, the whole AO got smashed with 8mm HE and 2 x 2,000lbs were dropped onto Mercie as well as 2 strafing runs. This enabled a rapid extraction and the lads were in the air within 40 minutes of wounding, which compared to the last time is fairly rapid.

[The] afternoon saw Russ and I cleaning Sim's weapon and packing his kit to be sent back to the UK. His lads are ok but clearly a little shaken. I will be stepping into Sim's shoes for the next couple of days until things have settled and then Iain will become the new OC8 until the new troop commanders arrive at the beginning of December.

How things change in a day! The end of the day is here and after a few cafe crèmes with Russ it's time to rest until I take overwatch at 0300. Winner! I feel it will be a restless night with so many thoughts running through my head after such a bizarre day. But as I said earlier over a cup of coffee, you live for the dit ... and today is one fucking dit!

20th November

Today I found myself in an unusual position as OC 8 Troop, [planning] for a patrol out in the early hours of tomorrow morning.

It was a good and interesting planning process with Sim's section commanders, but very muddled task organisation as a result of the injuries sustained over the last few weeks. After the planning I gave orders in a way that tried to make no big deal of it in order to reduce the ripples and make any transition to Iain as their future troop commander as painless as possible.

They went well and I felt like I had the attention and backing of all the lads before I left. The patrol however never happened because of two other potential contacts in other AOs so my close combat troop commanding would have to wait for another day.

21st November

I'm still OC8 and will be for a patrol late tomorrow night, back to Mazdurak! Iain will be taking over in a couple of days.

Helo came in tonight with 100 bags of mail, but it's late and so I'll go and get them in the morning.

22nd November

A long morning stacked with two sets of orders for the next two days. The job I was doing changed halfway through the second set as no-one informed me that I would still be OC8 and therefore I was a little threaders but just had to suck it in and say that it's all because of the injuries.

So anyway tonight will be another patrol to Mazdurak but under the cover of darkness so we don't expect it to be too feisty. We are providing a block to the south and a screen to the north-west and west in order for an IED team to move into Mazdurak and clear that village of PPIED's that 'Lucky John' managed to find [on] the last patrol up there.

The nerves from the 8 Troop lads are obvious and I did my best to settle them. Let's just hope to build some confidence and have a quiet yet successful patrol later on tonight. We leave at 2130hrs.

23rd November

Toady was a long day. First the IED clearance of Mazdurak, which began with me yomping out (a change) to the FRV [final rendezvous point] and then breaking out and assaulting cpds [compounds] 571 and 514 to put a block into the south and prevent infiltration from Barikjo whilst the clearance was being conducted of IEDs in Mazdurak. The clearance of Maz was slow but for good reason. They found the IED that 'Lucky John' had partially detonated. When John stepped on what turned out to be an improved pressure pad, he initiated the detonator and a stick of PE, which threw him back 4ft. However the main charge did not go off, which was another 2 sticks of PE and a Russian 100mm artillery shell. If it had have gone off it would not have been just John but the majority of the troop would have caught it up. As I said, 'Lucky John'.

The IRT [Immediate Response Team] helo broke back at Bastion and so we had to extract due to having no [medical] cover. The EOD team blew the explosive in a location [where] we discovered a blind AT4... We got back [at] about 0600hrs for a bit of kip before I was up at 1100hrs to give orders.

At 1400hrs we were out again to recce a route across the Spillway. The Spillway is a large gorge in the mountain to allow the water to drain into the Helmand River if the reservoir overflows. Another afternoon of yomping behind the IED team clearing the route and then back. It was a good patrol and we really did open up a good new route for foot troops up to the north-eastern edge of the North FLET.

I was understandably hanging out when I got back, but not enough to prevent me from playing a quality game of Risk. I didn't have much luck and was a survival game in Europe whilst Iain closed in around me. He had the luck of the cards and very soon had completed his mission by destroying all the black forces, after which I cried 'Is it because I is black?'

24th November

It's Saturday again already. Just crossed 7 days off my Chuff Chart. Where is the time going? A day off today and so I've been able to catch up on all my admin. Boots polished, rig clean, bed space tidy and a good gym session.

We did have a small task of taking the UAV [unmanned aerial vehicle] det [detachment] up to Shrine Hill for them to overfly the area we're putting a sniper into tomorrow. However the UAV crashed within about 5 minutes of taking off, and so we got back for a fairly early night.

Handed over responsibility for 8 Troop to Iain and so I'm back as OC FSG. Happy with that.

25th November

Orders this morning for a sniper operation onto Gasimor and Risaji. We went out to support from Blue Pipe compound but none of those little Taliban dudes were home.

26th November

Lie in this morning after the operation last night and then utilised a good opportunity to get my Dhobi [slang for washing] done. Received orders for a South FLET patrol tomorrow, which should be quiet.

A couple of lads from the *Daily Mail* arrived today. Matt (reporter) and Jamie (camera man) seem alright blokes and hopefully will get them out to see a scrap sometime this week.

With the lack of manning it now looks like both Daz and I will be out on the ground for every patrol. Will be disappointed to miss out on pipes and wets on the peaks but happy not to miss any action on the ground.

27th November

Began at a civilised time at 0900hrs for an Engineer task on the South FLET and some ANP loving.

An uneventful patrol, though we were all surprised by the level of civilian activity in the area. Daz also recce'd and as a result opened up a road route between Yellow Beach and Cpd 105. Now back at the FOB and straight into battle prep for a recce in force to BK leaving at 0220hrs.

28th November

A successful patrol that opened some new ground to the east and highlighted some good fire support positions of the future for a dismounted FSG.

A quiet extraction other than a couple of fly-bys by an F15 and a Harrier.

A few hours later the ANP were out to buy goats in Shabaz Kheyl when they were engaged by the Taliban. I was called out with the WMIKs and I was impressed with the speed of our readiness. The lads were buzzing when we left but despite our show of force, there was no further need to engage. The ANP extracted safely and we returned to the FOB in the first downpour of rain we've experienced in Afghanistan. It is just as unpleasant here as it is on Dartmoor and I fear now that the weather has changed for the worse.

We don't really know why but morale is high at the moment. I get an occasional pang of wanting to be at home with my oppos [friends], a beer and a warm shower – though not in that order and certainly not as a oner [all together]. We've been scranning a stupid amount of junk after our last load of parcels and due to the patrol pace we have done very little fizz. I am determined to smash it when I get home and reckon now that I should start preparation for SF [Special Forces] selection sometime around 2012, which gives me some awesome time to play with and of course get fit. You can never start too soon and therefore I consider it begun.

I'm currently reading *A Thousand Splendid Suns* by Khaled Hosseini. Another very interesting novel looking into Afghanistan in the 70s and 80s. I'm really beginning to understand fully why we are here and can truly see an end-state, unlike in Iraq. This country has so much potential and I only hope that I see it fulfilled in my lifetime.

I think a game of Risk will be played tonight. Then a day of battle prep tomorrow before a clearance of Khak-e-Jahnnam early morning on the 30th.

29th November

Today flew by. The morning was filled with orders and getting, marking and fabloning new maps. Then I led Matt and Jamie (*Daily Mail*) and Andy (schools) up the peaks for some quality photo opportunities, which many I featured in and have copies of. As soon as I was down I was straight into a back brief and then onto watch in the Ops room. I was relieved early by Rolly who couldn't sleep and I made the most of the extra hour in my pit. Up at 0230hrs for a patrol tomorrow to take Khak-e-Jahnnam. It's sure to kick off. Looking forward to it.

30th November

The 2 month point! Another day not to be forgotten. The plan was to clear Khak-e-Jahnnam, which is an area renowned for enemy activity. I would be on the high ground at Dorset Ridge whilst Daz went further forward to provide closer support to 7 and 8 Troops who were with a dismounted GPMG(SF) gunline. ANA (OMLT) would provide a block to the west.

Everything was going well from 0330hrs, when we left, until about 0600hrs. I was sat on Dorset observing 7 and 8 conduct their initial clearance of the 3 peaks when I saw, then heard, an explosion to my left. I thought and said that it must have been 81mm 5mk called in early and presumed that I had just missed it over the net.

Then some screaming followed by 'Amber 12 contact explosion Wait Out'; the ANA call-sign who were providing a block to the west were in the M3 wadi and had hit an enemy mine.

2 sections had already pushed through the known vulnerable point with mine detectors and were continuing north when an interpreter with the Reserve section found himself in the blast of what was believed to be an anti-personnel mine. He lost his leg from mid-thigh down, had a severe injury to the groin and other attached leg, [as well as] a large abdominal around where exposed intestine could be observed. He was dead before the Doc got to him. The Doc himself got caught up in the blast as he was in the ambulance which was far too close to the lead troops. So close in fact that Mr Hamilton, who was driving, became a second casualty as his cab was right next to the blast. He had shrapnel wounds to his right elbow and face but will recover and was very lucky (looking at the amount of frag [fragmentation] in and around the wagon).

Because the ambulance was fucked I had to [dispatch] my Pinz to collect the casualties. Coops and Will drove down there, and Coops ended up cracking CPR on the first casualty before he and Mr Hamilton were lifted out of the HLS on to Bastion. I then had to deploy my second WMIK (Pete and Jim) who went down to assist in removing the blown up ambulance. That left about 20 minutes with just me and Hodgey on Dorset Ridge until Daz yomped in to relieve us and enable our release to the explosion site. Pete and Jim did a hoofing job driving through the mined area and extracted the Pinz/ambulance out and back to the FOB. We remained and provided the Coy with rear protection during their move back to camp.

An annoying day. We've lost our first man in Kajaki, an interpreter. Revenge will be guaranteed and will be sweet.

1st December

Morning for orders and then I deployed back up the peaks with 4 new media who arrived today. Andy, who's from Bournemouth and was attached to me in Iraq, has come out to Kajaki along with a bloke called Peter from the *Western Morning* news. Two chicks join us too, which is nice to see, and they were hanging out their loop by the time we reached the top. It was a good visit and I was unfortunately involved in a number of chad photo opportunities.

Tonight we move at 2120hrs up onto Essex Ridge to support a sniper shoot onto Kajaki and Risaji. We have to move up the M4 wadi with no moon through a known PPIED area. If I'm honest I'm not looking forward to it and fully expect to find a device.

2nd December

Last night/early morning epic clearance of the M4 wadi, which took hours. Hodgey and Coops were the lads to clear and did a blinding job under significant stress. Made sure I thanked them afterwards and they knew that their efforts were appreciated. We cleared up to Essex Ridge and got eyes onto Risaji.

The weather had taken a cold turn and it was absolutely icers [slang for cold weather] being in the trenches and observing for heat sources. We did spot a couple of sentries but the snipers didn't get eyes on.

Just as we were about to extract a shot opportunity opened for sniper into a sentry position and they fired under the cover of a controlled explosion. In the debrief Ads described the sentry 'taking cover violently'.

Another successful sniper Op. Though a bloody cold one. I lost my Lower Alpine hat and ended up wearing my beret. It keeps me safe!!

Got my head down around 0400hrs until 1130hrs and then out on a short patrol to the north PVCP for a Engineer recce of a potential MOG [Mobile Operations Group] crossing point (MOG currently in Musa Qala deciding whether it can cross Helmand River here at Kajaki). Some more chad photos for the media and then back in for a quiet night.

3rd December

A day of battle prep for a recce of BK going on tomorrow early morning. A lot of controversy over this one, and a heated discussion from the CSM who thought that the plan was unworkable and dangerous. Mega frustrating but in the end we cracked on with the same plan anyway. This discussion all happened last night.

We move at 2140hrs and go to Shrine Hill to provide overwatch for a recce to the west of BK and then a plan to kill a sentry in compounds 405/406 on the eastern end using a section from 7 Troop who will climb the compound wall, engage any sentry seen and then extract under the cover of an 109 HE Grenade, smoke, 1 full bar mine, 3 claymores and possibly a double Javelin shoot if we can ID further positions.

4th December

Moved out with no issues to Shrine Hill and got eyes onto BK. We had fairly limited arcs and so I pushed further to the east on Shrine and got a good view onto the compounds of concern. We saw stacks of movement all around the area that Iain (8 Troop) was going to conduct his recce [in] and also a sentry was seen running away from Russ's location as he was clearing compounds, and so it seemed that both the recce and the 'sentry slot' had been compromised.

The focus quickly shifted to a sniper shoot and so Wilf moved closer to an individual that we had identified in Compound 394. As soon as he was in position he took the shot and hit before immediately extracting. Despite one of the Taliban oppos dying we could still observe movement in the area and so after a soak period Wilf and his sniper teams went back to his FFP [final firing point] to re-engage. We were giving constant updates to Jim Spiller (his RO [radio operator]) as he approached his FFP but literally as soon as he transmitted 'in position' we observed the sentry move into the compound and remained out of view during the extraction.

Arrived back in early doors and then up for a back brief and orders for a South FLET patrol tomorrow. That lasted for an hour and I got my Dhobi done ... before adopting my current position in the Ops room for the next 4 hours until 1900hrs. Wazzer!

5th December

A social start to what was an anti-social patrol to the south. We were positioned in our normal spot south of compounds 146/147 until later when Daz and eventually a wagon pushed south-east onto some high ground, which gained better arcs onto Big Top.

It was a feisty day and my SF gunline received some fairly accurate incoming throughout although we couldn't even ID the firing point. Daz and his WMIK got even more incoming with rounds landing at [their] feet and over and under the vehicle with Jim Hossle on top. So much so that after an individual with PKM nearly outflanked them … Daz withdrew back to me.

The close combat lads pushed further south than ever before and once they had reached their culmination point they withdrew having a massive weight of fire put down from both my SF gunline and the 2 x .5s. A GMLRS and Javelin had gone in beforehand and then mortars were used to afford my extraction from our fire support position.

We assessed the casualties on their side to be 2 but later the District Commissioner informed us that we had killed 4 and wounded 6 others.

6th December

This has been the first full day off for ages and I have been happy to just waste it away. Finished the book I was reading, *A Thousand Splendid Suns*, cleaned my GPMP and then just loafed. Called my Mum and discovered I had made national press with Tangye the dog.

Now I sit listening to Ludovica Einaudi's 'Svanire' and contemplate the rest of my evening. A cigar, a hot wet, start the new Sharpe *Trafalgar* and then hopefully get a phone call to Ian, who I'm hanging out to talk to, which in civvy speak means that I miss the little scrot.

7th December

A fairly dull day, except for a gym session with Iain and an epic game of Risk when I reigned as champion for a second time.

Tomorrow morning I'm providing security for an irrigation project by the north PVCP. I plan to take stacks of wets and stacks of dits.

8th December

Whilst I was out on the ground this morning for the irrigation project we could hear the explosions of the ANA assaulting through Musa Qala and a massive amount of ordinance being dropped. On the net was a lot of activity with helos destined for Kajaki being re-tasked to deal with casualties sustained elsewhere and a call for a Marine to be extracted immediately to Bastion for what was assumed to be a welfare case.

9th December

The day started early at 0120hrs and we moved up as FSG complete to Shrine Hill. Wilf was commanding FSG B (W3 & W$) and was hoofing throughout the day with decisiveness and accuracy in reporting. We were supporting a feint into the south of Khrolehabad, which went well though didn't push as far north as expected.

The shortfall in the move was short because of the sun rising and a small delay after Mne 'Tucks' Tucker stepped onto an anti-personnel mine, which didn't fully detonate. It would have been linked to a much larger explosive, which if it had detonated would have caused significantly more damage than a cut finger, a trouser leg black with carbon, a weapon a few metres away and a little bit of a shock to the system. Another lucky escape for 40 Commando and more specifically 8 Troop! Tucks should buy a lottery ticket at the first available opportunity as the Gods are clearly on his side at the moment.

Once a distraction device was placed (DRFD [remote command detonator] bar mine) and all FF [friendly forces] were extracting, the bar mine was blown and we engaged two identified sentry positions with 2 Javelins fired simultaneously, killing 3 EF [enemy forces]. Due to the fact that all our boys were behind us we had full arcs to our front and made best use engaging all enemy movement to our north.

The .5 was used to great effect and we killed another 4 Taliban in the space of 20 minutes without taking a single round of enemy fire. An extremely effective morning's work.

Apart from 7 enemy dead, Ricky Hatton lost his fight against Mayweather and yesterday United beat Derby 4–1. Life still goes on elsewhere despite all things Afghan.

10th December

Day of battle prep for sniper Op tomorrow morning, and a deception patrol to the southern AO. The deception patrol was dull but for the extraction when Mne O'Shea rolled the Pinz on his way to pick up the ANA OMLT from the north PVCP. Fortunately he was the only one in it and he was lucky to escape unscathed despite doing a full 360 degrees inside the cab. His helmet saved him.

We squared him away and the vehicle was recovered by Will Patten and able to be driven back.

This minor delay on extraction meant that we rolled straight into a sniper ambush, which due to the legalities of this theatre now have to be referred to as 'Domination Patrols with Snipers Forward.'

11th December

The ground domination patrol with snipers forward was uneventful and no heat sources were seen in the target area except for dogs.

I managed to drop my map as I was making my way back to the wagon and had a good quality flap as I went back into the night, which was successful. Tonight (this morning) I also proved my incompetence at rolling tabs (cigarettes) much to the hilarity of me, Luke (MFC B) and Mikey P who were in the trench with me.

The rest of the day spent catching up on sleep, debriefs and re-supplying the peaks. The OC also had a 'clear lower decks' and briefed the Coy on our successes, failures and the way forward, which was I'm sure good for the lads to hear.

Morale seems high today and we're now settling down for a quiet night and a DVD. The CSM lost in a card off for wets and I'm still waiting for my prize – 'my mug won't fill itself Royal!'

12th December

We have a good Op tomorrow! All planning and hob-nobbing had been done for a recce early tomorrow morning in preparation for a sniper-led ambush on the 14th and 15th. That, however, fell by the wayside for what now will be a tasty patrol to BK.

A warrior MOG to the north-west around Musa Qala is enemy route towards Kajaki with the plan to pincer the EF between 2 contacts. The MOG will push through a suspected TB re-supply route and inevitably get into a fight around 4km to our north-west, whilst C Coy clear into a good portion of the southern tip of BK.

We, as FSG, will remain in camp on immediate notice to move for the first 2½ hours of the patrol until first light when we will move to Shrine Hill to support the fight at approx 0630hrs.

We should have awesome arcs, which should be good but has obvious potential for receiving incoming also. Our BPT [Brigade Patrol Troop] is to move forward to an un-recce'd (by WMIK) ridge and provide closer fire support onto the western edge of BK. This will be a risky move but one that will be required if requested.

I have the position as Alternative Coy Commander again tonight and so I will be having to pay particular attention to the Coys movements for the 'just in case' scenarios, which I am sure will not occur.

Generally I am looking forward to an interesting and challenging patrol with the possibility of great success yet the ever risk of the obvious, which I won't specify as I wouldn't want to tempt fate. Break a leg to us all is the best comment I can make.

13th December

Currently I am sat in the Ops room as watchkeeper and to be fair I am hanging out of my hoop, having been up since 0330hrs and on patrol for a good portion of it. It was an excellent patrol, which exceeded all my expectations and I think many others.

We began it on immediate NTM [notice to move] sat in the briefing room, which was a nice change to the usual departure 10–20 minutes before the foot call signs. At 0630hrs we were called forward onto Shrine Hill but before I knew it I had the word from the OC to fulfil my BPT task and push forward onto a fairly bare feature to provide support into the east of BK where CCTs had been engaged by a heavy calibre weapon and small arms. On the route in we broke a drive shaft but still managed to find a route to the high ground and get the vehicles up it.

As soon as we arrived we identified a bloke running from a known FP [firing point] across a wadi but we were too late to engage and so, as I deemed it to be a likely route for enemy infiltration and extraction, I denied it to EF with sporadic GMG and .5 into the wadi itself.

Soon after we received an RPG round, which landed a little too close for comfort at only about 50m to my north. I reported and the lads engaged with GMG, .5 and I got behind the GPMG... Shortly after this incident Daz, who was on [the] west, ID'd EF in one of the compounds to our front and so Fletch put down some extremely effective GMG fire right into the compound. The enemy dude was truly fixed in his compound and was not seen to move out again.

Between us – FSG A on the high ground to the south-west of BK, Tel and Mikey (FSG B) on Shrine and Daz on west – we engaged with 4 Javelins. The number fired upset a few people due to the difficulty with re-supply and the cost of the missile.

Despite what turned out to be a frustrating issue it was a highly successful patrol that we all extracted from safely before we used fast air to drop one of the compounds that had been housing the high-calibre machine gun.

Today had been one of my best days in the Corps, until the de-brief following the patrol, which fundamentally changed my mood. It's about as threaders as I've been in theatre and am going to have to try harder than normal to keep a calm and cool manner over the next couple of days after the past 24 hours.

So what else today? Well the showers were crazy cold, I've got my first proper spots of the tour. I bit my tongue driving up the peaks re-supply today and at 2230hrs I'm so tired I have spelt the majority of these sentences incorrectly. I will get some sleep and I'm sure a new day will come with a refreshed piece of mind.

15th December

Morale has improved today and things have all seemed to go well.

First was a trip to Unknown Left with a few of the OMLT and ANA for a bit of local national relations. It went well and it was a nice two hours away from camp just shooting the shit with the locals.

On return it was a quick turnaround and out on what should have been a boring feint to Shrine Hill and then a small recce for a future hard arrest op, whilst snipers dug a 4-man sniper hide.

All of the above was as boring as expected, yet Dave, with me on the CLU, identified a known sentry position, which the Boss wanted me to drop during the night extraction. Fortunately at about 2200hrs the sentry wrapped and both of them got their heads down in a trench and so it would have been a wasted missile.

16th December

A memorable day as it is the day I broke and went down for a warm shower (although it was not warm it was significantly warmer than the shower in our grot, which is bordering on freezing).

17th December

Strange as this was two days ago (written on the 19th) but I can't remember anything that happened and so will move briskly on.

18th December

Thoughts of a patrol that would kick off as we moved into unknown ground around Shabaz Kheyl – an area which we haven't been engaged from before but have heard an HMG being used in the area. It turned out to be a quiet one with a good amount of atmospheric work done amongst the farmers south of Shabaz Kheyl.

Russ was called away to get onto a flight towards the end of the patrol and was whisked away on a quad to get onto his flight home. Troop commanders to replace him and Sim arrive tomorrow and we have the 'bite' [a trick] well and truly planned.

19th December

Wilf is the OC today and he is milking it. Got me to start banging out press-ups for being late to his 'winners' brief for Chris and Gareth, the new sprog troop commanders. The 'I' was particularly good – standing for enthusiasm!!!

Shortly we will have a mock mortar attack just to fully see them off before the real OC will end the 'bite' and introduce himself proper. A good value day for morale despite it pissing with rain for the entire day. It's been honking.

20th December

Still an overcast and muggy day, for which I spent the first half driving between all the ANP locations with WO2 [warrant officer] Quinton for him to do a bit of liaison work. Smoked a ridiculous amount and drank chai, but all for the good of British/Afghan cohesion.

The night was spent out on Dorset Ridge providing overwatch for an airdrop on DZ [parachute drop zone] Quimby. Surprisingly the RAF's part was a complete success only to be ruined by the engineers inability to drive at night.

On the extraction I was prepared to engage a pair of TB whom were a potential threat ... during the paradrop. Though as the aircraft had already completed and was out of the area it could not be justified.

For the first time on a patrol I decided to return straight to the FOB rather than wait to be the last call-sign though just as I crossed the bridge to the FOB I was called back out to assist the engineers recovering one of their dumper trucks. After a successful recovery we returned to the FOB, had a cold shower and then head down.

21st December

Today has been a hang out! All day spent on the peaks filling HESCO [large barriers of wire mesh and fabric liner, filled with sand, dirt or gravel] and sandbags in order to winterise the peaks. We built 3 Sangars for the guns and a galley [slang for kitchen] for the lads – all on west. I wasn't quite ready for such a sunny day and by the end of it I had a stinking headache.

Fortunately after a cold shower, stacks of coffee and some scran I felt much better and settled down to watch Ewan McGregor's *Long Way Round* before getting my head down for a whole ten hours. Much required!

22nd December

Battle prep was conducted for what will be a good Op into Khak-e-Jahnnam in the early hours of tomorrow morning. Orders to me followed by orders from me to the lads, then quickly up to HLS Lancaster to zero the .5s.

We did our usual back brief where we talk through each of our plans in turn so the whole Coy understand each other and the Boss is sure that we understand what he wants. This was the first proper Op that Fitzy (Gareth) and Taj (Chris) have planned and they certainly carried the confidence and tactical acumen that we've come to expect from their predecessors Russ and Sim.

I will be positioned on Dorset Ridge whilst the Coy (including Daz and SF gunline) move and clear the 3 peaks and Nipple Hill before moving north and clearing the first 4 compounds of Khak-e-Jahnnam. I have a keen eye onto 3 compounds in Khak-e-Jahnnam where I have spotted sentries before and not been able to engage. I am positive that tonight will be the night when I fire a Javelin into them at last.

The Coy clearance will all be done at night thought it's pretty sure to kick off as soon as the sun comes up. It will be the first contact that Fitzy and Taj will have been involved in and I'm sure they'll be fine, although only time will tell.

This evening I also discovered that on Monday (today is Saturday) a few from C Coy will feature in the *Sun* as a special feature on 40 Commando tashes [moustaches]. I know that Iain will feature in nothing but a red thong and a cowboy hat and the OC in his YMCA biker rig. In addition I found out from an email sent by Mum that one of Ian's batch oppos died a couple of days ago.

23rd December

Everything went to plan this morning with a successful clearance of Khak-e-Jahnnam and few rounds fired, most of which were directed at Daz and FSG B.

I instigated the contact with a Javelin into two blokes on sentry in Cpd 240. One bloke went to bits and we observed the other one crawl from the impact point for about 30 minutes until he was in the cover of another compound. Wilf killed 3 with his sniper and Daz got a further 3 with 2 Javelins and GPMG(SF) fire.

On the extraction Johnno and Will were awesome on the .5 and engaged 3 EF identified in Cpd 227. They were firing through our own smoke screen on Thermal and were putting rounds through doorways at 2.5km. After we had finished firing I had a comedy moment on the net and reported that 'I have checked fire on Cpd 227 as all pax seen have either dispersed or dispersed in situ. Am observing. Out.'

After extraction I got some sleep in preparation for the final 3 episodes of the *Long Way Round*. A quality programme and has inspired me to get my bike licence during POTL [post operation tour leave].

24th December

A civilised start at 1000hrs for us to travel down to the north PVCP and support the Engineers building an irrigation channel.

The first hour was good. Just gobbing off with the interpreter and drinking chai. But the novelty wore off and 3 hours later I was more than ready to go back in.

Received orders for the Christmas Day patrol tomorrow, which the *Sun* have taken a specific interest in and sent a reporter who arrived today.

The patrol should be quiet as I'm not thinking we're pushing the enemy enough for them to engage. However I'd like to think FSG will have a few more kills under the belt by Boxing Day. Once again we'll be on Shrine Hill and will be hitting anything that moves towards an enemy firing position and if the last patrol to Khak-e-Jahnnam is anything to go by they won't be doing it covertly. Merry Christmas.

25th December

Christmas Day 2007 will be remembered as the hardest Christmas Day ever!

The patrol was straight forward enough leaving at 0430hrs (except for one man who overslept) and all of us in position in good time. The clearance by the CCTs went well but despite a lot of movement we couldn't identify anything hostile and/or an immediate threat. We did however receive 3 good quality series of bursts from the enemy. The first was fairly civilised and they fired a few bursts well over our heads. The second lot of burst came a few minutes later and was distinctly anti-social with rounds whizzing amongst our heads. The final burst was just as we extracted.

It was absolutely freezing and I was pleased to get off the ground and fortunately had time for a luke-cold shower before taking over guard as an Xmas treat for the lads from 1200–1400hrs. My Xmas Day lunch was well nothing because straight after guard I was up the mountain with Daz to wish my lads up there a Merry Christmas. After that, back down to the FOB for meat and pasta before settling down to a Christmas Quiz. Very good value and a night not to be forgotten. I got my head down at 2359hrs only to be up again at 0300hrs to go on as watch keeper. Gen – the busiest day of the tour.

26th December

An unfortunate incident occurred last night with the Galley on Sparrowhawk East burning to the ground, which greeted me in the early hours of this morning when I came on watch. It was all over by then and after a quiet 2 hours I got my head down again with the intention of lying in for a significant period of time.

This was not to be and I was awoken early to climb up to the peaks and investigate the fire on East. I will not bore you here about my findings. Suffice to say that no-one was to blame.

On my return I took Fitzy and Taj up to Shrine Hill to [give] them a ground brief and deny a blind smoke from yesterday's patrol.

Tonight we had a Gurkha curry with the Gurkha Engineers. They had bought a goat which made a very tasty and satisfying meal.

27th December

A nice lie in before receiving orders for a patrol to Mazdurak in the early hours of tomorrow morning. I am taking FSG A up to a point just south of Essex Ridge. It should be much better cover than our usual spot but I imagine we will still take a lot of enemy fire whilst 7 Troop and ANA clear Mazdurak and 8 Troop clear Mercie. This is the least of my worries however as we will have PPIEDs. I have pushed my best men forward – Dave and Bungy, who I trust completely – yet I still have an air of concern in my mind which I hope I have hidden from the lads. The fact that I have requested the ambulance to follow directly behind me shows that I expect the worst though as the old saying says 'hope for the best'. I think it's the same for most when I say that it is not the bullets that scare [me] but the cowardly bombs.

Spoke to Mum and Dad tonight which was really nice and wished everyone a Merry Christmas and sent my love.

28th December

I apologise for writing my last entry as I was about to die. I genuinely thought that I would but clearly I have thankfully been proven wrong despite a few close calls whilst we were in position.

We survived the clearance up the M4 and dug ourselves in to a hill just south of the Essex Ridge. It was in a much more covered location to the east than Essex Ridge proper and so felt a bit more secure as the CCTs cleared through Mazdurak.

It was all quite quiet until some TB had infiltrated onto the other side of the M1 wadi (west of Mazdurak) and fired into the ANA and 7 Troop. Those boys reacted well and extracted under a heavy weight of their own fire. Due to limited arcs we just had to watch and suck up the rounds coming our way. The first seemed quite civilised (not really) and the following bursts were accurate and sustained, landing just in front of my trench. Despite a significant amount of two way traffic we extracted out of the TB killing area without casualties and were home mid-morning.

The afternoon I spent familiarising myself with the quad. Will took me out and we just smashed about around the dam for an hour or so.

29th December

All day spent planning for a patrol that didn't go ahead. Why? Well it was something to do with neither of the quads working! I hope nothing to do with me!

30th December

The Boss ran some training for a new vehicle that arrived yesterday, the Supercat or ATMP (all-terrain mobility platform). Daz and I were first on the priority list and I had a good morning cutting about before I was into the Ops room as watchkeeper for the rest of the afternoon and evening.

31st December

A South FLET patrol that was long and uneventful. On return our first experience of fresh scran in Kajaki, which was an awesome experience. I've never known salad to be so tasty.

The evening was filled with entertainment provided by Dozor in the form of a camel race. All very good banter but for me it ended at 2300hrs when I found myself once again in the Ops room as the duty watchkeeper.

1st January 2008

OK so being watchkeeper last night didn't really count as my first entry into this diary in 2008. Besides it would still have been 2007 back home [as they] are 4½ hours behind us.

This day will stick in my memory not because of the two patrols we went out on because, bluntly, they were a waste of time (though we didn't know that until we were out). The reason is of one passing comment from the Boss in the morning and a quality chat with him between patrols in the evening.

The first was simple yet fulfilling. 'Do you give your lads blowjobs?' he said whilst making the wets. 'Why do you ask?' He then explained that he'd been speaking to Durks last night during the camel races and that he'd been talking about how he had been singing my praises all night. Chuffed!

The second which meant even more was during a chat outside over a wet about future jobs. He basically said that he would recommend me for a job as troop commander on the YO [young officer] batch! Although that would not be a next job and would be one or two in the future it was about the biggest chuck up that I could imagine. RMYO troop commander is about as good as it gets in my eyes and to have the job would be the highlight of my career, so the fact that I have been considered in the frame for it has been the biggest boost in 'career morale' since the arrival at CTC [Commando Training Centre] in September 2004. The other thing he asked was if I had considered going on SF selection. 'Yes but not for a few years,' I replied. I had been conscious that I didn't ask him if I was right for the job but having him ask me gives me confidence that maybe he thinks I am.

2nd January
The morning spent cleaning my GPMG and the afternoon spent loafing. Essentially a relaxing and therefore enjoyable day off.

3rd January
Today was a simple task with engineers to improve a section of road on the M25. During the patrol one random round came through camp and got everyone a little excited for a while and then was forgotten about.

4th January
Kanzi atmospherics patrol, which gained good atmospherics but for me and FSG it was uneventful.

5th January
A little more excitement with the IEDD [improvised explosive device disposal] team clearance of the Chinah bypass. Doesn't sound too kinetic but due to our push into Khvolehabad it turned out to be!

(Last time we were in the same place we took 4 casualties on extraction.)

The contact began soon after we had pushed north of Chinah and was aimed at ANA who unfortunately for us were in a direct line between us and the enemy and therefore we got a generous proportion of the bullets into our position on Shrine Hill. They were also engaged from the west-end of MK and as it was in arcs to us I gave it everything we had.

We had to suppress the same target again later as ANA crossed some open ground into a compound they had taken fire from, but not until two Apache had smashed it with their cannons.

Fast air and Apache were with us then until the extraction and unsurprisingly Terry Taliban went all quiet whilst the IEDD team completed clearance of the Chinah bypass.

The IEDs discovered turned out to be vicious. The one which Tucks stood on and only partially detonated was connected to three mortar shells – one of which partially exploded. Tucks' luck! The other two located were just the actual 'Kajaki pressure pad' (only found in Kajaki) and looks like they were detonated by goats based on the bits of goat scattered around the local area.

6th January

Again another clearance for IEDD, this time to clear the area where the interpreter took flight. I thought it would be a quiet one but during the CCT's movements to put blocking positions in place they were engaged. Unfortunately the enemy fired from two bunker positions that we had identified, and as soon as we saw them fire Fletch engaged them with a Javelin which was observed by Dirks landing on one of the enemy's chests. (Probably the one we locked onto!)

Our arcs narrowed because of FF movement in front of us and so other than a bit of .5 we watched the rest of the contact whilst dodging the odd round impact around our location on Dorset Ridge.

We had a good amount of air tasked to us rather quickly, which were utilised on a couple of strafing runs into a compound that had been a firing point. Always good to see. Coops on the CLU observed a mortar direct hit and a 'heat source' become two 'heat sources' rapidly after impact. Another good patrol where we have got something from nothing.

It's currently 2355hrs and I'm watchkeeper until 0300hrs. I am knackered and I'm up at 0700hrs tomorrow for a patrol to clear G19. It's swamping it down with rain outside and there are weather warnings and flash flood warnings up the yingers. The Ops room is leaking and the constant dripping is driving me insane.

7th January

My gosh it rained all night and all day. We had a patrol planned in the afternoon which looked to be on the edge. So I went out with two WMIKs to assess whether or not we'd be able to use the wadis to get into position. Did I say wadis I meant rivers! There was no way looking at them that we could use them but I did a quick wade check. It was a strong current lapping over my gaiters and fast flowing. That wasn't even near the centre of the river and I was checking at the widest point. Upstream it would only get higher and faster so I made the call over the net that it was 'unworkable for vehicles' and so to the delight of the Coy the OC called stand-down. He came out to join me and have a look for himself. The only thing he could say was 'Good call mate'.

Should have played poker with the lads tonight but ended up in an officers' game of Risk. Stand-by for some shit tomorrow.

8th January

Got shit for not playing poker last night. Not surprised.

Airdrop re-supply which was on time again which is always good. ID'd three persons acting suspiciously about 900m to my north. Was very tempted to [fire a] Javelin at them and the Boss decided to clear the compounds they were in until I watched them for about another hour and assessed that they were picking up brass.

9th January

Recovery Day! Cleaned and tidied the grot today and received orders for a Pay Sang atmospherics patrol tomorrow morning.

Daz flies out on R&R [rest and recuperation] tomorrow also and so we've had to re-jig the ORBAT a little. We are the priority and so I get the pick of the bunch.

10th January

The biggest epic of patrols and not a round received [by FSG] in anger. All because of the bloody rain. The rivers running down the wadis have dried up but the power and sheer volume of rain has taken its toll and there are no longer tracks where there once were and indeed some of the tracks have become impassable, which we discovered the hard way.

We hadn't been out the FOB for 20 minutes when we got stuck crossing the M1 wadi. Nothing too serious and we managed to self-extract and get back on task, which was to support a patrol in Pay Sang from a new feature called Split Ridges.

We had just pushed forward of the ANA after catching them up when we found ourselves well into a patch of mud and truly stuck. We just about got out of what we thought was the worst and then discovered ourselves properly stuck, bottomed out, sinking the lot. I had been wearing my gaiters in the morning but decided to take them off because I wouldn't need them. How wrong I could be stood in thick mud that at times caused me to hold onto someone or something to pull myself out.

It took us well over an hour to get unstuck with another section from 8 Troop (Thomo) and Ads' snipers assisting. In the end we had to essentially build another road from corn and sand tracks to move our second WMIK onto the high ground, which eventually managed to pull Whiskey 1 free. Epic! We were very lucky not to have taken incoming as there was a time when W1 was bare from all ammo, weapons, missiles, the lot, to reduce weight and increase our chances of recovery. Only the ANA had a small contact just as we got the vehicles back onto hard standing.

There were times when I thought there was no way out and we would have to deny the vehicle or as someone suggested 'build another FOB around it'. However as bootnecks always prove – anything is possible.

The patrol got canned because of all the dramas and we dried out the wagons whilst I received orders for a South FLET patrol at 0500hrs tomorrow pushing fantastically close to Big Top. I hope for more success tomorrow than from today – Not Hard.

On watch now at 2135 and have until 2300 until I can get my head down. Today drained me dry – I'm knackered.

11th January

A recovery day mostly spent cleaning the mud caked on me, my weapons and my vehicle as a result of yesterday. Oh actually I forgot – it was also a South FLET patrol that pushed right up to Big Top. We found a new FS position, which proved excellent arcs, but despite 8 and 7 Troops smashing some PID'd persons in Big Top I decided not to join the fight.

12th January

Another airdrop into DZ Quimley though with a slight change. Firstly, rather than Dorset Ridge we pushed north of the DZ (on the DZ) to provide a block to the north and secondly, the air did not drop because of the weather.

5 hours in the dark and cold watching what we thought was a bloke but turned out to be nothing more than a big owl, for nothing! Threaders.

13th January

A nightmare sniper ambush onto Compound 180 [at] Risaji. I jumped at the opportunity to man-pack GPMG(SF) onto Cemetery Hill, south of Essex Ridge, which provided us good arcs. However the snipers could not get a shot off because of the poor ambient light and so we ended up extracting with no kill.

During the extraction the clag [slang for bad weather] came in and it turned into 'Operation *Cake and Arse*' as the vehicles attempted to extract across the wadis that have all been severely cut up as a result of the rucs that ran through them a few days ago.

14th January

Today turned out to be a good scrap but a bad day for me. I felt physically sick for the latter half of it and smoked more than I ever have in one single day. All because of an incident that was far too close to blue on blue [NATO term for friendly fire] for comfort. No one was to blame but as the commander I can't help but feel responsible.

The clearance of an area between Khak-e-Jahnnam and Gasimor was aimed to destroy a trench and bunker system in compounds 162/164. The ANA were tasked with that and were heavily engaged from several different compounds and the trench system itself.

7 Troop were in Mercie screening and blocking the western flank, whilst 8 Troop provided more depth support for the ANA positioned as usual between us and the enemy in compounds 166 and 167. We were on Dorset Ridge as usual and assisted with overhead fire from GPMG(SF) and later GMG into identified firing points in Khak-e-Jahnnam compounds 173 and 240.

The GPMG(SF) got through 3,000 rounds and was engaging for a good hour in order to support the close combat movements to the front. I had made the decision not to engage with .5 because of its low trajectory and so stuck with the safe bet of GPMG(SF) and GMG locked off and with a high trajectory well over the lads heads.

I was extremely careful with the GMG and fired well to the right to range it onto target before creeping it to the left. Once on it was safe to suppress with the fire support section commanded by Foxy directly beneath Compound 167.

Seb had put down well over 300 bombs onto target and then the lock that holds the GMG in place slipped just at the wrong time bringing the barrel down just as he fired a 3 bomb burst. I observed the rounds land metres away from the southern wall of Compound 167 where Foxy and his lads were. Immediately I checked fire and then heard the obvious call from Foxy informing me that our rounds had landed around his location. It was millimetres away ... from landing right on top of their gunners on the roof. It was a truly horrible feeling.

At times like this it is particularly important to acknowledge the error and so I made a particular effort to speak to Foxy and his boys explaining why they nearly got fragged. Also I brought it up before anyone else could in the debrief and highlighted the lessons learnt.

Despite that incident we all extracted safely under the cover of mortars and a 2,000lbs bomb dropped by a B1 Bomber. We observed a 1 x KIA with one of the mortars, throwing the bloke a good distance in the air, and it is assessed that 6 died in the 2,000lber that went into Compound 215. A good result but a bad day. Feels like we won 7–0 in a qualifying game but still didn't make it to the Euro Cup Finals.

15th January

22 days until I'm on a flight back to Blighty for my R&R and boy do I need a break. Days like yesterday remind me of how mistakes can cost lives and although it was no-one's fault, I take responsibility, possibly wrongly. I just look forward to fucking up and it just not mattering! That will be a good two weeks.

Today I'm cracking admin and writing a 'Near Miss' report for yesterday's incident. Tonight we plan to receive the first water airdrop since the Falklands War. Let's see how it goes? At the moment the weather will probably stop it but we shall see. I will have 4 x WMIKs supporting overwatch to the other shore. So a prime position for what is destined to be a very boring evolution.

16th January

A frustrating day, which should have climaxed with the first wet paradrop since 1982. However unsurprisingly the weather called endex to that and so instead we played Risk, where I beat OC C's recent run of victories with a victory of my own. Hoofing!

17th January

An uneventful day apart from my last patrol for 6 weeks to Unknown Left for a bit of Afghan lovin'! It was nigh on a white out for the majority of our time up-top, although we did get some quality snow shots whilst there and after some insistence Ray took a quality 'Facebook photo' – its upload awaits.

18th January

I spent most of today cutting around on a quad chasing helicopters. Literally. I was running the LS [landing site] for a re-supply and 26 blokes out, most of which were R&R ranks including the OC. We were waiting for a good hour before the first lift was called off. Then all back in the FOB we were told it would be on the ground in 10 minutes. Woz. So off I went collecting the lads together before having to get the Doc on the back of the quad to get him down to the LS (clinging for his life) and onto the helo seconds before it lifted.

Half an hour later it was back to drop a 4 tonne U/S [unserviceable], which I took a good hour to move to the FOB before I could relax for the night. Or not, as I now found myself as 2IC and so had to complete a new FLAPSHEET [emergency contact list] and PERSREP [personnel report] for all those in and out. I will try not to bore you with paperwork dits for the next few weeks.

19th January

Up early doors to man the Ops room in time for a patrol to the South FLET. The patrol itself was busy with a good contact and useful amounts of ammo going down range including one Javelin. My task throughout was to keep the BG [battle group] informed of all activities on the ground and to obtain air assets, casevac etc. It is an interesting time, a safe time and a warm time in the Ops room but essentially not where I want to be. Yes – it's a step up whilst the OC is away, but I am much happier getting rounds down on a two way rather than writing about someone else doing it.

As a 'salt into the wound' moment, Buck and Bernie came into the Ops room on completion and told me all about how hoofing it was. Hoofing.

20th January

Well I'm back in the Ops room for a dry airdrop, which has dropped without incident and we're just sending an F16 for a show of presence over the lads.

Today Iain and I smashed fizz for what must be the first time in over a good month. The weights were hard but the run after was ridiculous. Pledge to panic fizz before leave and again before POTL.

News also on my next job options. LCO [Landing Craft Officer] – No, CTCRM [Commando Training Centre Royal Marines], prefer not, MAOT [Maritime Air Operations Team] – but will involve a 6 month tour of Iraq before the job becomes available in April 2009, JTAC – but will mean no POTL because of JTAC course and then straight out onto H9. My position is currently 50/50. MAOT would be quality but with an alternative stop gap other than Iraq. JTAC clearly the other 50% but it doesn't look like the appointer is keen as there are already 2 junior officers in the job. It will be a quality opportunity and a financially sound idea. I should have news tomorrow so will see.

21st January

A successful sniper ambush onto Compound 150 Risaji. 13 rounds of .338 were fired and 5 IR Illum but the effect was one of three sentries dead. The snipers could hear the other two screaming before they ran back to the safety of the north.

22nd January

A recovery day, though I spent most of it cracking paperwork in the office. Proffers.

23rd January

Much the same as yesterday though with a peaks change and a phone call to the Adj [adjutant] that pretty much squares me away for the next three years.

On completion of OC FSG appointment I will complete a week's course before deploying with the UN for 6 months in Georgia. What do I know about Georgia? Well not a lot but when you're also on UN pay and clearing over £3,000 a month who cares.

When I return I will take POTL before taking over from my oppo Jay Knight (MC don't you know) as MAOT based in Yeovilton, which is very handy for home and cracking a variety of different tasks, including a sociable 2–3 month tour of Herrick every now and again. Two hoofing jobs! V pleased.

24th January

The Coy proved some new ground in a village called Pay Sang. A very quiet patrol which was a surprise although the village elders were clearly influenced by TB and simply didn't want us there. So we obliged.

25th January

A long watch from 0100 until 1300hrs in order to be present for a patrol in MK. Again proving new ground and putting pressure on the TB, but again a quiet day.

It really seems that the TB have wrapped in the cold weather and just don't seem to want to fight. They are guaranteed to warm to the fight as the temperature rises and so I am not counting my chickens yet... Not yet!

26th January

A simple working party to UKNL in order to finish a rebuild on the ANP accommodation.

27th January

A shura [Arabic for 'consultation'] was conducted [with] LNs [local national] from the local area and the evening involved another DZ Quimby airdrop. Successful and warm as I spent it in the Ops room, which was a nice change to the usual dark evening gathering.

28th January

During the night I had an epic with reporting and answering questions from the CO. All that happened was the peaks observed a few lads in Kajaki and then two vehicles arrived. My concern was that they may have been setting up an IDF [indirect fire] location and so I authorised warning shots into the M1 wadi. These were effective and so I reported it to the CO.

29th January

A South FLET patrol that was strangely quiet. We pushed right down to Compound 213 which is knocking on the door of Big Top. No received fire, which was due to the potential red phos reported between TB to [the] North and South FLET and we extracted without incident.

30th January

A recovery day. Though not so much, as most was spent in the Ops room completing R2.

31st January

The first amphibious airdrop since the Falklands. Very unexciting but a BZ was sent from the C130 pilots. Can't understand why, but thanks anyway! It was an epic recovering the stores before they sank with our limit boats, but was achieved eventually.

1st February

Irrigation project was completed on the South FLET with the assistance of some reluctant LNs.

2nd February

South FLET was cancelled because the IRT was grounded. Frustrating – so I spend the afternoon eating about 5 litres of cake! Not through choice but through losing a game of cards. Toppers! Couldn't eat evening meal because I needed to vom.

The evening we watched 9th Company being slaughtered by the Mujahadeen in Afghanistan. Tomorrow I expect the 2I/C will up the security measures, with the camp stood to permanently! Gen!

1st March

Nearly a month since I last wrote mostly because of my R&R but also because of being a little busy. Well maybe a lot.

I did have some dits to write about picking up dead ANA bodies in Musa Qala on the flight back to Bastion on my R&R. I did have something to tell of the last couple of days scraps before I left Kajaki and possibly something to say of the flight back into theatre. But it is all insignificant in comparison to the last couple of weeks in Kajaki.

The day before I flew I discovered that Kajaki had its first fatality when a corporal from the OMLT stepped on a PPIED as he moved through a mouse hole into Compound 167KJ.

Only days after, 40 Commando suffered its first loss with Cpl Mulvihill, also as a result of a PPIED.

Then on 28th February we suffered another bad day, which I will not forget. It began with 'contact mine strike!' Ben McBean had initiated a PPIED consisting of 3 x 82mm mortars; although only two detonated they still caused significant damage to Ben and two lads close to him – Yates the section commander and Stu McBreaty who had moved beyond it. The extraction of casualties became priority and they were all on a helo flying back to the hospital in Bastion within 50 minutes.

A tragic day! Stu took shrapnel into his arse but should be back with us in a few days. Yates took shrapnel but after some initial concerns he should be ok. Ben was unfortunately more seriously injured.

The following day we went back to the spots where the OMLT corporal lost his life and Compound 162 where Ben's injuries were sustained. It was an extremely big ask for the boys, but we needed to find out what had caused the two incidents with IED specialists moving forward to investigate.

The two devices were pretty much the same, the only difference being the one that killed the OMLT corporal fully functioned and was in a legacy mouse hole, whilst the one causing Ben's injuries was on the corner of a compound and only partially functioned. I suppose you could suggest that he was lucky to some extent.

In addition another device was discovered in a neighbouring Compound 166. This was smaller than the others with only a 60mm Chinese shell as the main charge, however its placement in a small, low mouse hole would have meant it would have detonated into a man on all fours, which would have caused even more damage than the other two.

So what do we do now? Well we stick two fingers up to Terry Taliban and crack on! This sounds very gung-ho and in fact we have learnt a lot from these two incidents and will try further to mitigate the risks, but essentially we must continue to dominate the ground and, when required, take it.

2nd March

Was hanging out for a change of scenery and so volunteered myself for an airdrop resupply on DZ Quintay.

What an epic that turned out to be! I walked out with TAC [Tactical Headquarters] and the drop was on time but the parachute malfunctioned on one of the four pallets and as certain as night is dark the only pallet of fresh rations piled into the deck. Then a Pinz rolled on the extraction, which took hours to extract. Finally the USP1 at one of the Ops decided to engage us just before extraction. Two good accurate bursts forced a competition to see how many blokes could hide behind a dumper truck.

3rd March

South FLET patrol to complete some works on the G11, which passed without excitement.

4th March

The Ops room and work in general are really getting me down at the moment. Just constantly seem to be playing catch up, with the HPW [High Performance Wave] (email) playing consistently and jobs and paperwork in an unending stream.

On a positive note I got my midterm report, which is hoofing and I'm going to read it again now. I hope it will make me feel better.

15th–16th March

I was getting incredibly bored with writing about shite in the Ops room and so I thought I'd wait until I was back on the ground and doing interesting stuff before I wrote again, hence the gap of 11 days. It's good to be back!

The last two days have been a patrol to dominate the ground around Khak-e-Jahnnam and it began very quickly with some excitement. Just as we arrived on Blue Pipe Compound to provide overwatch we were engaged by 2 x EF in Compound 703. It was targeted at us but quite inaccurate. Nevertheless we identified the two blokes moving back into the firing point and decided to put a Javelin into them, killing them both. They didn't try that again!

We moved to join Daz and FSG B on Dorset Ridge (similarly Daz had engaged a known bunker with a Javelin shortly before) and after a show of fire power (all weapons on the WMIK – rapid fire for 2 minutes) we set into night routine. I got a small amount of head down though broken by 2 long EF bursts ... which landed around us and dreams of scorpions, for some reason.

The next morning, day and evening were all quiet and we just moved around the area trying our best to keep active and taking opportunities to get out of the sun. All extracted after last light and I was asleep within seconds of my head touching the pillow.

17th March

I needed a rest day and I got one. Tanning, reading and fizz.

18th March

One of the most satisfying patrols so far. Down on the South FLET and all remained quiet despite us pushing further than ever before on the western flank (Tally Ally). Just before the extraction 7 Troop took some incoming from Big Top and the OC dropped a GMLRS on the bunker used as a firing point. Then more fire and another GMLRS. At this stage I had started to bring up my 2 x WMIKs to suppress the target whilst Cash on an GPMG(SF) gunline had already started to fire.

Just as we crested we took some fucking accurate incoming and then began to suppress the EF firing points with all we had. We didn't take any more accurate and after a third GMLRS and a rolling mortar barrage Terry had clearly lost the will to fight and the rest of the extraction occurred silently.

On return FSG were stood too, due to a nasty incident on a LN who had detonated a PPIED – ripping his calf muscle off and incurring additional shrapnel injuries. Despite the bad incidents, it had positive Information Operation implications for us; the TB indiscriminately injured a civilian, whilst the ANP collected the victim and we flew him out to hospital.

19th March

Nothing on patrols wise, just again tanning and fizz. I did however get to speak to Mum and my brother, which was good for morale and to make it better I had a phone that didn't cut out once in a whole half hour. Bonus!

Lieutenant Thornton and his friend Marine David Marsh were killed in action on 30 March 2008. Lieutenant Thornton was 22 and Marine Marsh was 23 years old.

OP *HERRICK 7* – OC C COMPANY

The OC C Company kept his diary until the start of December, 2 months into the tour.

1/10/07 – Day 1

Woke at 0035 loaded into transport with D Coy at 0100hrs to arrive at South Cerney at 0310 only to be told the flight had slipped to 1730, tedious.

Morale boost was four naked Marines cheering outside the 'Crossed Keys' pub with a Union Jack and RM [Royal Marine] flag – quality. Moved to transit accommodation at 0600 in time for breakfast then rest and parade at 1430 – standby for another delay. Moved to Brize [Norton] to confirm a change of aircraft, therefore fewer passengers. C Coy allocated 6 slots so had to thin 14 ranks back to Norton Manor Camp – a complete waste of a weekend! Fuc+*ng Crabs!!

Once in the air (2045hrs) all went smoothly to Bastion. Met Alex, Neil et al to get an update, and took the opportunity to send a fax bluey [slang for blue aerogramme]. Sorted kit and received 1st e-bluey from Dad. Started RSOI lectures, as well as a more formal introduction brief.

Provided a full HO/TO [handover/takeover] pack from Kajaki which was very useful but confirmed some fears regarding pattern setting and maybe an overly kinetic stance. Final point, discovered that the TQ [Troop Quartermaster] got in contact during his forward recce to Kajaki with 1 X KIA from him on a .50cal WMIK – no doubt we will hear the full story!

2/10/07 – Day 2

Second Day of RSOI so spent all morning in lectures – all OK much the same ground as OPTAG [Operational Training and Advisory Group] but greater Afghan focus. Post lunch to the ranges for a check zero. Zero not perfect, but will do – not a chance to Zero the CWS [Common Weapons Sight] as 140 firers and only 10 lanes! Remainder of Coy arrived at midday – good news but all looked tired. Missed ramp ceremony for Danish KIA but spent time sorting details for advance party flight tomorrow. All will get to go forward but remaining 14 ranks will need to check zero at Kajaki. Having received HO/TO FRAGO [fragmentation order] yesterday, I spoke to CO 1 Anglians in PM to get any final command pointers. His direction was he thought it would be hard to push the FLET any further particularly with fewer ranks. Other issues raised were the resupply problem, setting patterns and the state of the bridge – all V valid! Spent all evening moving accom [accommodation] – out of RSOI accom and getting more issued kit (Osprey, Mags [magazines for weapons], Pistol, FFD etc). The problem is how to get it all packed and decide what to leave behind – lots of hard choices. Stuck to 1 Bergan and a daysac rather than grab bag as well. This will allow a move of position if required – which boots to take is however still as issue…

TQ all over stores (as ever), despite 2 storemen being poached. Moved to camp 501 within Bastion.

3/10/07 – Day 3

Great sleep in air conditioned accom. Fairly chilled morning, with admin conducted to sort out arrival of main body, due to no one being on camp when the main body arrived. Orders/brief/direction given to Iain and CSM and Quad Training booked. Bde/TRF 'good ideas club' regarding tickets required for vehicles does not survive contact with reality – due to lack of vehicles. After a long wait on the flight-line flew to Kajaki (1hr!). State of camp better than expected but still room for improvement. Much bootneck self-help will improve the situation. Not sure whether an air of complacency has set in, or if the situation out to FLET is safe but all ranks within the camp are V chilled out. Long chat with Tony (OC B Coy) added a lot of meat to the bones of my earlier briefs. A very honest handover, but B Coy are clearly ready to end of their Op tour. Sorted webbing out, again(!) and went with Osprey with Pouches rather than separate webbing – tried to convince myself that the £120 spent on the chest rig was not a waste of money. Other personnel kit put to one side due to 0300hrs start for patrol. Could not sleep due to heat, full bladder (to ensure I was fully hydrated for ptl [patrol]) and a mind full with changes etc.

4/10/07 – Day 4

Early start – 3AM. 4AM depart, many 40 Cdo [Commando] ranks nervous as not sure what to expect. A simple action, which they have clearly done time and time again. Action on the ground difficult to follow due to lack of spotted maps, but very kinetic with automatic fire only inches from my head as I moved onto a compound roof to get the best views of the action. Command of GMLRS (2 fired) air (2 x F15 straf runs) and Mors [mortars] (460 bombs fired) was the largest lesson, but FLET easy due to movement constrained to compounds. No CIVPOP [civilian population] seen 2 confirmed KIA. Back on camp by 0940hrs.

Conducted a debrief, then walk around camp to make an assessment of improvements. Many identified – some quick wins, some larger projects. Walked to peaks in PM – hard work but worth the view – V good SA [situational awareness] provided by individual briefs and the commanders views of those in place. Admin tonight followed by initial impressions report. Need to work out Coy numbers possible, but it will be tight and rely on all company attachments pulling their weight – given that most will come from elsewhere in the Commando, this should be easier than it has been for the Anglians.

4 x 107mm rockets fired at camp landing just 4–500m north. Initial response was heavy weight of .50cal then Mor into sighted firing point. No BDA.

5/10/07 – Day 5

A reasonably chilled day with a chance to get out and about and see the FLET from a number of different positions – ANP PVCP, and unknown OP1 & 2 – a good chance to see the ground from a number of different angles including forward. Also got inside the hydroelectric station itself – V impressive and clearly much work still to be done if the 3rd turbine is to be fitted. The Brigade plan to move the turbine in Jingle trucks up the 611 appears barking mad, but worth a try?

Received orders in the afternoon which were deliberately comprehensive for our benefit, especially the ground para. Got x 3 SH [support helicopter] resupply. Just as well as we are down to 200 x 81mm Mor rounds and just 1 day of rations. The mortar issue is the real crux and needs to be solved if the constant demanding cycle of resupply is to be nipped in the bud, as it will constrain Ops. Spent PM cracking admin, including a first impressions report for the CO.

To bed early due to an early start. Woke with a mouse in the top of my daysac eating my biscuits fruit – neck of a giraffe!

6/10/07 – Day 6

Early start (0300hrs) to be out by 0400 – nearly got timings wrong as we just finished crossing some open ground before first light. Intel indicated that they knew our presence. Troops in contact (TIC) started with 2 x GMLRS then a B1 on station. Much incoming fire with multiple FPs ID'd (x20) so ptl went heavily kinetic early with 7 x 2K JDAMs [Joint Direct Attack Munitions], 6 x .5K JDAMs, 1 x Javelin, 2 x bar mines and 614 mortar rounds fired. Understandably the Anglians did not want to lose anyone on what was to be their final patrol. Patrol Modus Operandi appears to be to move forward until in contact, stand off from EF and engage with a heavy weight of fire then withdraw. I am sure I can do better with more manoeuvre and less fire – albeit with a little more risk. Movement at night I think is the way ahead especially with our better optics. C2 will be harder as we will [be] using indirect fire on hard to ID FPs. Enemy is very tenacious. Even after 2,000lbs JDAM dropped on 1 position the enemy got up 30 seconds later and fired again! Tony (B Coy OC) reckons this was one of the most kinetic North FLET ptls they have done. Remainder of the C Coy advance party were not impressed with the individual skills seen by the Anglian rifleman – a contributing factor to their high ammo consumption rate.

7/10/07 – Day 7

A relaxed day of admin. Spent most of it continuing with my initial impressions report for the CO and doing the interviews/chat for the Force Protection review. A major issue I foresee will be the Cdo HQ reaction to manning the front gate (currently by ANA) and wearing CBA [combat body armour] 24/7. Both are unsavoury due to morale and degrading effect.

Got out on ground on Shrine Hill to see the Fire Support position and North FLET – good to see.

Detailed Cpl Cameron and Dirkin to look at sniper ambush of Building 7 in north – a good first option. Need to make a decision on who has priority for RIP [relief in place] – given to Iain but SH 'bums on seats' versus stores will be an issue.

Camp wearing body armour and helmets after 1800 due to threat from indirect fire 107mm rocket attack which was gained from 2 sources – a follow up from the previous nights' rocket attack. Just spoken to Ops who again reinforced the problem of the mortar ammo resupply is having with the G4 boys. Better and more accurate control with reduced rates I think will solve this drama.

8/10/07 – Day 8

Sorted kit out for return to Bastion and work more of the force protection review – still lots to finish. Visited ANA sentry post to the west of the FOB to find it not manned – Shit-oh-Lah! After being informed that this gives the best protection to the west, to find it not manned is not ideal! Clearly a point for the report.

Listened to the first part of Tony's orders for tomorrow's patrol to M4 and BK. It is supposed to be a feint with minor Mor support, time will tell...

Was supposed to fly out on a US flight KAF-KJI-BSN-KJI-KAF but after a 2 hour delay we were informed the BSN [Bastion] part had been cancelled – the plan of then flying us on a C-130 to BSN fell over as we were dropped off at the US end of the runway and had a 3km walk to UK flight Ops to get loaded on the 2230 flight. In RSOI accom from 1600–2150 – it was like a scene from a Cambodian refugee camp – kit and personnel as far as the eye could see – a situation made less ideal by an inability to finish my report as the sockets are US type in the accom. Tedious.

9/10/07 – Day 9

Arrived in BSN at 0130 – utter waste of time!

Got up and gave the CO my initial impressions report – no time to proof read it as he was off to Sangin. Kajaki patrol last night was uneventful as the AH [attack helicopters] scared off the TB. Briefed and chatted to the CSM about Kajaki and my brief to the Coy – no dramas. Went to the range to watch the lads fire. All good stuff No/minimal safety for HE/RP range, snipers, 51mm Mor and UGL [under-slung grenade launcher] plus section attacks all running concurrently. All seemed to enjoy it. Troop attacks followed – again, good stuff. Some minor points to iron out like weapons in the air for movement. After dinner wrote and delivered Coy Attack orders for tomorrow. Brig McKay will be watching, so no pressure!

Finished late sorting kit.

10/10/07 – Day 10

Woke this morning icers with the air-con an overmatch for my summer weight sleeping bag. Wish I brought my bivvy bag. How am I going to cope in the winter now our Chacon with our winter kit has been lost? Bit of personal admin, then sat around waiting for transport to ranges – 40 minutes late!

After a bit of a delay troop commanders gave their orders then a Coy ROC drill – still consider it a good idea. Attack went OK – very controlled and methodical but a little slow. All informed net will take some time to get used to. Not helped by doing a compound clearance with PRR [personal role radio]. Royal Marine Video Production Unit filmed the action and should have some good footage. Still photos provided were OK, but not that impressive. Got back late so Dhobi, scran (lots of it – will be last decent food for a while) then JOC daily update. Discussed plan for 14th Nov with Alex [2IC 40 Cdo] at the update and was convinced to conduct day assault/patrol with AH overhead. Difficult to vary the Scheme of Manoeuvre (SofM) too much. Detailed troop commanders to look at south AO (Russ), sniper options (JT [John Thornton]) and feint to north (Sim). Cracked a bit more of the Force Protection paper before a late night. Rest of Coy drew ammo.

11/10/07 – Day 11

Last day in BSN before returning to Kajaki in afternoon. Spent morning in JOC listening to 2030 update and trying to book/deconflict air for patrol on 14th – told this was impossible but 15th would be OK for AH. So have changed the programme hoping to put off bde [brigade] comd visit.

Briefed Coy at 1100 on rules of the FOB, SOPs [standard operating procedures] etc – all looking forward to getting in – eventually. Mega rush to get to flight with dead ground trace and $5K being thrust into my hand on LS! (for Afghan projects).

Arrived in Kajaki with less than ideal coord [coordination] by Sgt Joyce to get all personnel together for a critical brief – poor anticipation. As it was, most were side tracked by oppos. Getting peaks up was a priority with 2 x guards briefs given by Tony, the second to the main body.

Night of Eide meant much 'celebratory fire' into the air – maybe a little unnerving for those on the peaks, as some of the fire was close [to] their position. Intel indicating a 107 rocket threat immanent, but never came.

12/10/07 – Day 12

Bit of a rush in the morning before B Coy departed – final handover parts. Fortunately camp had been swept of gash [slang for surplus or rubbish], but this did not stop C Coy working like ants to clear, move, mark, unpack etc, etc. Ammo store in particular involved all ranks on camp in large human chain as we moved it to a more appropriate and safe location.

TAO [Transfer of Authority] conducted at 1000hrs – should have been 0930 but poor comms meant I could not get through. All decisions now mine and lots of ranks (217 in all).

Wrote 2 sets of orders for 14 and 15 South FLET patrols – almost identical – 14 seen as a feint and ground domination with 15 being a TIC. Will be hard to coord times especially with AH on station for only a short period – best they are on time! Wrote J2 and ISTAR [Intelligence, Surveillance, Target Acquisition and Reconnaissance] documents – lots of work for Cdo HQ – unless they bat if off.

Much firing at night – looks distant and unable to ID where it is. Some loud bangs also!

A late night, but at least spoke to [my wife] and the boys.

13/10/07 – Day 13

A manic morning with orders bought forward to 0930 to give more time to Troops. CSM did not get the message so a mega rush for him. Orders went OK. WO2 Quinton informed me that ANP Station was attacked last night! TB as close as 300m – need to stop that as that is audacious! Will place a standing patrol in due course.

Conducted force protection walk around – a few points ID'd mainly in ANP camp – swill and stagnant water about. Lunch was followed by Tp [troop]/Coy minus training in Tangye – a chance to see Afghan architecture and try the all informed net – worked OK, but was limited by the ground. Moved to Royal Crescent for a ground brief. Intent to move commanders and FSG to Unknown Left stopped as Pinz was taken by CIMIC [civil-military cooperation] and peaks resupply – pissed off as an opportunity nearly wasted.

Sgt Smith identified the problem with the mortars. They had not been dug in properly and as a result the baseplates were unstable – a basic error. Much hard work by the mortar det to dig out the pits and provide stable platforms. This should reduce consumption by providing more accurate fire.

Stand to rehearsal at 1830 then 1915 'show of force' – woke up TB when they moved into Mazdurak, although they soon sussed what was happening.

14/10/07 – Day 14

A day that seemed to blur into itself. Woke at 0300 to depart camp at 0400 (the plan) but after numerous snags left at 0420 and whole Coy not complete until 0600 in the DOP [drop off point] for a South FLET patrol. Lads were a bit nervous, but they got on with it. Started to clear compounds by first light and seemed to take an age. Aim was ground orientation and ground recce for FS locations as well as a feint. The morning seemed to drag with the Coy still not reaching the LOE by midday. I stopped it at this point as the blokes were clearly hanging out and we had achieved enough. A long hot walk back. Enemy PID at Big Top and encouraged by WMIK .50cal not to return fire or move forward. Got back to a whirlwind of lunch, debrief, orders, admin. Informed that AH for next day would be at 0640 therefore need to be up at 0100 to depart at 0200. Got the call to phone the CO at 2030 (I had just got in my pit!), as I walked out I heard then saw the 107mm rocket overhead land 400m away! CO happy with my intent (from initial impressions report) and will push more snipers my way – great news!

15/10/07 – Day 15

0100 awake for a 0200 depart for a South FLET patrol. Leaving the camp turned out to be an epic. Having emphasised the need for all Tps to conduct the necessary prep to ensure a swift departure, everything went wrong. First the MPs [military police] lost the keys for the Armed Pinz, which slowed the ferrying of [personnel] to the north PVCP, next the back gate was locked after the first wave had gone – not sure why Cpl Allison did that? Having returned from a second wave, Mne John tipped a Pinz onto its side

– luckily no casualties as he just jumped out! This again slowed procedures. Given the complete lack of ambient light, and our lack of NVG [night vision goggles] driver training a not unpredictable accident!

Once underway all went well with a very quick clearance by 7 and 8 Tp on the 611 despite the dark. Due to time delay Tps were not in contact before AH arrived which meant all TB went to ground. Having cleared to LOE, I called the extraction with 20 minutes of the MR2 [Nimrod] remaining. As we started to extract 2 shots (107mm or RPG) were fired, probably at 7 Tp. .50cal engaged followed by Mor (57 rounds), Cpl Rees engaged (and dropped) TB at 1,300m and Mne Prentice fired 1 x Javelin at 1 x TB seen with a PKM. A controlled extraction ensued with WMIKs covering the withdrawal. A relaxed rest of day.

16/10/07 – Day 16
Visit to ANP station.

A late start – 8AM followed by a trip to the ANP station to see the Chief of Police. All part of a stating patrol recce. Visit went well with him clearly pleased to see us. Also helped by today being pay day – they were all in uniform – a first! Defences were OK although it appears the ranges the TB attacked before were exaggerated. Actual ranges were 800m not 300m. Unknown Left next. A sorry state of affairs with V poor accommodation, an easy, quick win CWA [consent winning activity] engagement. In particular they complained of a leaky roof. Scavenging at Roshan Hill should suffice to rectify the problem. Got a bit of a rifting from HQ for not submitting the CONOPs [Concept of Operations] early enough – fair one. Therefore spent afternoon writing 2 sets of orders and thinking of a programme 5 days out. Had to make changes to allow time to watch the rugby World Cup final. 7 Tp deployed at 1700 for their first standing patrol to ANP Station, Unknown Left and Roshan Hill. All went well except mortars illuminated the snipers. Mortars initially mistaken by the CSM and I as incoming fire! Novice.

Spoke to [my wife] and sent e-mail.

17/10/07 – Day 17

Tired this AM after some early starts – gave orders at 9AM – no dramas – for tonight's North AO Patrol. Then spoke to 2IC and CO reference my concerns over the learning account for the Pinz (by the letter of the law one is not required), the results of the 40 Board of Enquiry – OCs to ensure correct Vehicle Night Driving training and seat belts (not worn or conducted by us), the granularity of the ISTAR products (these I requested for the sniper Op are of the compound, and not the area in front). CO and Alex were happy and very supportive of all my efforts and encouraged us not to get frustrated by the bureaucracy required by the HQ. Again he emphasised the lack of pressure on me to push the FLET – all reassurance I wanted to hear. Finished Force Protection review and sorted personal admin before tonight. Received 2 x incoming mortars at 1740 near the Tangye Police station – this is a lot earlier than usual. Peaks ID'd the FP and mortars were again very quick to get up to speed – rounds south of target (Compound 24) which were adjusted. Norm [the forward air controller] called for air. 2 x F15s talked onto target in the Ops room. No TB identified, but mortars claimed 1 enemy KIA.

Night Patrol went without incident – a silent move in and clearance of Shomali Ghulbah and Kanzi. Good drills from the Mnes. 1 x dog KIA (it was just about to attack) and a bar mine used to deny a tunnel. A little frustrating not to go Kinetic, but it bodes well for the first sniper Op. The movement co-ordination and compound clearance with very little ambient light was the key lesson identified.

18/10/07 – Day 18

A quiet day of planning, prep and personal admin. Conducted debrief at 1100, then orders for standing patrol, followed by complete SITREP [situation report]. No lunch due to chef's move of the galley [kitchen] – therefore Noodles and Boil in the Bag. Tried to sleep again, with no luck so chilled and replied to HQ queries over vehicles and sniper Op. In particular the CO's question about the distraction device – which he has not come across before.

Wrote 2 letters and an e-mail. Tried to phone CO with no luck, so sent an e-mail on a number of issues. Spent the evening with the

Gurkhas for their annual festival and had a fresh Goat Curry, which was killed this AM – 1 chop to the head!

Early night to prep for sniper Op.

19/10/07 – Day 19

Morning seemed to disappear in a whirl – orders at 0930 followed by SITREP, Read Downrep [written back brief from the HQ], lunch, wrote orders for 21st North FLET patrol then checked previous e-mails. Found one to all Coy Commanders reminding them of the need to write a Friday ASSESSREP [assessment report] – Shit-Oh-Lah! By then it was 1600! Banged out 3 pages, all quite simple in retrospect but on top of orders a bit of a brain frazzle. Came under 107mm attack again, 2 (or 3?) rounds on ANP station and on peaks between Athens and Sparrowhawk. Quickly wrote the South FLET SofM which will involve a feint, withdrawal, Guard and Block, intent is to wear the enemy down by remaining in position. Will have to thin the ANA platoon out as they will be combat ineffective after some time.

Tried to phone CO, with no luck so reassured Alex instead. CO must be getting a complex that I do not wish to phone. Called [home] – spoke about school.

Sniper ambush went OK. Enemy appeared to have been warned off! Move in good, but hard to identify the firing point in the darkness. Very dark so IR Illum requested – 5 shots, but no BDA so withdrawal called, enemy stood to, and intel suggested a follow up so claymores fired followed by GMLRS. Given the low light levels, it would have been a nightmare to have conducted a fighting withdrawal. A sergeant took it upon himself to fire 2 rockets (rather than one). Not Happy, and I explained the difference between Command (me) and Control (him). Regardless, the MO appears sound.

20/10/07 – Day 20

After the early morning return to camp at 0500 (?) the remainder of the morning until 1100 was spent asleep. Had to wake up to crack the SITREP before 1200 then into a patrol debrief. From that to lunch and some personal admin time. ANA Chief of the General Staff was due to visit the OMLT which I was informed would not require any C Coy involvement. Started to crack into a set of orders when a number of VIPs with large entourage arrived at the FOB from the HLS with the OMLT in tow. Walked over to introduce myself to the OMLT CO to find myself in front of the Brigade Commander – Ahhhh! Not prepared! Took him to the briefing room and gave him the standard brief which he seemed happy with, although I was wearing trainers, so looked very relaxed! Called for the CSM, who was also in the dark and therefore turned up in shorts and t-shirt – all on a back foot. He appeared to depart happy, so turned out alright after all.

Afternoon cracked more admin then watched the rugby – nightmare, try not given therefore South Africa win. Good to be all around to watch it, but disappointing nevertheless. Also had MP dripping about driving the Pinz at night.

21/10/07 – Day 21

Had a bit of a lie in followed by orders at 0930. All OK for a North FLET patrol. Rob Grant had to be casevac'd due to the possibility of a fly laying an egg in his eye. Buck took advantage and loaded the SH with 6 bottles of gas for the galley – just as well as we were down to 24hrs worth.

North FLET patrol left at 1530 which I think surprised the TB. Intel suggested they did not know where we were and once they ID'd us, it was dark. They were clearly not happy playing at night. Cleared Mercie (7 Tp) and compounds 18–20 (8 Tp) and went out with new ANA/OMLT team. All went well, extraction called, then all hell broke loose. 'We are taking accurate, sustained and heavy fire' – Sgt Joyce. Recce snipers ran out of ammo. 1 x Javelin fired, Mors and peaks engaged. Norm had a B1 on station and dropped 1 x 2K JDAM on Compound 10. All lads happy! BDA = 8. The company performed well in this highly kinetic contact.

22/10/07 – Day 22

What was supposed to be a busy day turned [out] V chilled.

AM gave orders for a 1500 South FLET patrol but after a Crypo change [secure codes which enable secure communication] we have no

TACSAT [tactical satellite communications] ability so no air or HPW. SIR [serious incident report] not sent from last night so minimised Ops room work. Cancelled patrol at 1200 and changed programme so 7 Tp conducted a river crossing recce with the REs [Royal Engineers] to Unknown Left. This has left a large hole in the day. Cracked another set of orders for South FLET penetration, got my hair cut from Sully (not bad!) – paid him 6x gofers for his efforts. Iain will be out tomorrow with the Engs [Engineers] and MPs (with snipers doing a ground orientation).

Gave a verbal brief to Alex, who was happy. Upon the return of 7 Tp had the first night of the FOB Zeebrugge Cinema. I am very excited, although the Mnes have been watching films on their laptops for a while. Clearly Grash dug out blind on the cinema and the effect was awesome. Unfortunately, the *Borne Ultimatum* did not work, so had to settle for *300* instead – a good night regardless.

23/10/07 – Day 23

Iain excited by his day out of the office and set off by 0930. Spent morning sorting the SITREP knowing that it would be requested eventually and then the Ptl Matrix out to 3 Nov. CSM conducted R&R admin while I wrote 2 sets of orders. Movement then an explosion seen south of Essex Ridge which peaks fired into – mortars tried to adjust, but the whole thing was badly reported by the peaks – I stopped it. I think they had actually watched a failed mine laying incident. Engineer task on Unknown Left went very well with ANP officers helping. They are very happy with their new roof and forward defences – amazing that it had not been done earlier. Snipers and OMLT conducted a Zero and ECAS training and historical photo of the kit they take on the ground. Comms still frustrated by Crypo which should be sorted by tomorrow on US CH47 in flight – UK CH47s are unserviceable.

24/10/07 – Day 24

Visited peaks with Cpl Raj and Sgt Euan QGE [Queen's Gurkha Engineer]. Aim was to make an assessment of the accommodation and defences, walk up remains hard work as ever, it is easy to forget how much of a killer on the legs it is!

Once up on top I discovered a dramatic improvement in the standard of the accommodation and defences. Our lads have clearly worked very hard to improve their situation. West is still in need of work but the main problem is stores and a lack of engineering experience. Tangye followed us up – he had only gone down that morning – mad as a fish!

On walk back we stopped and visited Russian House, just outside the back FOB gates – a morbid site especially considering the amount of bullet holes on the inside of the building. It must have been a horrific final battle.

Cracked some admin in the afternoon and watched *Munich* in the 'Mess'.

Helo brought in stacks of mail for the lads (and the 2IC!).

25/10/07 – Day 25

Conducted orders and battle prep for most of the day, before moving out at 1530 for a patrol on the South FLET. Idea was to move out and conduct a feint withdrawal. This was supposed to prompt EF sentries to relax and allow our snipers to engage. As it was, it took longer than expected to move south and clear sectors, and meant we were not in position until after dark. EF did not relax battle discipline and remained in trenches. After a 2½ hour Mexican stand-off, which did nothing but eat into sleep time, the Coy withdrew.

26/10/07 – Day 26

Late start after the previous late finish.

Spent day cracking backlog of admin and battle prep for next day patrol.

27/10/01 – Day 27

Deployed from FOB at 0400 and pushed into Shomali Ghulbah. Move in and foothold V swift although intel suggested they knew – made easier for them after 3 x bar mines were used to make entry. Snipers quickly in position but unable to ID known sentry positions.

This meant for a frustrating period of waiting. Patrol canned as there was little to be gained despite numerous ambush warnings we received. Potential threat to CH47 from 'Stingers' meant FSG had to deploy to cover the high ground.

28/10/07 – Day 28

Back brief at 1400 for a South FLET [patrol] departing at 1400. Today was supposed to be the 'big push' – a shame therefore that we had no air allocated. Regardless, the march out went fine and the 'new' route north to Talley Alley worked OK although was a little slower due to ground. Once at the top of Talley Alley the Coy came under contact. Thought to be Pay Sang but may also have been from [Compound] 261. En PID in the Big Top with RPG and intel suggested SPG-9 in the area. Due to lack of air and the threat to the WMIKs I called for GMLRS. WMIKS suppressed Big Top while 7 Tp sector was cleared allowing ANA to push through. GMLRS eventually hit the target but 100m from WMIKs identified firing point which again fired with RPG. Air on station (2 x F15) by the time ANA started their clearance by which point poor comms and poor light made FF ID difficult. Some confusion with the snipers and with Air IDing friendly forces convinced me that it was time to withdrawal. A strafing run on Big Top hit the target but link up with 7, 8, ANA and Tac HQ was a nightmare in the dark. Got back to camp to toast the corps' birthday – started de-brief then got fired at with 5 x IDF (107mm or mortar). Also informed of Doc's slack drills – no dragon light, helmet, or weapon while walking about…! I engaged.

29/10/07 – Day 29

A Marine told [me] about his Grandmother (she died) = utterly gutted. CO's line in the sand remains, making life hard for the Marine. A rushed set of orders (due to activity last night) which eventually went OK. Lots of admin, SIR and SITREP, which combined with a helo resupply and everyone wanting to get on the new HPW slowed the process. Before long I realised I had missed breakfast and lunch!

Lieutenant John Thornton, Royal Marines. (Courtesy of the Thornton family)

The interior and exterior of the Kajaki hydroelectric dam, situated 55 miles north-west of Kandahar City in Helmand. The dam has a dual function, to provide electricity and to irrigate the land. Part of C Coy's mission while in Afghanistan was to ensure access to the dam and protect it. (Photo Sgt Anthony Boocock © Crown Copyright)

An Afghan National Army soldier investigates a possible IED during a road search. Since C Coy's 2007–08 tour, the British Army has handed over more and more responsibility to the ANA, including such activities. (Photo Sgt Rupert Frere © Crown Copyright)

A Royal Marine throws a smoke grenade to provide cover for a counter-IED team, tasked to safely dispose IEDs in the area. (Photo Cpl Barry Lloyd © Crown Copyright)

A view of the green zone along the Sangin River, photographed from the high ground surrounding the Kajaki Dam. (Photo Sgt Anthony Boocock © Crown Copyright)

A Desert Hawk UAV is launched from a WMIK Land Rover. It can be used for numerous tasks, such as force protection for convoys and patrols, route clearance, base security and reconnaissance or target tracking. (Photo Dave Husbands © Crown Copyright)

A mortar platoon team fires 81mm shells at Taliban positions in support of a patrol from FOB Zeebrugge. This photo shows paratroopers from 2nd Battalion, Parachute Regiment, but the Marines would have used the same equipment and techniques on their tour only a few months earlier. (Photo Sgt Anthony Boocock © Crown Copyright)

A grenade machine gun is pictured here being fired, mounted on a WMIK Land Rover. (Photo Cpl Russ Nolan © Crown Copyright)

British and Afghan flags fly side by side on a Royal Marine patrol in Helmand. The Marine is manning a .50 cal machine gun. (Photo Sean Clee © Crown Copyright)

Land Rover WMIK, shown here on patrol in Iraq. It saw use in Afghanistan before being replaced with the Jackal armoured vehicle. (Photo Cpl Ian Forsyth © Crown Copyright)

LEFT: Pictured here are elements of the Manoeuvre Support Group from 42 Commando, Royal Marines, based at Bickleigh Barracks Plymouth, whilst conducting live firing of the new light forces anti-tank guided weapon Javelin. 42 Commando Royal Marines were the first UK Armed Force to live fire the new Javelin system. The weapon went on to see extensive use in Afghanistan, including with C Coy. (Photo Sean Clee © Crown Copyright)

RIGHT: A foot patrol of Royal Marines, 40 Commando, pass near Kajaki in 2010. (Photo Si Ethell © Crown Copyright)

Troops from 45 Commando, Royal Marines, discovered this weapons haul, including RPGs, rifles and bomb-making equipment, January 2009. The Taliban's weapons have changed little during the course of the war. (Photo CSgt Baz Shaw © Crown Copyright)

An Apache AH 64 helicopter firing a Hellfire missile in an exercise over the Arizona Desert, USA. The Apache was the attack helicopter that C Coy relied on for air support during their tour in Helmand. (Photo Graeme Main © Crown Copyright)

An RAF Chinook CH-47 comes in to land in Helmand. The Chinook has been used throughout the war in Afghanistan to transport troops. (Photo Sean Clee © Crown Copyright)

Terp problems have re-emerged – after an impromptu boxing night two nights ago and accusations being thrown about it came to a head again today. It also does not help that one of them does not speak Pushtu! He will be backloaded ASAP.

Deployed at 2030 for D18-20 and E43-45 sniper ambush. Despite poor comms, and an inability to speak to the UAV the route out went well with all C/S [call-signs] being in position at 0300. Snipers A could not ID the target. Recce snipers moved to a mounted position and got eyes on Compound 45 – sentry ID'd, IR Illum called. 6 shots – 1 kill and a Coy withdrawal. A good nights' hunting.

30/10/07 – Day 30

Despite getting in at 0400 the day started early for the CSM with the Terps fighting again! Remainder got up for a 1030 patrol debrief – admin – the usual SINCREP [significant incident report]. Patrol report, then 1400 orders for a standing patrol.

Admin still taking time with HPW computer but Iain will now have to use the welfare computer for work. Marine still very upset about his grandmother but despite another call to the CO he remains adamant that he will not return home for the funeral.

A day of admin and prepped for the VIP visit. Watched *Transformers* but was interrupted by a call from the RSM [Regimental Sergeant Major] which the CSM took. Long and short, the RSM was backing the CO's line as to why our Marine should not return to the UK – a real shame, and difficult to sell.

31/10/07 – Day 31

No diary entry

1/11/07 – Day 32

The whole day was supposed to revolve around the VIP visit which after doing the usual SITREP admin was supposed to transition into the normal patrol programme. Due to the number of visitors (17) all our vehicles, plus the ANA 4x4 would be required – the flight continued to be delayed which impacted the programme by dropping lunch. I asked for some deconfliction with the resupply flight – also from KAF [Kandahar Airfield] – but in the end, they all arrived together on the wrong LS! Ahhhh.

After a small hijack from [the battle group] and a poor (misguided) brief on the security situation, the VIP party came to the FOB for the C Coy version of events. All went well – next to the bridge then to the power plant, then discovered their return flight had been delayed so had time for Athens. Once on Lancaster flight again delayed 3 more times – just after last light 1½ hours late a UK 47 arrives. It lands with the TQ, 30 bags of mail and Mne Howe (+ a new MP).

Wrote the ASSESSREP in a rush and watched *War* in the mess – utter shit film! A Marine has been diagnosed with suspected malaria – shit on all of us if it is confirmed.

2/11/07 – Day 33

Another admin day – great.

'Kwick Fit Fitter' arrived in time to watch Mne Patton fix the 4x4 and the mini bus.

Marine casevac'd out with suspected malaria. Dr made 'have you taken your Malaria drugs' signs – now all over camp. Got a 'down load' from the TQ on life in Bastion and his frustrations – a thankless job!

Continued with the security review, but difficult to make real progress.

3/11/07 – Day 34

A day of light activity although seemed to get lots done. Tps went to the range and check zeroed. Also some intro to dems [demolitions] was conducted by the AE's – not sure how many rules they broke!?

Visited the range to see a number of rules being bent – had a word with the HODs [heads of department] during the debrief. One to watch!

Uncle Buck (TQ) cracked a G4 huddle and squared lots away ref weapons and WOCS.

Conducted orders and back brief for North FLET patrol also started Sims' OJAR [officers' joint appraisal report] and some more work on the security review. Had a little sleep – not sure why – lots on my mind. A hot night due to the cloud cover.

Also, boats arrived on the CH47 – all manner of possibilities are now open...!!

4/11/10 – Day 35

After an early start (0200 reveille) the move out of the North FLET went well with Tps getting in to the Chinah bypass without difficulty. ANA broke into Chinah without a problem and the remainder pushed forward into Khevalabad without entering the bypass. Clearance of sectors went well and all Tps moved beyond their LOEs to get better eyes forward. Withdrawal given after snipers engaged 1 EF in Compound 1. Then all hell broke loose.

A number of persons were seen well to the north. 81mm Smoke dropped to discourage dickers. Started taking fire from north and west and received 3 x T3 causalities (8 Tp gunshot to ankles and lower legs whilst on a compound roof top) started causality evacuation south with the intent of using Chinah bypass. Then fire received from the east and 4th causality sustained (in arse!). CAS on call (2 x F15) which dropped (2K lbs) on Compound 1 Risaji – within 400m of Coy HQ – it felt very close! Started to move back and ANA report EF to their north between us and them (effectively encircled). Epic!

7 Tp sent south to clear, but could not ID the EF. Decided to move east of Pyramid Hill which was a high-risk strategy – then received fire from Barikjo. 81mm Smoke called into M1 to cover extraction but soon began to run low (all too quickly down to last minute of mortars which resulted in a 'bake and shake' mix of HE and Smoke – some called very close to friendly forces). AH on station neutralised to west of Bypass with SAF [surface to air fire] to cover east across M1. All casualties back on EHLS [emergency helicopter landing site] for recovery, but the SH was very short of fuel by this point. 15 firing points identified during the debrief, and assessed to be 15 enemy KIA. 3 x Javelins fired. In short, a highly kinetic patrol, with the casevac under fire testing the mettle of the whole company – lifting the 4 casualties

(and all their kit) took most of 8 Tp, and turned out to be a highly demanding and very physical exercise. To a man the company pulled together and I could not have asked for more. The co-ordination of Air/AH support together with the deconfliction with mortar support was especially impressive. Under fire, and exposed after a lack of smoke, the CSM took considerable risk moving forward to collect the casualties.

5/11/07 – Day 36
Bit of a later start due to the aftermath of the day before. Standing patrol went out at 1000 rather than 0800 to Crater Hill with 1/2 Troop rotations.

EF seen in Khaka Keyel and Kaji, and some movement in Risaji. 429A agreed with haste and .50cal used to disrupt a heavy weapon which was looking like it was preparing for a shoot.

ANA went out for their standing patrol to ANP Station and Unknown Left. Seemed to go OK.

Reports from casualties are good (considering) and 2 will be flown back to the UK tonight.

6/11/07 – Day 37
A day of battle prep, due to 3 hectic days ahead.

Delivered order for South FLET patrol (push on east) and nearly all FOB ranks involved. Engineers very excited by their smoke deception device. What I considered to be a crude device is in fact quite sophisticated and sizeable with 12(?) smoke grenades on 25-second delay fuses then PE4 and a petrol bomb to make it sink. All floating on 4 x AT4 end caps made into raft. Cpl Raj told me that it was in fact a whole slab of PE4 and an RPG.

7/11/07 – Day 38
Up early and in position with no EF knowledge of us being forward. Had to hold for 30 minutes while light improved, but had bypassed quite a long way! ANA on east of [Compound] 611 and 7 and 8 Tp to west. All ranks made good progress and it was not until the first bar

mine was used that intel suggested that EF had stood to. After this, I gave the order for the smoke distraction device to be placed in the river and set off. Concurrently the Gurkhas had dems on large poles to make noise on the east flank. The floating device required one of the Gurkhas to wade up to his chest in the river to ensure it rode into the centre of the current. Unfortunately, I could see none of this due to the green zone between our location and the river. Troops cleared to their LOE and then ANA had an RPG fired at their location. Initial lack of EF movement may have been due to PREDATOR overhead. Once TIC declared a French Mirage came on station and GMLRS stood-by. Heavy indications of EF on Big Top combined with intel was sufficient justification for GMLRS to be called on Big Top. Still receiving fire, so called for Mirage to allow us to extract. Mortar HE and Smoke used to suppress, but talk-on for the Mirage took forever! I think not helped by the poor level of English by the pilot. Eventually dropped.

After extraction EF fired a 107mm rocket at Sparrowhawk West which missed by about 40m – returned fire at rocket firing point with mortars.

8/11/07 – Day 39

3 Para Recce (to take over after 40 Cdo) and BBC (to film our remembrance service) arrived.

A very busy day of briefings and briefings and briefings!

Non-stop questions and much ground covered. Recce programme lasted until 1115hrs by which time they were over briefed.

BBC amused themselves in the afternoon.

Rockets fired at the FOB, but landed next to the ANP station. Mortars returned fire with the BBC filming them. SO3 media made a comment like 'you don't do much here do you?' – words she'll regret as I then decided there was no need for her to go on the ground with the BBC as Mr Warrington could escort the film crew.

9/11/07 – Day 40

Completed Para visit, but had to change plan with a trip to Athens and [the] dam rather than up the goat trail – they left happy.

RSM, Adj and OC Mortars, Padre, CCT and EOD arrived with Bugler and PO Photo.Briefing start all over again! All seem happy.

Had to change EOD clearance patrol based on EOD chat so timings had to allow more time to clear.

Back brief had to cover changes and had to thin out some 'hangers on'…

10/11/07 – Day 41

North FLET EOD patrol.

Departed at 0930 – blocks to south Essex Ridge (8 Tp and RSM and Adj and OC Mor), ANA to block on Mercie and 7 providing security for EOD. Within 50m of stepping off. REST found a device in the M4 and disabled it – this appeared to take an age, but the results were worth it – a pressure plate IED with mine and Arty [artillery] shell attached. Almost as soon as the ANA were in place they started taking in-coming from the north and east (Gasimor). Mortar and W3 used to suppress. Clearance continued up Essex and more on top with fire taken from Risaji. BBC came away with some good footage (including them running downhill under cross-fire) and EOD did a good job of clearing all four fire bays. The ATO was then directed to another 107mm with wires in the nose. Extraction called and ANA collapsed. As they did SAF increased and 8 Tp, 7 Tp and W3 especially vulnerable on the east of Essex Ridge. Mortars worked hard to suppress multiple targets as no air or GMLRS was available. Very dangerous especially for 8 Tp who received accurate fire. Peaks .50cal used to kick up dust in M1 to help. 4 Javelins fired, but only 2 EF KIA confirmed.

11/11/07 – Day 42

Focus today was Remembrance.

All walked up to the top HLS after 0830 orders. The BBC was already set up with flags flying and a lectern in place. The atmosphere was spot on. In place early, but the service itself went very well. Mne Worths' drill was more than a little ropey, but all in all a success. All beamed live to London but not sure how much was shown? Conflicting stories…

[My wife] told everyone to watch, and the boys missed rugby – all to be disappointed – Bugger!

Rest of the day was a bit lazy – phoned home, wrote 2 letters and chilled. Given that there are still a number of HQ ranks at the FOB, this is possibly a wrong message to portray?

Back brief for South FLET patrol in the PM.

12/11/07 – Day 43

A sociable hour to start a South FLET patrol, as we stepped off at 0800. The rationale being that if we left too early the dam overspill would be an epic. Far more CIVPOP than ever seen before – which is both good and bad – all seemed content with our presence. 7 and 8 Tp blocked south on 611 while the ANA went to report line Silver on Talley Alley. EOD cleared all 3 PPIEDs on 105, finding 1 x PPIED and destroyed the AT [anti-tank] mine. This was after a long wait in the sun! HQ ranks who came to visit (RSM, OC Comd and OC Mortars) got the RAF treatment with also a long wait on the HLS. AH turned up to escort and flying very low got an RPG fired at them. 'Pity I couldn't stay longer as I'd have killed that mother fucker', said the yank pilot as he extracted. EOD then cleared 163 and 174 with no finds before everyone extracted. An 8 hr patrol with a worthwhile result.

Remainder of the day in admin including intro for 2 x BCRs [battle casualty replacements].

Officers Mess played Risk – I won.

13/11/07 – Day 44

Gave orders for Black 18 Clearance and conducted a peaks change.

Usual admin then wrote the Compound 40 clearance orders.

After lunch the CSM, 2IC and myself went to the spillway to make an assessment of whether it could be used to get a vehicle across. Had a good ½-hour climb all over it and came to the conclusion that although the ATV [all-terrain vehicle] or ATMP could, it would require much prep work and should therefore only be considered for a foot move. Back of Athens also looked at, and discounted it as a loading point into boats in the lake; too precarious to get into the boats from the bank. Back brief then HODs and clear computer in-tray before an early night for an early start.

14/11/07 – Day 45

Departed at 0500 for an EOD clearance patrol to M4.

Route out went well with all the Tps into blocking positions as planned. EOD went forward to clear the out of bounds area in Black 18, and although the task was supposed to take 30 minutes, it took a lot longer as 1 x PPIED was soon discovered by REST. 1 x AP [anti-personnel] mine (half gone off) attached by det cord to a 81mm mortar. In addition S50 (snipers) found an unexploded RPG. ATO blew them together. Intel suggested a follow up and troops received some inaccurate incoming fire. 81mm Smoke used to cover 8 Tp's withdrawal and all Tps extracted. Back by 1030, our shortest patrol to date.

Troops now see the benefits of the Op *Barma* drills and the used REST visitors to revise their drills. EOD called away for a PPIED task in Sangin after an OMLT officer was killed – exploitation required.

Officers and CSM had another Risk night. CSM = 2 wins against my 1.

15/11/07 – Day 46

A day of admin.

Finished the RN.com blog – gave orders for a Compound 40 clearance.

Wrote orders for the Amphibious Recce/standing patrol and did the long-cast.

CO's visit on the 18th looking unlikely – a shame he must be threaders having not had the opportunity to visit yet.

Wrote an e-mail [home] and tried to phone – no luck.

Back brief conducted for tomorrow's Op. All in all a long day of admin followed by an early night (2140).

16/11/07 – Day 47

Up at 0245 to depart at 0330 for Compound 40.

Route out went well with a remarkably quick move to compounds 28–30. Cpl Borthwick (MP) had an ND [negligent discharge], which turned out to be an accidental discharge – trigger caught on side of the ambulance. All C/S in overwatch before first light to allow ANA and 7 Tp to cross open ground and clear compounds. Very interesting to see the ground from a new perspective and the route opens the possibility of moving onto Nipple Hill from this flank. Returned by 0900 with no contact or sign of contact from TB.

Spoke to CO, who apologised for not visiting. He had to visit Dan, after the OMLT KIA incident. Admin in afternoon including looking at a new mapping proposal. If it goes ahead, then we will need to change the way we report all current compounds – it will take a while to get used to...

17/11/07 – Day 48

Up early to give standing patrol orders at 0830, cracked some admin, including re-writing Mazdurak orders after a USB stick virus was wiped by my computer. Back brief was conducted shortly before patrols started to leave at 1430.

Commando HQ asked for a 'formal risk assessment' after someone got cold feet about our use of the Mk5 RE boats to conduct an amphibious movement in the lake. I guess the concern is a lack of life Jackets – risk assessment rapidly written and sent – had to ask for a response for a go/no go.

UAV to Athens to get eyes on – very useful and a good product but they crashed the UAV north of Spillway and [were] unable to recover it.

Iain saw the lads' version of Top Trumps, which was made up of members of the Coy – not happy as he is dressed as an angel.

Iain went on the ground, leaving the Ops room – all went well with the other patrols (standing patrol to north PVCP and Unknown Left ANA and 7 Tp). While Amphibious Recce patrol was quicker and achieved far more than expected – very good arcs onto South

FLET and Big Top. Definitely one to use in the future as it enabled a quick and unexpected movement onto the southern flank.

Phoned home.

18/11/07 – Day 49

A battle-prep day so little to report. Had a relaxed time in the morning conducting orders prep before giving orders at 1000 for Mazdurak. Everyone knows this will be kinetic, so more interest than usual. Collin (OMLT Comd) was supposed to fly out today but got changed at the last minute – as did the 2IC and RSM of the Artillery Regt. Flight delivered a new chef, also some more 10 man rations and bottled water. A bit odd as it is mail and fresh rations which are actually needed.

Spent the day looking ahead into the long-cast, getting a rough plan for the next 10 days and writing 2 sets of orders. A bit frustrating as my 2 gig memory stick appears to have a virus – super tedious! I now have no record of November's Orders.

Early night, due to another early start.

19/11/07 – Day 50

A shit day in the Office!

Left at 0330 up the M4 a clearance of Mazdurak. WMIKs in place in overwatch with no problems. Troops move in OK with a new route from the south. ANA lead and started break-in. 8 Tp lead up Mazdurak followed by 7 Tp.

Intel indicated that TB at Risaji knew we were there. 7 Tp was being watched by dickers from Kaji who were engaged by GMLRS, just before they were about to start engaging. Kaji also engaged with Javelin. Then a long wait before the enemy returned fire. When they did it was ferocious, with FSG on Essex taking most fire, but also into Mazdurak and Barikjo. Far more RPGs than usual (9), with 1 landing 10m from the WMIKs and Sgt Joyce. Air seemed to take forever to come on station and just as long to get talked on – I guess not helped by the poor light levels. During 8 Tps' break-in Cpl Kersey stepped on a PPIED which partially detonated! He was blown back 3–4ft – shit! A very lucky escape.

At this point the element of surprise was well and truly lost, and it was clear where we were on the ground. Clearance told to continue but with metal detectors forward – still before dawn, this slowed the clearance considerably. 45 minutes into the start of taking fire, an RPG hit 8 Tps' position. Mr Quintin (standing in as the Tp Sgt) took over and sent a casevac request. I guessed Sim had been hit, as 20B was prominent on the net at this point. Very calm and collected, but I could sense the atmosphere at the other end. Risaji was smoked off and CSM arrived on his quad to extract Sim and Cpl Kersey at speed. Withdrawal was called but I still had snags getting FSG from Essex and ANA out of the killing area. F15 dropped 2 x 2K JDAMs plus 2x strafing runs which helped FSG extract. Mortars working non-stop on three flanks, which required a helo inserted CCL [combat configured load] request for more mortar ammunition. CSM came back on his quad to accompany the Coy during the extraction. There was blood all over his trailer stretchers. It would appear an RPG entered a room through a window they were in.

26 firing points counted and 15 enemy KIA accounted for. Once back at the FOB, another Marine also declared a casualty with frag in his arms and back, he had walked back to the FOB and not said a word! He was extracted with the CCL. A sombre conversation with CSM as he cleaned the blood from his stretchers.

20/11/07 – Day 51

A subdued day after yesterday's events. Cracked two sets of orders this morning for the Engineer 611 repair task and a second for the South FLET patrol. Asked HQ about the 3 casualties – a positive update, with a rapid turnaround to get [them] back to the UK. Spent the remainder of the day doing admin. Wrote the orders for the Gasimor sniper ambush to be submitted for 429A approval, then started on the H&A [honours and awards] write ups. This job is made all the harder with the lack of Sim, to get his views on 8 Tp. After cracking the debrief got a call from the 2IC to request we bin the patrol due to the chance of a contact in Musa Qala and Sangin, which would result in little support for us. To bin the patrol would mean cancelling tonight's also as we would have to leave the Hesco-

Bastion containers in place. Decide instead to limit the LOEs, and therefore avoid the chance of a contact. After yesterday's epic, it was important to 'get back on the horse'.

Left Engineer task at 1830 with a vehicle move to north and south PVCP. Good illumination meant task went ahead at a good pace helped by Cpl Raj's enthusiasm. Intel suggested a revenge IDF attack which matched movement on the ground. Mortar HE fired. 2 men run into Mazdurak carrying something heavy. They were engaged with Javelin by the peaks. BDA =1 (reported to be 'the expert').

Finished all 611 repairs at 0030, so binned the next day's patrol but kept the mortar line on station in case of another revenge attack.

21/11/07 – Day 52

A bit of a late start, but someone did not pass the message about the late breakfast, so had to get up to eat.

Conducted back brief at 1100 for last night and wrote the SITREP plus read CO's ASSESSREP for BG(N). All good stuff and gives an indication of the pressure he is under. IEDD team inbound so had to re-write the patrol programme to clear Mazdurak – back into the 'rats nest'! Also had to write orders for the spillway clearance so a long day in the office.

4 x SHs scheduled, but last 2 arrived very late and slipped into 1 x SH and 1 x Blackhawk. Briefed new arrivals as they included the Engineer RSM and OMLT Coy commander. More time away from the computer.

Expecting 100 bags of mail. As the helos come in suspicious movement is seen to north – another attempted IED attack? They must have shit themselves as the AH arrived on station having not been here at night for so long!

22/11/07 – Day 53

Got two sets of orders completed back to back with a joiners brief beforehand for CSgt Rolland, Cpl Taylor and the new dog handler. Orders went well although it turned into briefings until midday non-stop. Spent PM cracking admin, including H&A and writing to the villagers in Holford to thank them for all their gifts. Realised by 1700 it was Thursday and there was an ASSESSREP to write before the 1830 back brief – shit! Quickly cracked it before getting some personal admin and battle prep done. We have run out of 10 man rations and so now on ORPs [operational ration pack] – odd having had a flight in.

Night patrol went well. IED clearance of Mazdurak. Took an age to get there after numerous metal objects found in the wadi. Also took a long time to clear building 522 which has a Russian 100mm shell with pressure plate in it. Only cleared ½ of the rest of Mazdurak as IRT helo went US at 0330 so had to call a withdrawal EF had no idea we were there – got back in just after first light at 0630 – all very tired.

23/11/07 – Day 54

A rapid turn around and back out again. Up at 1130 for breakfast. Back brief and debrief before out for 1400. Just enough time to write the OC comments.

Despite leaving at 1400, it took an age to start the clearance for the LS to spillway and north. C/S bounced through each other with the IEDD team moving north. Nothing found which was reassuring, but again a long day due to the slow progress made, ANA/OMLT took far too long to get out on the ground and were only just in position to block. Got in at 1830 – again V tired. Rapped on all admin and ate!

Played Risk – Iain won.

24/110/07 – Day 55

Conducted the debrief for the route clearance – no dramas. Reviewed the orders for the Gasimor sniper Op and incorporated Risaji Compound 14.

Spent most of the morning writing letters to the 6 lads who are now back in the UK injured and getting them right. This included writing to thank for 2 x parcels received – one from Mrs Munday whose husband was in 40 Commando and captured in Dieppe. Revisited H&A write ups.

Went to the District Commissioner's for dinner, which went OK. He seems a decent bloke. Food OK although no doubt I will have the runs tomorrow!

Lads did some metal detector training and painted the ambulance (sand rather than green). Also sent off the UAV det to overfly Gasimor and Risaji but unfortunately it crashed into Kaji – not sure of the reason. HQ asked if we will be collecting it... No chance!

25/11/07 – Day 56

Informed by the HQ that helo re-supply today would be reduced to 1 cab and the next will not come until the 3rd Dec. Ahhhhhhhh. Not sure the food will last that long.

Conducted orders for sniper Op, then cracked remainder of admin. Another look at the OJARs plus H&A. Finished SITREP and sent Key Leader Engagement report after scran with the DC [district commissioner] last night.

Spoke to Alex after the CSM ripped a strip off CSgt Simkins for not supporting the FOBs, listened to the pressure the HQ is under with 2 x MOGs out, one soon to deploy and D Coy soon to move location. Also asked to consider options of MOG moving west and attacking Kajaki AO – will need to expend some calories on refining this plan.

26/11/07 – Day 57

Wrote two sets of orders and briefed the *Daily Mail* journalist.

27/11/07 – Day 58

0900 South FLET patrol. Aim to complete Engineer task, recce route up to Compound 175 and get ANP on the ground (for the first time).

Route in went well. Lots of local nationals seen on the ground – far more than normal. ANP bit went well with lots of interaction and mixing with CIVPOP who appeared happy to see and talk to the ANP. Some J2 gained. Engineer task went well with a rapid completion of task as did the recce. OMLT team got on the ground and saw Talley Alley – an added bonus.

Back in by 1300 – enough time for admin, a late SITREP, wash, debrief and back for tomorrow. Early to bed for an early rise. The DC visited to give Intelligence on BK – timely!

28/11/07 – Day 59

0230 deploy for BK recce. An early start!

CSM quad broke on way out through Tangye = stress on time. However, it all worked out in the end. ANA cleared Shomali Ghulbah, 8 in sector black (Iain on the ground, with JT in the Ops room) while 7 Tp pushed forward. No sign of life, UAV had a bad launch and crashed, hitting the bloke on the back of the head!

Good recce completed by 7 Tp with obvious break-in point found. Reluctant to push forward due to report of a sentry in position and an impending electrical storm which would shut off all comms. Started to extract as storm hit – lots of dust, then came the rain! First so far on the tour. An F15 show of force used to help the extraction in daylight.

Once back, the ANP went out to buy a goat at Shomali Ghulbah and Shabaz Kheyl. This was 2 hours too late and as a result they came under fire. Mortar smoke was used to cover their extraction and WMIKs went out to cover the wadi and demonstrate some solidarity. A lot of risk for a food buying foray.

29/11/07 – Day 60

Admin Chadmin!

Orders at 1000. SITREP till 1300 – then look at the long-cast and predict future patrols. This took some time.

HQ asked for 2 x paragraphs on the *Daily Mail* drug story – ie what's their angle?

Post lunch discussion with Mr Quinton regarding the ANP and Shura and then the ASSESSREP followed by a back brief, dinner and a write up for the next sniper ambush.

A frustrating day in which I felt I had achieved nothing!

Up at 0250, so early to bed.

30/11/07 – Day 61

Up at silly o'clock and departed under brilliant moonlight. 7 and 8 Tp moved up M5 while ANA up the M3. All going well with 7 and 8 moving to and beyond Compound 40 with no problems. 7 Tp were half way up 3 peaks when the explosion broke the silence. It was clear even before the radio message that a mine-strike had occurred.

The message from Warren (OC OMLT) was bleak; 1 x T1, 1 x T3. It was only a little consoling that the T1 was not a UK call-sign, but not much given the MIST report: 'missing a leg, severe abdominal and head injuries and missing his hand.' Shit. Situation made worse as he also said the ambulance was US. Plan had to stop and focus on a withdrawal as attention shifted to casevac. This took forever due to the requirement to clear the minefield. The next problem was the armoured Pinz. First reporting was also depressing, 'we could destroy it with GMLRS'. I dispatched the CSM to provide greater clarification which indicated that it would tow OK. 1 x WMIK and 1 x Pinz dispatched to tow it back as the Coy withdrew. Doc informed me that the Terp was dead by the time he started CPR. A good effort by Mne Goldie (the AE) who went forward to clear the route to the ambulance.

As 4 reporters arrive from south-west regional papers, the *Daily Mail* reporter extracts.

1/12/07 – Day 62

A slightly later start for a Risaji/Kaji sniper ambush. All in position without a problem and no EF knowledge. Snipers B route out was hard and dead ground to the west of Essex, [which] turned out to be unsuitable. 8 Tp recce to the north of Essex went well.

7 Tp block in Barikjo and Mazdurak OK, but no target ID'd in Khevalabad. IR Illum used to ID a target for snipers B, and a distraction device used to highlight sentry position enabling the shot to be made.

All happy with the result, although only 1 BDA, not 2.

2/12/07 – Day 63

Recce of irrigation project.

Conducted a recce of the planned irrigation project with the 2IC, DC, OC Engs and CSM. A very straightforward task, but provided a useful first story (and photo opportunity) for the 4 journalists.

The UAV det conducted another overflight recce north of Shomali Ghulbah. Less than ideal that they crashed it, resulting in 8 Tp having to dash out in 2 x Pinz to retrieve it.

Many questions from the journalists on the sniper ambush Op.

3/12/07 – Day 64

Orders and planning for a break into BK and recce to the west.

CSM not happy with the plan, as clearly involves a degree of risk with imagination used to defeat a sentry before the break in. As the sentry was on the roof with good arcs, this would have involved a shoot at close range whilst on a ladder. 7 Tp were well up for the task and Cpl Dawson volunteered himself as the key ladder man. Plan, prep and rehearsals went on all day.

Out at 2200 with movement into position going OK. However EF knew we were out. As such BK was like Piccadilly Circus. Once we arrived 5 sentries were identified. The 8 Tp recce was called off and once 7 Tp had started the break-in, there were indications that the EF were aware (one person seen running away).

Cpl Rees, called forward to attack the sentry – a quick move in and kill – little further reaction from other known positions, so he was sent back for a re-attack. As there was no target present for Cpl Dawson, I called withdrawal. Back in a 0500.

4/12/07 – Day 65

A late start, then straight into orders and battle-prep for a South FLET patrol.

Another press interview and finished the link up estimate as best I could.

Also completed a write up of our sniper Ops so that the HQ had a template of how we conduct these 5 phase operations, as well as the top tips gained so far.

IAIN SUTHERLAND'S RECOLLECTIONS

My first real memory of JT was on an exercise prior to deploying. I, as well as JT, were both new to C Coy and were being put through our paces by the Company Commander.

I was steeping up as OC and he was commanding his troop. We attacked a series of objectives (buildings), and once complete, moved onto the next task.

I still remember thinking at that stage that JT's leadership and command style were his best assets – he also had a great and logical military mind, better than my own.

JT had just come from his first posting as a troop commander with the D&D's [Devon and Dorset Light Infantry], in that we shared something instantly – joking about 'Pongos' and the Army's way of doing things.

The remainder of PDT [pre-deployment training] is pretty much a blur.

The next memory of course is the deployment – the OC and troop commanders had deployed with the advance party. I, as the Coy 2IC was the last to deploy, and so came out to find everyone fully up to speed and tanned – except for JT – he never tanned, he reddened!

Once we took over the FOB from our predecessors, we began to patrol. I took up my place in the Ops room while the Coy deployed onto the ground. JT commanded the Fire Support Group (FSG) comprising of 4 WMIK variant Land Rovers each with different weapon systems – Javelin, HMG or 0.5 Browning machine gun. Their call-signs (C/S) were Whiskey 1, 2, 3 and 4. JT was always Whiskey 1.

As the 2IC in the Ops room – I rarely actually saw what was going on – more just piecing together the patrol from the understanding of the plan, and from listening to the SITREPs given from each C/S on the ground as they gave them.

Of all the radio reports I listened to, Whiskey 1's (JT's) were always clear and simple – regardless of what was going on. If you simply listened to his voice he could have been anywhere – certainly not taking fire or engaging the enemy – unflappable. Probably my strongest memory of him.

As time went by, and as we were living on top of each other, I got to know JT better. He, like myself, also became a bit of a 'tour smoker' the cigarettes were so cheap out there that it almost made sense!

Smoking time was the 'set the world to right's' time. He and I were the only officers who smoked in early stages of the tour, so a fair amount of time was spent either sat outside on the Ops room or outside the accommodation 'having a tab'. We would also use the pack of Top Trumps cards (I forget which type) to decide who was going to 'get the wets in' (make tea or coffee) to drink while we smoked. I lost that one quite a lot!

JT also had a pipe, can't remember whether it was from the start of the tour or whether he bought it on R&R. Either way, that was another great way to pass the time. He took great pleasure in the preparation phase before he smoked it. The whole pipe smoking event took around 40 minutes to complete – it was a great post dinner wind down before bed!

In the UK, JT and I lived next to each other in the Mess annex (now called the Thornton Annex), and although we were in the same company we did both do our own things in the evening. However, one night I wandered into his room and asked him what the name of the track was he was listening to (the walls weren't that thick!) – it was a song I'd heard from the latest BBC *Planet Earth* series. 'Hoppipolla' by Sigur Ros. JT thought it was a hoofing track –

I couldn't agree more. After his funeral I found out that he had requested that it be played after the service. Great choice mate.

My diary entries were rather intermittent throughout the tour, and only written for about 2 months in total. The first entry was on 11th December 2007 – and was a synopsis of the bits I could remember from the first 2 months of Operation Herrick *7.*

11 Dec 07

I've been putting this off for far too long. I've now got a decent notebook, and wish I'd started writing sooner. The Company 2IC job that I'm in may not be the most steely eyed I've ever done, but it's a great job and I've learned so much already; about this country, the job, the blokes and myself. Emotions have run high on a number of occasions, not the least when we have received casualties in the Company. Those were 2 pretty shit days.

But what can I remember from the last 2 months:

The day we left. 5 Oct 07 was a fairly tense day. Caroline (fiancée) and I had spent the previous night in Cardiff at the St David's Hotel and Spa. We had a great time and I remember thinking how lucky I was to have her with me, and that once this tour was over we would be getting married. I always think back to Iraq and think about the lads who had girlfriends while they were away – 'what a nause' I'd think back then, just something else to think about and someone else to worry about – how wrong I was. I have needed Caroline and her support throughout everything since I've known her and especially now, all the time.

Anyway, the transport from Norton Manor camp left at around 0330 I think. I remember saying goodbye to Caroline – I tried to keep it as non-emotional as possible – she was staying over at the camp so I left her in the room as I went to get on the bus. She was very good and only a few tears. I kept telling her I'd call her in the morning to wake her up – just to keep the conversation as normal as possible! She seemed OK when I left, so strong.

I remember there being no clouds in the sky as I walked across the parade square – I remember thinking ' I must put this in my diary'. The stars were bright and in their thousands – I hadn't seen a sky like it for ages, a nice send off from the UK weather – typical … always when you're leaving the country does the weather perk up!

Once in country we got ourselves and admin sorted and flew out to Kajaki to meet up with B Coy Royal Anglians, a good bunch of lads who'd had a decent tour, with a few rough spells thrown in. We had a few days of handover with them before they headed off home – we'll be in their shoes in a few months – hopefully after a job well done!

So we settled in nicely over the next few weeks, clearing up and redesigning the camp to suit our needs. Royal Marines are so ingenious when it comes to making their lives more comfortable – tables, chairs and beds all seemed to spring up out of old wooden boxes and pallets. They're an awesome breed of men – pro-active and energetic to the last – regardless of the situation.

My life has been confined to the Operations room for most of the time. Daily routine is from 0700–1300 in the Ops room, during which time I'll write up and send our daily logistic requests, Daily Personnel reports and the daily Situational Report. The Boss usually gives orders at around 1000 which breaks up the morning. I'll also stay in the Ops room when patrols are out on the ground, which is normally about 4 days out of 7 – so a busy time… Well I say busy – I'm not out on patrol with the lads, which is pretty disappointing, but hey – that's not my job at the minute, besides I'll get my chance when the Boss goes on his R&R.

4 Nov

4 Nov was our first real taste of a fire fight. The Coy patrolled up to Chinah and Khvolehabad with the intent of looking for future routes to push further north. The last time the Anglians went up there, they got into a fight, so we were expecting something similar to happen.

It was all fairly quiet to start off with – we moved out at 0330 and used the darkness to cover movement as much as possible. Come first light the ICOM chatter started up and they knew we were out. The peaks started getting a few sightings to the north as we were clearing compounds, but nothing that they could really have an effect on. Then at 0730 8 Tp started to take some fire onto their position from the north. Then the enemy seemed to spring up right in the middle of the company, with a couple of men who started shooting at the ANA/ OMLT but they soon went away. I remember it being fairly confusing in the Ops room to begin with, but as the reports came back, we soon had a good idea of what was going on, and where. We constantly sent reports back to the headquarters explaining where we were taking fire from, and making sure that they were organising air support for us if we needed it.

Suddenly it came over the Company net that we had 3 casualties. I didn't quite register it to start off with, but that went away in half a second. We heard from the Company that all 3 casualties were T3 – casualties are grading on a T1–T3 Triage status, T1 being Very Seriously Injured (VSI). All casualties had received lower leg injuries, it later transpired that they had all been in fire positions on a roof when a burst of fire hit them all at the same time – the same bullet probably did the damage to all of them.

I sent the casualty extraction report (called a 9 Liner, due to the 9 items of information required ... such an imaginative name!), and was told the Medical Emergency Response Team (MERT) would be with us in about 35 minutes. However, at that time we didn't fully appreciate that the situation on the ground may not allow them to extract the casualties that quickly. The company was now surrounded on 3 sides and were taking heavy fire. 2 x F16's began dropping bombs on targets but the enemy firing points are so difficult to see that this became a tough task for all on the ground. During the extraction, one of the guys carrying a stretcher was hit in his groin (missed all the important bits!) and the bullet came out of his left cheek! He now became a T1 casualty as the blood loss was significant.

They eventually extracted all the casualties to the EHLS which require the Sergeant Major to do 'dash of death' in his quad bike, across open ground and in front of the enemy to pick up the casualties – definitely deserves recognition for that one – legend. The helo had been holding nearby for some time now and was eventually able to come in and collect the casualties. The rest of the company by this point had extracted to a safe distance and it wasn't long before a very tired and battle hardened Charlie Company were back in the FOB. The whole thing lasted 7 hours.

I had a cigarette with the 8 Troop Commander whose men had been injured. He was clearly a bit shaken about the whole thing and about losing 4 of his blokes, but we spoke for a while and I re-assured him that he did everything right, which he did, and that shit like this will happen, and sometimes there's no way you can plan or predict every eventuality. The good thing was that all of the lads were alive, and the casualties were back in Bastion and safe.

The loss of those first four didn't really affect our business much, we all know the importance of getting on with the job in hand. Although the boss was more wary about putting 8 Troop in a position where more casualties were likely, but we soon got replacements for them, and it was business as usual.

8 Dec

We got an urgent call on the 7 Dec (1st day of an operation to take Musa Qala) that we needed to extract one of the OMLT (who teach the Afghan Army) who were part of 2 Yorks Battalion. This was an Operational Welfare Case and as such was of highest priority. The lad's name who we needed to get back to Bastion was Johnson, and it was with a slow and sickening realisation that it was pretty likely that his brother, Sergeant Lee Johnson (who had left us 4 days prior) had been seriously injured or worse. Sgt Johnson had cancelled his leave to go home in order to carry on with the Musa Qala operation – a real tragedy. It turned out that he had been killed by an IED. It hit us all pretty hard that day, especially Sergeant Morrison (Johno's replacement when he left Kajaki). We all knew Johno well and it was a bitter pill to swallow to know that he was gone. His body was repatriated on 13 Dec.

15 Dec

Daily routine started much in the same way as usual – with a 0630 start and ready to be on watch for 0700, we had watched *Casino Royale* the night before in the 'Officers' Mess' cinema – a projector on a wall, and it hadn't finished until late so I was feeling a little groggy! As I was walking across the Ops room I saw Charlie, one of the 2 dogs who stays in the FOB with us, sprinting past me with a stick in its mouth – they don't normally get active that time in the morning, so I was interested to know what he was up to. Then I saw Sully (a 22 year Marine) throwing a stick for him. It was a very clear day and crisp day, and the whole scene looked quite surreal, like a bloke in the park with his dog – we could have been anywhere in the world.

19 Dec

New troop commanders arrived today. They both seem like good lads, we got them on a few bites though. For a start we had Corporal Reese (Wilf) acting as the Company Commander, so the real boss had to maintain a low profile. Wilf, who has no front teeth, gave them his OC's joining brief over lunch, this included his own special acronym – WINNERS.

W – Warrior spirit
I – Inthusiasm (deliberate spelling error)
N – No Surrender
N – Never give up
E – Exceptional Leadership
R – Ready for Anything
S – Surprise… 'I'll be surprised if you last 2 months…'

We were all trying not to piss ourselves laughing.

Later that evening our mortars fired some illumination rounds over the known enemy positions (a regular tactic), and for anyone who has never heard an 81mm mortar fire before it sounds like you're receiving incoming fire, they're so loud. So we acted like we were under attack and threw the troop commanders in the 'Bomb Bunker' – a small cave in the side of hill, and told them to wait there and not cause any trouble – they were shitting themselves, so we fired a few more illumination mortar rounds and left them there for ½ hour. The real OC then went an introduced himself!! I think they were slightly relieved.

20 Dec

More battle preparation today, our first stores air drop is taking place tonight, so the troop commanders are writing their first set of operational orders. The two troop commanders seem to be getting on well, pretty sensible in their outlook and with a good sense of humour. JT has taken them under his wing and is showing them the ropes and explaining the pit falls they should try to avoid when leading their men.

I spent most of today mulling over the wedding guest list. Caroline is organising the whole thing back home and needs me to finalise who I want to invite – not an easy thing, but it'll get done. I mean it's not like I've got a lot to do for the wedding, other than organise the honeymoon – still not sure about that one – but I'm certain that my Op Tour bonus will be entirely spent on it! Worth every penny.

Managed to speak to Mum and Nan today, so big morale all round!

21 Dec

Productive day today. The Company went up to the peaks in its entirety to finish the winterisation of the positions up there. We had to man handle all of the kit across – no mean feat but it'll mean that those up there will be a damn sight more comfortable. Also had civilian casualty today, 2 of the Afghan workers from the dam had a row over some bread which resulted in one of them shooting the other – a slight over-reaction! In through his hip and out through the left cheek. He was losing blood at a rapid rate and it took forever to release the MERT helo to come and pick him up. The Doc had to drill into his bone to cannulate him – the femoral artery had been shot through as well so blood was everywhere. Fortunately the Doc managed to stabilise him and by the time the helo came in to pick him up he was in a pretty good and stable state – well done Doc!

Spoke to Caroline this evening after finishing my watch – had a really great chat, it almost felt like I was back in the UK on my mobile. Although I still miss her terribly, I think I came off the phone feeling so much better – just hope I get through on Xmas day!

23 Dec

Moustache competition in the sun today!! We had our pictures taken a couple of weeks ago for the 40 Commando 'Tash competition' my cowboy hat and red thong went down a treat (Brokeback Mountain cockduster!).

The patrol that was due to go ahead today was cancelled late last night as we were lacking in blokes – HQ just keep turning off our helos – the pain of sending men away on R&R and then not getting them back would be easier to bear if we had a full explanation, but they never come!

The Engineer OC was due to leave today (he's been due to leave for 2 weeks) but he's managed to stay out here a little longer. A good thing as he's a cracking lad and his Gurkha soldiers are awesome – I've never met blokes who are so cheerful and eager to crack on, I've never seen an unhappy Gurkha – they're all legends.

Nothing much else to report – had a flight put on at late notice for us which is coming in tomorrow at 1750 with 19 men on board … high morale all round!

25 Dec

Xmas Day. Another early start at 0400 – Santa hat on all day. When I went on watch we reported to HQ that we'd seen a heat source through the Thermal scope moving along the road stopping at every house and dropping off parcels – chuckles from the other end of the radio, 'Acknowledged. We've had other similar sightings, confirm he was wearing a red suit, over.'

'Roger, red suit and snowy white beard.'

'Acknowledged. Merry Xmas Royal.'

The Patrol for the lads went well – the enemy don't seem interested that much at the minute – don't think they like the cold much!

Good stash of presents from friends and family! Best ones from Mum and dad – catapult, juggling balls and tomb raider for my Playstation Portable ... feels like I'm a kid again!

Spoke to brother Matt and Caroline today – great to speak to Matt. Caroline sounded sad wish I could have cheered her up more – it's her birthday next on 22 Jan so more presents required on that one!

Really starting to notice the weather now as well – those new warm showers we have are tempting now – think I'll move from cold to hot showers tomorrow – think I deserve it!

26 Dec

Bugger – showers frozen this morning, although I can crack a manual cold shower – body was numb once finished (half an inch and a dozen wrinkles springs to mind!!). More mail today, from the flight which came in yesterday – some great stuff in them again – people are so thoughtful and kind when they put parcels together – I must never forget that.

Bit tired today. Was on guard until midnight last night (officers and SNCO's) cracked the guard for the lads on Xmas day. Had goat curry with the Gurkhas for dinner as the Engineer OC's leaving do, apparently it wasn't a hugely dignified death for the goat – tasted great though.

31 Dec

A patrol to the southern part of the AO today which gave the troop commanders a chance to see the green zone – it was pretty limited in its scope, deliberately so to give the new commanders a chance to get acquainted with the ground, without having to fight through it! Dinner was fresh rations, well a hot dog and some sweet chilli sauce. The main fresh meal comes tomorrow. This will be the first time we've had fresh rations since starting the tour in October, up until now it's been 10 man rations – which are fine in the hands of a good chef, but can get monotonous!

Sgt Conway and 7 Tp had organised the camel racing night for 2030 – so we piled into the galley where they'd set it out – broomsticks and cardboard for the camels, and the jockeys had made their own rig. Once the racing was finished it was time to introduce the new lads to the Company, so they all had to stand up and spin a few dits about themselves, followed by one of the older marines standing up and regaling us all with how he got his best friend's mum pregnant – amazing...

Midnight came and we all downed a non-alcoholic beer, shook hands with everyone and then went to bed! Happy New Year.

1 Jan 08

Interesting day today – 20 hours on watch due to a large number of small patrols going on (again familiarisation for the troop commanders). However I did teach myself to juggle! Must show dad when I get back!! Dinner was fresh rations a promised – steak chicken, cauliflower, chips and pepper sauce – fantastic!! Although it was only a few hours later that I found myself running for the toilet where it quickly came out the other end ... apparently the doc tells us that because our bodies aren't used to digesting fresh food – that's likely to happen ... good job it's not food poisoning!

Oh and the water stopped working today froze again – Gurkhas will be having a look at it tomorrow.

2 Jan

Bit of a recovery day today I caught up on a fair bit of sleep – nothing much else to report, still juggling, and the water is fixed!

4 Jan

Flights came in today with the IED Disposal team for the IEDs we have been finding on patrol and marking – they arrived whilst we had a patrol out on the ground conducting atmospherics.

Civvys seem happy to have us here and claim to have good security in their village but I can't help get the feeling they just tell us what we want to hear. Whilst the patrol was out we heard a radio intercept which said that the locals were not to cooperate with us or they would be taken out of their houses.

The local police gave us a dog today. He's completely white and has been named 'Phos' – he looks like a mini polar bear – must take some pictures!

5 Jan

Good day today. The IED Disposal team went to clear the Chinah Bypass and found 3 IEDs. There was a bit of heavy scrap – we had Apache and fast jet support throughout which was well received!

During the contact, Tangye (the black dog who lives with us) spent the whole time cowering under the table in the Ops room. The dogs usually let themselves out of the camp when the company goes on patrol and follow them throughout. We had to keep the dogs back in camp today because there was a sniffer dog on the patrol who would have been distracted if the others had got in the way. Plenty more juggling cracked – coming on well!

7 Jan

Terrible weather today – all of the wadis were flooded and the rain has been coming in hard. It had been raining all night – the peaks had terrible night of it – must have been honking.

The patrols were cancelled for the bad weather, as none of the vehicles could move through the wadis and so a decent casualty evacuation plan was not viable. It's certainly not something we're willing to risk.

10 Jan

The weather has cleared up a little and the rain has stopped [but] the ground is still totally water logged. Our patrol to Pay San had to be cancelled part way through due to the vehicles getting bogged in again. Although we did speak to a fair few local nationals throughout. They are still keen to speak to us but are so scared of the Taliban that they won't accept any help from us, or medical supplies as the Taliban will take it from them. It really hit me hard today – how are we supposed to overcome this problem, we can't provide permanent security for the villagers as we can't be everywhere at once, and they won't accept our help when we offer it. It's a real kick in the balls that the Taliban still have a grip over the locals. I hope we can change that a little by the time we leave here.

We got our summer leave dates through today. We're supposed to be back to work on 26 Aug – just as Caroline and I go on honeymoon! I spoke to Mark the Adjutant about it, he said it shouldn't be a problem – better not be!!

Started Snowing!

11 Jan

Early start as it's another patrol today. The snow covering the ground is only a thin layer and most of this has gone despite the cold. It's freezing now though! I'm currently in the Ops room and the lads are having a tactical pause out on the ground.

To be honest not much else to report today. On the plus side, the Boss has allowed me to go out on the next air drop tomorrow night and command the Coy. At least it will get me out.

12 Jan

I'm not going to say much – other than 'we love the RAF' day, has been cancelled. We spent 7 hours on the drop zone today from 1700 to 2300. The drop was put back from 2112 to 2235, and when they arrived the pilot said the cloud cover was too low and they couldn't drop, although we had been trying to tell them that... It was also snowing and raining at this point as well – hoofing!

15 Jan

Well, we were due our wet paradrop tonight, but the weather has been pretty crap all day –raining and low cloud cover, the peaks were in it all day – they could only see 20m in the freezing cloud – I didn't envy them.

Getting excited and a little nervous about Company command, the boss will no doubt sit me down and go through the Dos and Don'ts when out on patrol, although I'm pretty sure that I've managed to pick up much of the way he operates. As always, and with every plan and patrol we've undertaken, we don't take any unnecessary risks. There's always tomorrow to push a little bit further into the AO, and if you don't have to take the risk in order to complete the mission, then don't bother. Sounds like a slightly risk averse method of planning, but it isn't, we continue to push further each patrol we go on, we just don't go further than we plan to … simple really. That's what a limit of exploitation is for…

The air drop was eventually cancelled today due to bad weather. Anyway up at 0300 again tomorrow morning after some furious shift swapping, post-wet paradrop cancellation!! Must get my head down.

19 Jan

The boss left on R&R today leaving me as OC C Coy – nice. The patrol programme for the next few days has been written and orders for the southern AO patrol tomorrow have been given. In passing moments I guess I've been apprehensive about commanding the company. SO much to think about, in addition to fighting the Company – I'll be interested as to how I get on. Assess the risk and make the decision.

On the positive side the boss didn't give me too much of a pep talk, so I'll take it from that that he's happy I'll be fine. Tomorrow's patrol is going to push further than we've been before and so should be interesting to see how the Taliban react to us. Time will tell.

20 Jan

A freezing cold morning as we set out at 0800. We cleared all the way down Talley Alley and I then went firm [static on the ground] with the snipers to watch the clearance south. The lads' drills were slick and it wasn't before long they had cleared their objectives. Not a shot fired thus far. I pushed up to the front troops, 8 Tp had good arcs onto the main enemy position we always get fire from – 'BIG TOP' (a small copse of trees which looks like the Big Top of a circus tent). They were pretty close, but still no fire from the enemy. The ANA and OMLT started clearing further towards the LOE. While searching the compounds 7 Tp came across some unexploded ordinance (mortar bombs mainly, which can be used in IEDs), which we decided to blow up in place. Then the ANA got a short burst of fire from the enemy sent their way. Nothing too accurate, but they certainly knew we were there. We finished clearing and searching the compounds. There were a few locals around, but not many – not really the time of year to be out farming!! Once we'd completed the search, we began to extract, always the normal time for an attack to start. It feels like they open fire on us as we're pulling back anyway, which almost makes it looks like we're running away from them when they begin engaging us, it's happened a couple of times now. We had got about 800m away when a burst of fire came ripping through us – I heard the whizz of bullets come through us and then 8 Tp turned and executed a perfect anti-ambush drill – I heard a fire control order from one of the lads and they began putting down fire onto the firing position, although I have to say there wasn't a lot coming back at this stage. We fired some mortar smoke to cover the extraction and moved back to the FOB.

The patrol itself was a relative success, we achieved our mission, but I do hate the enemy's tactic of firing on us only when our back is turned and we're extracting anyway.

I'm also bothered about the lack of interaction we have with the civilians population at the minute, although I know it's normal for them not to be out in force at this time of year (they're all farmers after all), but I wish there was more we could do to provide security for them. Of course ideally they could move back into Tangye village, just across the river from the FOB, that way we could provide protection for them. But the village is destroyed form all the previous fighting and getting anyone back there is going to take a lot of work – I hope we get there.

21 Jan

Air drop today – all went well.

I noticed that one of 7 Tps' lads as been looking pretty threaders lately – spoke to the Fitzy about him – he said he hadn't been right for about a week. Apparently the lad's a bit worried about getting married in August – aren't we all!!

12 Feb
Not been so good recently with diary entries – a busy time as Coy Comd didn't really lend itself to regular writing. The boss got back on 7 Feb so I'm back as the Ops Officer. To be honest the 2–3 weeks went V quickly – not as much enemy action as I expected, and the weather often conspired against achieving the best plans – so what have we achieved, well quite [a] bit.

We conducted an amphibious air drop of stores into the Kajaki Dam – apparently the first for the Royal Marines since the Falklands – or so I'm told. Whilst it was great to do, it was actually a pain in the arse, only half the stores we asked for could be dropped and of those about 20% we unusable due to water leakage – despite being packed V well by the RAF! That said it was less man power intensive, and gives us another option should our usual drop zone get compromised in future.

With my R&R fast approaching we've got a second Ops officer flown in to assist JT while I'm gone, so he's arrived to learn the ropes. JT is more than squared away with the process, but he's got a troop to run as well, so the extra body will help alleviate some of the pressure and time he needs to spend in the Ops room.

I didn't make another entry into my diary after 12 February. However, the following is what I remember about the 30 March.

30 March
Once Whiskey 1 had been hit by the IED and the Zap numbers came in it was clear who was injured. It took everything I had to maintain my composure, and send the information up to the Headquarters.

Dave Marsh was confirmed as dead very soon after the MERT landed at Bastion, but JT was still holding on.

For the rest of the day I wrote up the patrol report, it was later that evening that the Doc came in to the Ops room to make a call back to Bastion, during which he was told that JT had passed away. Once he told me – I left the Ops room, walked into the dark outside and wept for about 5 minutes – I couldn't believe he was gone.

I remained on watch that night to complete the patrol report, and at some point called the HQ to speak to the Padre, Stu Hallam, who was with JT when he died. After talking through what had happened I felt better that Stu had been with him, someone he knew and trusted.

A service was organised for a few days later, the CO, RSM and Padre came up to Kajaki to be there. I read JT's eulogy, which he'd written himself before we left the UK. The whole service was very fitting and moving for both Dave and JT. The last part of the service was a song played on one of the lads iPods entitled 'Hymn to the Fallen' and sung by Katherine Jenkins – apparently Dave had thought it was Hoofing. I think we all struggled to maintain dry eyes at that point!

Loosing JT and Dave so close to coming home was a bitter blow for the Company, but the lads picked themselves up and ensured that the handover to the Paras was conducted in typical bootneck style. In some ways the events of 30 March made us even more dedicated to ensure we passed every lesson we had learnt onto them. I think they appreciated that.

There is no doubt that the loss of JT and Dave changed my outlook on our tour completely. In my mind, there is nothing glamorous about conflict, although the adrenaline rush will sometimes confuse that. The 'glamour' and attractiveness of this job comes from the time spent with like-minded men, all striving to achieve the same goal, all pulling in the same direction, and placing ultimate trust in each other. Despite being in the profession of arms and understanding the risks we place ourselves under, I have never stopped asking myself, 'was it worth it'? We achieved our mission professionally, we didn't take any unnecessary risks and we left Kajaki in a better state than we had found it. But I would feel so much better about that 6 months if I were still able to share a beer with JT and Dave.

CHRIS FLETCHER'S DIARY

Monday 15th October 2007

'Winner' a 0100 wake up and it's freezing outside. Cold at night and boiling in the day. Our start is early due to the lack of air support we were supposed to have. Our windows are blacked out, partly because the sandbags stop the in-direct fire coming through our windows and any other spaces are covered to stop any light escaping. It helps us gain advantage by not being seen by the enemy. We're on the north side of a mountain where the peaks are our observation posts. Any light we do let out can be seen for miles.

We head out of the rear gate and as fire support group (FSG) we move first and leap frog forward while the gravs [slang for riflemen] follow. Due to the darkness and only driving with a night vision goggles one of the lads rolls a vehicle but he's ok and another gets the wheels caught in razor wire. Driving in the dark definitely takes practice.

We reach our fire support position shortly before first light. The lads get out and start mine sweeping their way up to the fire support position, our vehicle moves slowly to keep the lads protected and drives cautiously past the PPIEDs.

Once we reach our position Mikey P dismounts as well and sets up the Javelin and we all scan our arcs, looking for suspicious movement and hopefully positively identify the Taliban.

The intelligence we've been given suggests that the Taliban won't move around with weapons. Instead they leave them in trenches and previous firing points (one minute a farmer, the next minute Taliban).

The attack helicopter flies overhead for an hour searching and scanning, looking for the same as us before engaging targets in an area known as 'Big Top'. I've never seen anything like it and it's an awesome show of power.

The gravs are moving slow and cautious as they should. Rushing the compound clearances could lead to casualties.

Mikey P is still behind the Javelin and constantly scanning and searching the likely enemy positions and previous firing positions that were given to us on the handover by the Anglians. We were told on the handover that the vehicles act as bullet magnets so I'm glad we don't have them crested on the hill just yet.

We hear that the Taliban can see us and are waiting to be told to fire. This intel gets passed on to us and I can't help but feel nervous at the thought that we could well be in a contact at any moment.

We get the call that the gravs have cleared as far as they needed to today and start to head back but almost as soon as their backs are turned the Taliban open fire with a few RPGs to initiate the contact followed by some burst of AK-47.

The boss asks for the first vehicle to move up and Coops is top cover on the HMG, he immediately starts to fire at Big Top where the RPGs came from, his rounds needed little adjusting and he was on. The boss asked for our vehicle to move up (probably because I'd been dripping about not getting the chance to fire). I aimed at Big Top and fired a spotting round to make sure I was on, I didn't see my fall of shot first but Mikey P did and said it was on and he had PID'd at that location. Mikey locked onto the target [with a Javelin] and engaged, and it was a perfect hit on the Taliban and the compound they were in. I fired a second shot which again I didn't see but Mikey confirmed it was on target. We stay watching for movement and Bernie and Jim engage with GPMG from a bit further away and their rounds are really accurate. Wilf had a confirmed from 1,300m so FSG had a good day all round.

Once the gravs had moved past us we collapsed our position and made our way slowly back to the main road. We keep pace with gravs with our guns facing rear toward the enemy to cover us all as we move back in.

Saturday 19th October

Up on the peaks now, what an epic climb that was. It's almost vertical in some places and there are a few bits of rope in other parts but it was a man test getting up here. We have to carry our kit up for the week and plenty of warm clothes too, as it's even colder up here at night. The routine is ok up here, just sentry for 2 hours in the day and 2 at night. It's really basic though, with a solar shower, hand washing clothes and having a turd in a barrel. I think the smell of burning crap won't ever leave me.

The view is amazing though. I'm glad we've got these peaks here as observation posts.

It's good to be able to keep an eye on the sneaky bastards as they move from position to position. It's weird because a lot of the villages close-by are uninhabited and yet the only people that move near them are fighting age males. I can only guess what they're up to. You can see 60–70 buildings all connected in a big mud walled mass. But from up here you can see some of the trench systems that the Taliban have used previously. All I can think of is that I'm glad I don't have to walk around down there and I take my hat off to the lads that do.

It's boring up here on the peaks and time does go slowly but I get the feeling that after a few close contacts and towards the end of the tour the lads will want to be up here more and more as its relatively safe.

An OP went out in the late afternoon/early evening and the lads moved north. We've got a really good vantage point from up here and watching the lads through thermal they look like lemmings, all bright green from their body heat. A small contact did occur though and Daz got a Javelin on to an enemy target whilst I got 150 rounds off on the HMG and the other gun got 100+ rounds off too. A JDAM was brought in on top of an open compound with a few Taliban in it, I've never seen anything like that before.

Sunday 4th November

As usual a very slow and cold move out, this time it's an early start with us up at 2am moving by 3 and in position by 4, all under the cover of darkness. We know they can hear the vehicles but with the lights off they can't tell how many lads are on the ground or where exactly we are. It was freezing at our position and we had the 2 vehicles out of view with someone on the guns facing rear while we set up our position with Javelin and SF kit. Once we were sorted we took turns facing watching our arcs, me, Bungy, Steve and Dave Marsh were all spooning on a roll mat to keep warm. I couldn't help but look at the sky, no surrounding lights to blot out the stars. I never knew there were so many!

Bungy and I were on the SF gun I was the number 2, Dave was on the Javelin and was all set up ready to go. Our main area of concern was Risaji as there were always high numbers of Taliban infiltrating from the north. The sun came up but it was still a bit cold and then it started. 'Contact wait out' was called over the net, but we knew already as there were rounds going everywhere. The gravs had been ambushed and were getting shot at from loads of positions at the same time, but they were in some dead ground … and there were loads of trees and [we] had no idea where they were. We heard there had been 3 casualties from gunshot wounds. There were still loads of rounds being fired but not from us, even though we were getting overspill from the ongoing contact. Bernie fired a Javelin from the peaks into Risaji as he had PID'd 2 Taliban there. We were hanging out to fire and it seemed like forever until we could engage. We had spotted targets but because we were unsure of where the gravs were we couldn't engage but they managed to fire some flares so we knew where their furthest forward men were. I unlocked the pins on the SF and locked them off when Bungy had a target in his sights then he let rip. As he was firing I was preparing new boxes of ammo and oiling it to avoid stoppages. Every so often I changed the barrel and at one point it set my daysack alight as it was redders. Bernie engaged another target, this time near Pyramid Hill and once again his Javelin was a good hit. As the casualty extraction took place we upped the rate of fire and Dave had pinged a group of Taliban and locked on and fired the Javelin with a near perfect hit that wiped out a good few of them if not all of them. Bungy pinged a target near where we had been mortared from before and we changed targets and locked on to them, two Taliban PID'd on the corner of the building. After one or two bursts of GPMG Bungy dropped one of them [from] 3.2km away. As he slumped against the wall the other ran into dead ground chased by GPMG rounds and he never reappeared. Mortars started dropping all over Risaji which stopped the infil and exfil of the enemy. Bungy and I traversed across Khaka Keyel, Mazdurak, and Barikjo. This enabled covering fire for the casualty extraction.

Dave ended up on one of the other guns and I took over the SF from Bungy and he went on the Javelin, (as tankys we were all hanging out to fire the Javelin). Bungy found a but as he went to fire the missile misfired and nothing happened. He was threaders! Straight after that a 2,000lb bomb was dropped by the air support that had arrived, it landed just outside Risaji and was one of the most amazing things I'd seen. The Apaches were there too, in support of the Chinook that was there to casevac the lads. During the route back to the helicopter, an AE corporal, who was helping with the extraction, [was hit], so he too needed extracting to the HLS. The Apache started firing Hellfire missiles into enemy positions. After the casualties had left it started to calm down a bit with mortars providing smoke as cover.

We were last back into camp and an ammo state was given, 3 Javelins, 2,000 HMG rounds, 4,200 7.62mm from mine and Bungy's SF alone, 730 mortars, a 2,000lb bomb and few Hellfires. The lads doing ok though. They're back at Bastion and waiting to go back to the UK.

It's been a pretty quiet five or six weeks, no real major ops going on. A few weeks ago the other half of FSG had another good one on Essex Ridge, the gravs were clearing Mazdurak which had potential from the start but it didn't last long though. Someone stepped on an anti-personnel mine but only the first charge went off putting him on his arse; he was really lucky there. The lads got a lot of incoming on Essex Ridge funny old thing there were about five or six rocket propelled grenades fired and loads of small arms coming in from Risaji, Kaji, Khevalabad and Khaka Keyel. Unfortunately an RPG went into a compound [that] some lads from 8 Troop were in. OC 8 Troop got hit quite badly and we don't know how bad it is just yet... John Kersey also took some shrapnel to the face and an assault engineer had shrapnel to the legs and body but they were alive. I remember sitting on the peaks listening to everything on the radio thinking how helpless I felt and how much I wanted to be there to help.

Bungy was talking me on to Gasimor and Mercie with the HMG firing out between 3 and 5kms. The FSG lads were getting loads of accurate fire on Essex Ridge. So much so that they couldn't get into their vehicles. As we were high enough, we could put down some harassing fire to keep the Taliban's head down just enough for them to get some rounds back at them and extract.

After the change-over of the peaks we didn't do much on the ground so it wasn't much fun, but I'm back on the peaks again now and an early morning OP. Bungy and I get up for the OPs and sit in the Sangar with the HMG, radios, maps and optics. The other lads up here then only do one hour sentry as we have the other arc covered. It's quite surreal watching the lads patrol from up here. Sometimes you want to be on the patrol with them and sometimes you'd rather watch from a distance. The lads on the Op were cleaning up the M3 wadi which has loads of dead ground from the peaks; it's a good infil/exfil route for the Taliban as it has so much cover. At black spot 19 (which was where a mine strike occurred for the Anglians and cleared one week before by our EOD), the interpreter who was with the lads stepped on a mine on route to Khak-e-Jahnnam, the poor bloke was in a bad way with one leg missing, one hand missing, his body all over the place and some shrapnel through the chin. He was still alive, barely; he suffered a cardiac arrest and died on the extraction. After the area was secured, the gravs extracted back and that was the end of the patrol.

The southern Op that ensued was good. As usual Bungy and I were in the Sangar, but it was the south facing one which gets a bit warmer in mornings. It's good to sit there and watch before the lads go on the ground as you can see the movements of people change on the ground. We could see a few people moving around the area before the lads left the FOB. But as soon as they leave the atmospherics change too. It didn't take long for Bungy to PID at Big Top and he talked me on to the target ready to engage. Compound 261 got hit by a GMLRS. Once the gravs got close enough the Taliban opened up with a few rounds and Bungy told me to engage Big Top. He talked me on with small corrections until he was happy. I was shooting on single shot from the HMG at about 3kms, I couldn't see all of the rounds but Bungy had better optics and could see that they were landing in and around Big Top. We smashed Big Top with good accurate for ages. We were still smashing Big Top when the other half of FSG were in a gun line down south and they were hitting compounds 221 and 220 which are to the right of Big Top with 7.62mm. There was a bit of incoming for the FSG on the ground. As usual, shortly after the contact started, the gravs started to extract back with the FSG in vehicles giving them good close support while we were still watching in depth positions. Everyone back safe and sound.

Back on the ground again now and a slow start to the week, I've realised that weeks and days don't matter out here. We work when we work; there are no weekends or days off. It's full on and all the time. There are battle prep days, then ops and then re-servicing and cleaning weapons. We do get some time to ourselves but it's really full on!

The gravs were moving north this time and clearing Chinah which just looked like a maze of open top compounds with small buildings inside that all joined together. They cleared Chinah with no problems but Tucks from 8 Troop (lucky troop) stood on a mine which again didn't go off fully and the primary charge burnt his trouser leg. How do we get so lucky!

The lads start to clear Khevalabad and this was always going to be where the problems started.

We spread out on top of Shrine Hill as usual with the wagons on the rear side of the hill to minimise our profile on the feature. We have some good arcs on here across Baka Kheyal, Maka Kheyal, Mazdurak, and Khevalabad. We had two Javelins with us this time so Mikey P and Bungy set those up and sat behind them. They didn't have to wait long and had soon PID'd individual targets. They were given permission and fired at exactly the same time. As a tanky watching that, it was amazing; both missiles in flight at the same time and crashing down within seconds of each other. I managed to get a box of GMG off much to my own satisfaction.

Thursday 13th December

The gravs were moving towards Shomali Ghulbah to the west and slightly north to Baka Kheyal. We moved to Shrine Hill again and were there at very cold first light. Just as we were set up on Shrine and the gravs almost at BK our FSG vehicle was ordered to move as a 'TIC' or 'troops in contact' had been called. We could hear the rounds from the Taliban and they sounded like they were coming from a large machine gun. Bigger than their usual RPKs. We peeled round a cuffed route and Will Patten, the vehicle mechanic, was driving. We were going over some real tough terrain and the rear drive shaft had snapped. Luckily Will is a hoofing driver as well as AVM [armoured vehicle mechanic] and he managed to get us up onto a hill where we were told to act as a cut off to the enemy.

Bungy set up the Javelin and Will was on the SF gun, I was on the GMG and Jim was on the HMG of the other wagon.

There was a wadi to our front that I was putting bombs into it to cut off the enemy on their extraction. Our position was good but BK is on high ground so we can't really see into the compounds, and have to rely on the lads on the peaks. An RPG was fired at us from the front, and landed about 50m from our vehicle, I saw the smoke trail and started to fire and the other lads joined in shooting where bombs landed. The lads on the peaks saw 2 Taliban in an open compound about 1km from our vehicle, luckily the GMG lobs the bombs [in] rather a straight line to the target like a gun would. It took a few bombs but I got the range right and traversed the compound with the bombs... Occasionally I could make out movement in the compound so I was chasing them left and right for a bit. I could make out [a] small roof in the top right corner of the compound, I heard over the radio that the targets had gone there so I followed them up with a couple of bombs in the doorway and around the frame.

Dave Marsh told me later on that he was on the peaks and they were trying to get mortars on that position to which he replied, 'there's no need, Fletch is smashing the fuck out of it with the GMG.' I felt pretty good hearing him say that as I couldn't see exactly what I was shooting at, I was just going on what they could see from the peaks.

Bungy fired his third Javelin of the tour and Jim's HMG rounds were smashing a few targets and likely enemy positions with hoofing accuracy.

On our way back we had to do a dash of death in the wagons across an open road that the Taliban kept shooting down. It was a case of one, two, three floor it. We made it across but it wasn't a nice feeling.

The FSG bravo on Shrine took quite a bit of incoming ... it's the highest feature around so it makes you a real target. Luckily these Taliban aren't so good when it comes to accuracy.

A Harrier dropped a 2,000lb bomb on BK where the HMG position was and followed up with a few smaller rockets to make sure.

A few Javelins were fired and I had one box of GMG left after firing 450 bombs. No casualties, I think this was my favourite day yet.

Monday 17th December

There was another mine strike, this time a sergeant from our company. I can't believe how lucky we've been as a unit and a company; we've had 5 mine strikes here so far. The interpreter died and so did an army sergeant who was working alongside us. The three bootnecks that have stepped on the [mines] have only had tiny charges go off with no injuries sustained.

There's a lot of time to think of things while we're here, particularly when on sentry. I can't stop racking my brain [about] how the luck works. Who, if anyone, decides when, where and who dies? Is it fate? Do we make our own luck? Was it something that someone else said or did that stopped or prompted the other to take a fatal step or a life-saving step? It's definitely made me appreciate life more being out here when you're so close to slipping either side of the decision that can save or end your life. I had to write this down as it was driving me crazy.

Sunday 23rd December

It's a nice and cold 0330 departure from the FOB [and] we're man packing the SF guns and the Javelins but luckily Daz has got the quad bike and we've put a couple of missiles on that and a load of link for the guns so we take more to expend later. FSG Alpha with the boss are off to Dorset Ridge with 2 wagons and FSG Bravo, with Daz in charge, are off to 3 peaks to give cover for the gravs as they attempt to clear Khak-e-Jahnnam.

It's about 3km away at least and we're all carrying a lot of kit despite the quad being there. We finally reach 3 peaks and are set up and ready to go before first light. Wilf is on Nipple Hill with Quinny as a sniper pair.

There were loads of blokes in Khak-e-Jahnnam and Jim pinged me in particular on the crest of a hill next to tree about 800m away. It was just getting light and, as I was on the Javelin, I was using the thermal sights and looked to where Jim had mentioned. There were 3 Taliban crouched next to the tree all carrying weapons. It was the most blatant enemy I've seen all tour. They hadn't seen us but they did have eyes on the gravs. Daz asked the OC if we could fire but we were told to wait. One of the three ran off to the right down the hill and out of sight but two remained crouched next to the tree. Daz asked the OC again if we could fire and this time I got the go ahead to fire the Javelin. I activated [it] and waited for what seemed like ages. In a moment of over excitement I called out 'hang fire' as the symbol appeared through the CLU. This actually happens all the time but I'd forgot this time! I flipped through the sights a few times to make sure that what I was locking onto was the enemy. I got a final lock and pulled the trigger. The CLU dropped forward because the missile leaving meant there was no counter balance, I quickly pulled the CLU back and switched to day [sight] just in time to see one of the Taliban looking up at the missile as it came down and hit him vertically through the collar bone. He pretty much exploded on the spot and the other Taliban was nearby but didn't get the full force of it. Wilf made short work of him as he staggered to his feet with his weapon.

We started to get some real incoming from our half right which was pretty accurate. I loaded another missile, changed the battery and started scanning again. I could see where the other lads were firing and getting fired at from and could see 2 Taliban popping up and down on the roof of a compound. They would fire a few shots then get back into cover. I told Daz and he told me to fire so I activated the second missile and waited for the whistling noise to quite. It was still quite cold and they gave off good heat as they were close together so I managed to get them both in the same box to lock on to them as one heat source. I still checked through the sight pictures before pulling the trigger. It was a good hit but I didn't get to see as much of the carnage as before because as soon as I fired we were collapsing.

As the guns were getting packed up and we took as much stuff as we could down the hill to the quad the rounds were really starting to come in from the north-east. Bungy was firing his rifle and I joined him; we had a small trench that we were kneeling in and shooting from. Bungy made a magazine change, and as he did the rounds were really close, splashing in front of the trench. We were waiting for mortars to fire smoke bombs in front of us to cover our extraction but it was taking too long, so we all started throwing smoke grenades which had the desired effect. As we were leaving, the fast air that was covering us dropped a bomb on the bunker that was just to the left of our position on the hill, just in case any Taliban tried to fire at us from there on our way back in, or use it again against us. We all made our way back to the FOB and it felt a lot shorter on the way back. Probably because we were all buzzing from what had happened. I could tell we all wanted to relive it and spin dits but until we were back in the FOB everyone was still alert and awareness was high until we were safe.

Monday 24th December

Christmas Eve! Nothing really to celebrate here [although] the Sgt Major has tried to make it a Christmassy as possible which is a good thought. There's a sods opera and we're meeting in the galley later for that. Obviously it doesn't feel like Christmas Eve but we do what we can while we're out here. I think we're all just thankful it's been a good tour for us. I'm still on a high from yesterday but then I think about how easily they could get the upper hand on us. If it weren't for the professionalism of all the lads out here it wouldn't always be our way on the ground. Everyone stays focused and knows their own job, the work just flows naturally. No one needs checking on to make sure they're doing their jobs. It's a great company to be in.

Tuesday 25th December

There was a bit of an incident on the peaks last night, well on east there was. The lads were making wets in the galley before they went on sentry. They think that some of the embers might have got blown around when they had finished making it and were on sentry. The fire got pretty big and there's not much left of the galley by the sounds of it. It'll be interesting to hear the whole story!

A helo came in last and dropped off loads of parcels, I got about 6 and in one were some much needed thermals! Plenty of the usual stuff too, sweets, biscuits etc. Grandad sent me some tinned ham. Thank God it's cold otherwise it might have exploded in the heat. I think I'll take that with me on the next long patrol as a bit of morale [boost]!

The sods opera was ok last night, there was a bit of a quiz too. It didn't feel like Christmas until the parcels came but it felt a lot less like Afghan! There was a little bit of booze that some lads got sent out but it was pretty much just a sip.

Merry Christmas.

Friday 28th December

Quincy and Steve stayed up on the mountain as they were rebuilding the galley after the mishap the other night so me and Bungy stayed down for a few more patrols. We went out on an early hours patrol to the north this morning. 7 Troop cleared Mazdurak while 8 Troop cleared Mercie. FSG Alpha were on Essex Ridge and FSG Bravo were at Blue Pipe Compound. As usual it was freezing, I was glad when we got to Essex Ridge as we were digging trenches which was a great way to get warm. Me and Hodgey were digging our trench and setting up our SF gun position. Bungy and the boss were to our right, the boss was on the radio and Bungy was setting up the Javelin. The vehicles were reversed up just short of our position in case we had to make a quick getaway.

Royal Marine SA80 rifles hang on a wall above a Medical Section kit, ready to be grabbed in the event of an emergency. This is a typical scene across forward operating bases in Afghanistan.
(Photo Cpl Rupert Frere © Crown Copyright)

A Royal Marine from 40 Commando is pictured here, in 2010, using an L129A1 Sharpshooter rifle on operations in Afghanistan. His colleague is photographed with a GPMG. (Photo Cpl Barry Lloyd © Crown Copyright)

Empty cases from a general purpose machine gun litter the floor at a FOB in Afghanistan. (Photo Sgt Anthony Boocock © Crown Copyright)

Royal Marines from Fire Support Group, C Coy, 40 Commando, engage Taliban positions with a mortar and Javelin anti-tank weapon near Kajaki. (Photo AJ MacLeod © Crown Copyright)

A foot patrol of Marines from 40 Commando pass near Kajaki, Afghanistan, in 2010. (Photo Si Ethell © Crown Copyright)

A Medical Emergency Response Team (MERT) recovering a casualty from operations in Helmand Province in 2007. (Photo Sean Clee © Crown Copyright)

Troops carry a wounded comrade to a Blackhawk medivac helicopter following a sustained contact with Taliban fighters. (Photo Cpl Dan Bardsley © Crown Copyright)

A Royal Marine commando engages Taliban insurgents with an interim light anti-armour weapon, a rocket launcher designed to be operated by one soldier, in the town of Barikiu, Helmand. (Photo Sean Clee © Crown Copyright)

A plume of smoke rises into the evening Afghan sky as Allied air support brings an end to an operation. (Photo Sean Clee © Crown Copyright)

LEFT: The sign at the entrance to Camp Bastion, Helmand, the main headquarters for British Forces in Afghanistan. Within its perimeter are an airfield, offices and accommodation. (Photo Cpl Steve Blake © Crown Copyright)

RIGHT: The British forces outpost overlooking the Kajaki Dam, 2007. (Getty Images)

Signpost atop a British observation post near the Kajaki Dam. Home is a long way away. (Getty Images)

Afghan National Army soldier photographed over the Helmand River in Kajaki in 2007. The ANA, along with British Marines, patrolled the area near the dam. (Getty Images)

An Afghan National Army soldier (right) standing guard alongside a British soldier from the NATO-led International Security Assistance Force during a patrol of Musa Qala, December 2007. (Getty Images)

A British Army digger helps in the construction of a vehicle checkpoint on the outskirts of a town in Helmand Province, 2008. The use of HESCOs is clear to see. (Photo Sean Clee © Crown Copyright)

Taunton, July 2008: soldiers lower their heads during the homecoming parade for 40 Commando, Royal Marines. While the soldiers celebrated their homecoming, the three soldiers who died during their tour were also remembered. (Getty Images)

As usual once the sun came up and it was getting a bit warmer the gunfire started. 7 Troop were engaged with machine gun fire from the west of Mazdurak, 7 Troop smashed it with return fire. I think the whole troop was firing at the same time. It sounded hoofing.

I don't know if it was a bit of overspill from 7 Troops' contact or [if the] Taliban could see where we were – we couldn't see them – but we were getting some really accurate incoming. The rounds were hitting the front of the trench so me and Hodgey crouched down to avoid a bullet through the swede. I've not had rounds that close, I was flashing quite a bit out of frustration because we couldn't see where they were to fire back. Hodgey was just laughing at me though! We both felt really uneasy about the whole situation. When there was a lull in the rounds headed our way we'd pinged the direction they were coming from and locked the SF gun onto likely enemy positions and traversed those targets to give us some breathing space. Bungy had pinged 2 Taliban in Risaji and fired the Javelin and smashed them both on top attack. Mortars had been given grid [references] for their bombs and once they started we began to extract back. We extracted back to the FOB with no casualties and no real dramas.

Sunday 9th January 2008

Just came off the peaks to do a Gucci EOD patrol, the one they did north of Chinah saw the ANA mainly in a small contact which resulted in quite a funny and slightly cuffed fire and manoeuvre in ripple effect. Our patrol was to be a fairly quiet patrol with the boss' famous last words of 'we never get any incoming from Dorset Ridge'. We made our way up there which didn't take long and cleared the route and the area on top of the ridge with the metal detector. We had a sniper pair with us and the rest of FSG were to our east. I was stood in the vehicle on the GMG and Tel had the Javelin in with the boss and the sniper pair in a small trench they had dug. After about an hour and a half I asked Tel if he wanted to swap on the Javelin for a bit. It's quite a strain sitting there, scanning and searching with all the kit on for hours on end. Some lads swap every so often and some sit behind it for the whole patrol in the hope that they might get to fire. Most of the time though you'll sit behind it for an average of 5 hours and then pack up and extract back. But when you do get to fire it's an awesome feeling. Tel swapped with me after about 2 hours and took the missile off and changed the CLU to the surveillance head. I said he should leave the missile on just in case but he took it off anyway.

I was now sat in the trench between the boss and the sniper pair scanning and looking for movement and suspicious activity. The sniper team had some good optics with them and they pinged two blokes in a bunker that had a wall leading off to the right. The bunker had 2 holes in it and I could see the 2 people moving around in the bunker. I reported back to the boss that I could see the two moving around and he asked if I could get a lock on with the Javelin and I said yes I could. They were about 2.2km away and out of range of the snipers. Then as I watched them, I saw the picture go blurry in front of the trench. As I was telling the boss 'I think they're firing', we heard the shots. There was a delay from the distance so I saw the dust then heard the shots a few seconds after.

As quick as I could I took the CLU off the surveillance head and put the engagement head on. I did think about just firing from the seated position with no tripod but the heat source was small and I really needed it to be as still as possible so I didn't miss. As soon as I put the missile back on I had the seeker activated. The shots that were fired weren't aimed at us and as far as I knew they didn't know we were there yet. There was a fire-fight going on between the two in the bunker and the lads on the ground. The boss had already got clearance for me to fire and as soon as I got the lock on I fired. After firing previously at 800m the flight time for the missile seemed to take forever. I thought I'd missed it took so long but then finally it came down on top of the target. I asked the boss if it hit and he said it did. A signaller further forward with a sniper team confirmed that it hit and said it hit one of them in the chest.

It was a great feeling firing the Javelin. Not for taking life, but there was gun fire going in both directions. Once the missile hit, it was silent, [which] gave a brief respite to the lads on the ground and allowed them to begin extracting back. The gun fire did start up again as they were extracting but I like to think that the Javelin gave them a little breathing room to get out of there. A few stray rounds came our way and by this point I was back on the GMG waiting to extract.

One round came very close to the lads in the trenches and I saw it ricochet between them. We started to extract shortly after and made our way back to the FOB. Another good day.

Saturday 19th January

Another day another boring southern FLET patrol. The gravs are pushing down 'Talley Alley' as far as they can while some of them are moving direct down the 611. FSG are on Electric Hill and as always we have the peaks looking in depth to the places we can't see. Buck is out on this patrol and he's commanding our vehicle. Once we get to our position I dismount and set up the Javelin at the top of the hill with the vehicles behind me. As usual there are already people moving around Big Top. Then we get told to pack up and move to a new position slightly further down. It's a good position but a pain to get to. We found it on a recce a little while back but the routes are a pain. One goes direct off the 611 but between two compounds and past a graveyard which is all in dead ground. The other route is a bit more dangerous... The lads driving do a really good job getting round it. If they get it slightly wrong the vehicles could roll and at a weight of 4 tonnes plus ammo it could be deadly. We use the second route and our back end slides out a little as [we] drive along the contour. I was half out of the vehicle but we managed to keep it on track.

Once we got there we set up our positions again and I took up arcs towards Big Top with the Javelin. I was scanning for ages until I found a heat source in a trench about 50m in front of the trees at Big Top. It doesn't take a genius to work out why someone is in a trench in front of a known Taliban strong point when there are lads on the ground. I kept watching him and passed it up to Buck that there was one person ID'd in a trench. No sooner had I said that when another person joined the first. Buck told the OC that there were now 2 people in the trench at Big Top. Buck called to the top cover and asked him to use single shot on the HMG to see what their reaction would be. I watched the rounds ping in and around the trench. After the first round went over their heads the people inside dropped down in the trench and waited. After about 10 minutes they popped up again and stayed for a few seconds before ducking back into the trench. Each time they were up I told the top cover and he put a round in or near the trench and they would duck back down again. That sequence of events kept repeating for a few hours and then when the gravs started to extract a contact started with the rounds coming from Big Top. It instantly gets suppressed from 2 GPMGs, a GMG and an HMG. I could see the tracer going past as I looked through the CLU. The 2 that I had spotted in the trench earlier were still there and popping up and down much more franticly now and putting bursts of fire down towards the lads. I'd activated the seeker and Buck gave me clearance to fire. I finally got it though and fired as soon as I had it, and shortly after the missile went crashing down on top of the trench. Straight after firing I changed the battery and got a new missile and continued to search for new targets as the lads continued their extraction. Once they were a good distance past us we collapsed behind them and went at a walking pace in the vehicles giving rear protection all the way back to the FOB.

Monday 4th February

We set out at 0345 which gives us enough time to get down to our position before first light and as usual it's bloody freezing. Today we set out to push all the way to Big Top. Something we haven't done before and it has the potential to kick off from the start. The route we take is normal, as it's down south and we're in vehicles there is only one route we can take and it's straight down the 611. FSG move down to the newly named Thornton's Crest, which is the new fire support position. This time we went between the buildings in dead ground. The weather has been pretty wet the past few days and the hill was all churned up so only one vehicle got up the hill which was ours. The trials team were with us today and they bought with them the new 60mm mortar that is hopefully coming into service. The other vehicles were just back from us slightly and they dismounted the SF kit and set up some trenches at the top of the hill. The other half of FSG were behind us at another fire support position. Coops was on the CLU while Dave dug a trench. FSG Alpha moved back down the hill in our vehicles and set off south further down the 611 than we've ever gone in vehicles. We were looking for new fire support positions which we would need if we were to push down any further in the future. We got to another re-entrant on the left of the 611 which lead to some high ground. Then I dismounted from the vehicle and began mine clearing up the re-entrant wide enough for a vehicle. It was the worst clearing I'd done. We'd never been there before, and I could see that the sides were peppered with holes and blast marks from previous explosions and bits of metal scattered the ground making it even harder to clear. As I neared the top of the hill, rounds started going over head, so I kept low and kept moving. I was getting redders as well as I had my warm kit on. Mortars started firing too, so there were even more loud noises which made me feel even more uncomfortable. We finished our recce of the area quickly and moved back to Thornton's Crest to continue with fire support. On our way back an RPG hit the other side of a wall as we drove past it. It was so loud but we just kept driving back to our position. We got up the hill in one attempt and as we got there the SF guns were already firing. We started getting some accurate fire coming in at us and it was passing really close this time. I was on the GMG and as soon as the vehicle had stopped, I started firing. The [enemy] rounds stopped for a bit [so] we didn't have a firing point to lay on to. Then the rounds were coming in at us again and [were] just as accurate and hitting the ground around the vehicle, but we managed to get a rough direction and distance and started to put down some effective fire. I was stuck firing on my own, Dave was lying in the trench he'd finished digging and a good thing he was too – he told me after that he could feel the rounds going over his legs. Coops was laying in his trench behind the Javelin, Daz was behind the vehicle on the radio and Mikey P and Johno were laying down in their position. I put down a good amount of bombs in likely enemy positions in the directions the rounds were coming from. I kept firing and changing boxes until the SF guns had collapsed but by then the gun fire was dying down in our direction. We stayed a bit longer in our position until the gravs had moved passed us, then we collapsed on to the 611 and tailed the gravs covering them until we reached the FOB. 5 enemy RPGs fired that all air burst. Two Javelins were fired, one was from [the] west and Johno fired one from next to our vehicle. I managed to get 380 bombs off but all in all that was a honking patrol. The closest rounds so far and a horrendous bit of mine clearing. Didn't realise until after the contact that I had my ear defenders in during the contact, so the rounds I thought were close were actually even closer. Winner, not a nice day.

The following part of the diary is written from memory.

Sunday 30th March

The paras are starting to turn up now as it's nearly the end of our time here. We've been doing a couple of familiarisation patrols to get them used to our routes and tactics to help them in their handover. It's a Southern FLET patrol this time and we set off in the afternoon. We set up as usual and lead the gravs out. Our task is to provide fire support to the gravs so they can conduct the familiarisation to the paras. FSG Alpha are at the front and we caterpillar forward on our way to Thornton's Crest. As we move down closer using the only route available to us we reach our turning for Thornton's Crest. FSG Bravo are moving behind us and will be stopping short at a different fire support position. As we turn left off the 611 we pause and take out the metal detectors ready to mine clear our way up the hill to our position. I passed a metal detector to Bungy and made sure it was working and he took it and checked himself. Ray had the other metal detector and they set off side by side with a bit of space between them on the way through. The first part of our route off the 611 leads between two compounds that are about 13–15ft high, the gap is narrow enough just to get the vehicle through and I can touch both walls as we go past. After the buildings it opens out to the right and the wall continues to the left, the lads keep clearing and checking for enemy or anything strange. The boss asks me to turn around and make sure the vehicle behind us was close. As I did so, it went black. I woke up on the floor near the vehicle. I was dazed and asking for a rifle, I found one then stumbled over to where Mikey P was already starting CPR on Dave. I tried to help and started checking for secondary injuries as his legs looked quite cut up. A stretcher came and we put him on it and rushed back to the ambulance. At this point the Sgt Major grabbed me and told me to sit down. The realisation of what happened started to hit and I broke down in tears. As we were bringing Dave [to the ambulance], Bungy had found the boss on the other side of the wall and was working hard getting tourniquets on him and bringing him back to the ambulance. I watched as the ambulance left and the lads who were directly involved in the blast were taken back to the FOB. We stood in silence as we moved back there, I don't think anyone could really understand what had happened. We were all checked out by the medical staff when were at the FOB to check for any injuries sustained in the blast. I was knocked unconscious by the bar that went between the boss and Dave, it struck my helmet as I was thrown from the vehicle, Ray was hit by the bonnet of the vehicle and also knocked unconscious.

When everyone was back at the FOB, the OC got everyone together and told us that Dave had died. Even though I knew he was dead, it didn't become real until I'd heard it. I went straight to my room and cried. I knew something like this could happen out here but I didn't think it would. Wilf came in and sat with me. I think he knew that nothing he could say wouldn't help, so he didn't say much. I went outside where the other lads were sat. The gravs and anyone else who had little bits of booze saved for end of tour gave theirs to us as troop. Then it happened again. We knew the boss was alive when he left us and, as we sat around the table where both men used to share a pipe, we found out that the boss, our friend died at Camp Bastion. This broke the whole troop again.

No one really slept that night. We stayed up and spun dits and funny stories about the two friends we'd just lost. No one really knew how to act about the situation and the next day. I remember people's eyes on me, knowing what had happened to me but not understanding how they should feel or what they should say.

Time is a great healer, but no amount of time will ever make me forget the memories of the two legends, Spartans and friends that we lost that day. My heart goes out to those who knew them, those who loved them and those that were ever lucky enough to have met them. I think about them every day and will continue to do so forever.

A parallel translation of the favoured John 15:13.
'Greater love has no one than this, that someone lay down his life for his friends.'

REVEREND STUART HALLAM'S MEMORIES OF JOHN

Wednesday 12 March 2008

I spent the last few days up in the far north of the AO at Kajaki. This is the home of Charlie Company and one of the most strategic of bases guarding the hydroelectric plant at the head of Kajaki Lake. This is such a beautiful place – most of Afghanistan is beautiful as are its people – but this is a special place as it stands in the foothills of the Hindu Cush (the first mountains of the Himalayas) to the north and the desert plains of Helmand Province to the south. The base had been a royal palace at one time and then, after the Russian invasion, one of their bases.

The day before I had spent with the Doc on patrol, which had been great and thankfully, uneventful. Today I was going to visit the lads high in the hills above the base with their OC Lt John Thornton or JT for short.

JT is a brilliant young officer just 22 but full of potential and genuinely loved by his lads. Although only 22 he comes across as someone much older – he is very mature and wise beyond his years and I like him very much.

We would be leaving the camp by the back gate and then climbing the notorious 'Goat Trail' which leads up to the top of the hills where a troop of lads lives for a week at a time in the most austere of conditions. From there, they had overwatch of the whole area.

This was the only place in Afghanistan where you could genuinely say that you were going for a walk without having to take a whole troop of Marines with you, as it was deemed safe enough because of the hill positions above. Even so, it felt a little strange as JT and I left the base and headed out along the road south in full view of the Taliban positions just a couple of kilometres to the west.

The Goat Trail is aptly named as only a goat would be stupid enough to use it. Basically, the track heads straight up the mountain through a minefield (a legacy of the Russians' time here) and with two stones of body armour and helmet on, by the time we reached the top the both of us were 'hanging out' and in need of a 'wet'. JT remarks as we get to the summit, 'Parish visiting is a little different for you, eh Bish?' How right he is!

We spent the next few hours with the guys who were in great form, the Afghan winter was over by now, a couple of weeks before and the temperature would have been about minus 15 up here, but now it is warm and sunny and the lads were spending all their down time 'panic tanning', ready for coming home.

There is a track which runs from one side of the mountain to the other, and as we walked JT spoke to me of his faith and about what he believed in. It was clear that his faith was very deeply rooted and informed everything that he did. We felt like kindred spirits as we eventually wandered back down the hill and back to the base.

That night, JT and I smoked our pipes as we looked out over a beautifully clear Afghan night and talked utter rubbish to each other – laughing all the way.

Sunday 30 March 2008 Camp Bastion
RIP JT and Dave

Sunday started off pretty normally. Dave, an Army chaplain colleague of mine, and I took the main service, me leading and Dave preaching on the theme of Thomas. It went well. Dave preached very well and there were a good number there. Afterwards, there was the usual banter, me and Mick went out for a fag and chattered about how determined he was to become an Anglican priest, something he felt very strongly called to. We had all gone to lunch and then I came back down to the accommodation and was chilling with the guys in the tent when Matt came in and said that there were two seriously injured coming in from Kajaki. I asked if they were ours and he replied 'yes'.

Immediately, I left to go to the hospital and waited. The Adj turned up with more information and it didn't sound good – there had been a mine strike and the guys were in a bad way – no names by this stage. The CO called and asked me to stay at the hospital and keep him informed. WO2 Gaz Langworthy also turned up as did a number of lads from Charlie Company – Charlie, Tiny and Stretch.

The medical team's helo turned up and I was told that both were in cardiac arrest. As the first ambulance drove up, they carried the first stretcher out – the medics were doing CPR. I could see that it was Dave Marsh – Dave and I were in the same troop during commando training (838 troop). Dave was already dead.

Soon afterward, the second ambulance drew up and again the medics were giving CPR – my heart sank as I saw that it was JT. I couldn't believe it, I had only been talking to him a few weeks before on my last trip to Kajaki.

They rushed him straight into theatre and started working on him – what they call 'aggressive massage'.

Dave was taken straight into one of the trauma bays, but there was nothing they could do. He had probably died straight away but they had continued to work on him out of a sense of utter despair. They pronounced him dead a few minutes later.

The lads were still outside. They had seen JT and Dave come in so I had made the decision to keep them there, rather than let them go back to the accommodation to be interrogated by the rest of the lads – with the risk of OP *Minimize* being compromised.

I came out to them and informed them of Dave's death. Tiny took it the worst, but they all took it badly. So late in the tour, [with] so few days to do (Charlie Company would be going home in less than 2 weeks' time).

I went back in and watched as the trauma team busied themselves on JT. I could see that he was clearly in a bad way. Both legs were in a mess and his hips had been blown open by the blast. Yet despite his horrific injuries, JT was still alive and had been conscious and chatting to the lads on the ground up until they put him on the helicopter.

I gave last rites to Dave and then stood outside the operating theatre and prayed for JT. Adam, the trauma consultant who was working on him, called me in. 'Do you know him, Padre?' 'Yes', I replied, 'very well, he's one of mine and a friend'. 'Then can you come in and hold his head – talk to him ... please, it may help.' I did what he asked without hesitation. I talked and prayed simultaneously.

For two hours, JT battled for life, the hardest battle he had ever fought, but this battle was one where the overwhelming odds were against him. He didn't really have a chance. Eventually, Adam turned to me and said, 'There is nothing more we can do, it's over to you, Stu.'

I thanked the team for all that they had done and prayed for them and then gave last rites to JT. The operating theatre was awash with his blood but JT just lay there looking utterly peaceful – he was in a better place – certainly a better one then the rest of us...

I remembered that the lads were still waiting outside for news – but I was in bits, so before I went to see them I found a quiet room and wept...

Then I went outside and told them that JT was dead.

LIEUTENANT IAN THORNTON – DIARY OF OPERATION *HERRICK 15*

C Company, 1st Battalion, The Princess of Wales's Royal Regiment, left for Afghanistan on Operation *Herrick 15* on 11 September 2011 – the 10th anniversary of the 9/11 terrorist attacks. I had been a fully trained infantry platoon commander for just 3 weeks. After conducting an RSOI package at JOB [joint operating base] Bastion, I began a diary on the day that we deployed forward to the Nad-e-Ali district, some eight days after arriving in Helmand. The first half of our tour was spent maintaining security and building relationships in an area that was just about ready for transition to Afghan National Security Forces (ANSF) control. Just after Christmas we moved to the Nahr-e-Saraj (North) district, an area of operations still heavily contested by the Taliban. During six months in Helmand, the Company conducted over 500 patrols and was required to engage the insurgents with every weapon system at its disposal. We succeeded in supporting the transfer of a number of checkpoints to the ANSF, as well as the construction of seven new ANSF checkpoints and the establishment of an Afghan Local Police force to help secure the farming communities to the north-east of Gereshk. The last entry in my diary is on 25 March 2012, the day we left Afghanistan. After a brief period of 'decompression' in Cyprus, and two days of 'normalisation' at our barracks in Paderborn, Germany, I flew home to the UK on 30 March 2012 – the fourth anniversary of the day my brother, John, was killed in action in Helmand.

20th September 2011

I woke at around 0730 and went for some breakfast before spending a bit of time on the Internet. Then it was back to the tent to finish my packing before the transport picked up those flying out on the first lift to Nad-e-Ali. We reached the heliport ('Little Heathrow') checked in and then waited for the two Chinooks to arrive. Once they rolled up we lifted all our kit aboard and with body armour, helmet, eye protection and gloves all donned, we strapped ourselves in and waited. The nerves began to build as I suddenly thought back to the Chinook that was shot down a few weeks ago with the loss of many lives and thought about just how a big high value target we presented. However, due to a problem with the engine we never got off the ground and we had to unload the helo, which was apparently unserviceable [u/s]. With a major Op going on in the Upper Gereshk Valley, a further Chinook going u/s this morning, and a further two being shot yesterday, we would have to wait for the one remaining Chinook to lift their passengers to Nad-e-Ali under escort, before coming back for us. This then turned into being told to report five hours later for a 1900 flight as it had been re-tasked for a repatriation flight and also to lift some Marines of 42 Cdo to Bastion for the vigil service for the Marine killed in Nahr-e-Saraj yesterday. When [we came] back at 1900 our one Chinook had turned into two Merlins and, yet again, one of them had engine trouble and failed to get off the ground. With a steadily building backlog we eventually took off at 2240, with the remainder flying at 0010. The flight brought home the sheer scale of Bastion, which literally looked the size of a city from the sky. Fifteen minutes or so later we popped chaff as we slowed to descend into PB [patrol base] Samsor. The helicopter felt incredibly vulnerable at this point and I was literally braced for an RPG or small arms fire to wing its way towards us! Once on the ground we were briefed on the current threat level (low) and the situation on the ground (pretty benign). At least I can sleep without fear of a night time mortar surprise. I moved into a tent with the O/C, 2IC, Int Officer, ANA Advisor and the outgoing OC from 45 Cdo, and it is now 0200 and time for some head down. I have been given no timings for the morning other than 1100 for brunch. With both the OCs out for a shura at 0700 that I'm not required for, I think I will treat myself to a lie in before finding out whatever it is I'm meant to do tomorrow. Hopefully getting out on the ground. Goodnight.

21st September

Last night it was freezing! Massively regretted leaving my winter sleeping bag back at Bastion to be brought forward on a CLP [Combat Logistic Patrol] in a month's time. Had a pretty bad night's sleep what with the cold and all the thoughts of getting out on the ground whirling around in my head. Got up around 0745 and after a wash and a shave headed for the Ops room. Spent a bit of time familiarising myself with what goes on in there and then met up with Sgt Pitman from 45 Cdo, who is currently commanding the patrols multiple in Samsor and thus who I will be taking over from. Cpl 'Coops' Cooper (my 2IC) had already gone out with the Mastiff [an armoured fighting vehicle used for protected patrols] group as a top cover gunner, so I spent a great deal of time with 'Slim' Pitman discussing the local AO, how his blokes had covered the ground and the composition of his patrols and equipment carried. The AO sounds really quiet at the mo, with hardly any IED finds or small arms shoots in the last six months. Bad for those who want a scrap or two (me included), but good for those who want to come home in one piece (me included also!). Anyway with no patrols out this afternoon I squared all my kit away for a 0700 patrol down to the ANCOP [Afghan National Civil Order Police] PB at West Gate – which the insurgents have hit a few times. We shall see how that pans out. Coops came back to say that, despite having stones thrown at him as they drove past some locals, the locals seemed pretty onside and it was so busy everywhere that they could move about pretty freely without fear of IEDs. Apparently the biggest danger here is DFCs – essentially homemade claymore mines set to the side of the road and filled with nuts, bolts and ball bearings. Sweet. My kit is now prepped and after adding two extra tourniquets to my shoulder pockets that are prepped for one handed use even in the case of missing fingers, I tucked a photo and copy of John's last letter to me inside my body armour and will now get seven hours in before getting up for my first patrol on *Herrick 15*.

22nd September

I managed to go to bed with a t-shirt on last night and so remained marginally warmer than the night before. Got up for a shave and as I didn't fancy eating much just smashed down a cereal bar out of a ration box. I then double checked all my kit, put it all on and then went out to meet Cpl Cooper, Sgt Pitman and the Marine lads by the front gate. We patrolled out using a tarmacked road and then a prominent track before jumping across an irrigation ditch and cutting through some fields. The locals were generally pretty friendly, especially the kids who all wanted to shake hands, high five and of course ask for chocolate or pens – to no avail. Coops had a pen stolen from his admin pouch whilst taking a knee! [Kneeling down on one knee to adopt a lower profile and a more stable fire position – we do this every time we go static to make ourselves a smaller target.] After being stopped by some farmer who claimed an ISAF [International Security Assistance Force (NATO troops)] patrol had damaged his cotton field we met some others who threatened to start growing poppy if they could not get water to their fields (poppies don't need much water). These issues will all get passed up the chain. We reached West Gate and spent 10 minutes or so inside the ANCOP checkpoint. I met the commander and then we left to head back to the PB. Patrol 1 done with not so much as a sniff of the enemy – though you can bet they had eyes on us the whole way.

After the patrol I received my radio, GPS and best of all – my pistol. Hopefully I'll never use it as that will mean things really have gone tits up. Had a bit of time to kill after lunch and so did a 30 minute run on the treadmill – which less than 2 hours before a second patrol was probably a mistake! Anyway I then nailed dioralyte [rehydration salts] just to be on the safe side as going man down with dehydration on only my second patrol would make me look like a bit of a fool! At 1600 we left again, this time with an 8-man ANA call-sign in the lead – who looked genius, particularly the guy carrying an RPG launcher with a load of warheads sticking out of the top of his daysack! A quick patrol to the main local population centre took us to the central ANCOP checkpoint. Where the ANA put in a VCP [vehicle checkpoint] on the junction, we went inside so I could meet the commander and get a bit of a brief on the village. We took chai with the main man plus a few of his random lads and they passed us some pretty vague int [intelligence] about a possible DFC device kicking around. They seem pretty onside anyway so I will make sure I make the effort to pop in every now and again. It was soon prayer time so we had to take the ANA back to Samsor. There was a bit of excitement that evening as Sgt Ferguson's lads in PB Silab PID'd some insurgents digging in an IED on route Somerset. As I watched the live UAV feed of the dicks in action and listened in on the Ops Room radio net, the Americans had an Apache on call which fired 2 Hellfire missiles. Unfortunately they must have heard the launch as they Usain Bolted it across some fields just in time to escape with their lives and hastily blended in with some other local nationals, it became impossible to ID them and thus they will live to fight another day. Thankfully one of the Hellfires took the IED out, so there is one less for us to worry about. The blokes all arrived today and seemed genuinely happy to see me, which is nice. Tomorrow I'm taking them out on their first patrol and, to be honest, they seem pretty nervous. Hopefully all will be fine and that will give them confidence to push forward. Had a mega parcel from Vic today plus an e-bluey from Mum – very good for morale. Anyway I'm hanging out so will speak tomorrow.

23rd September

I jumped on a 3 x Jackal vehicle move to FOB Shawqat this morning. Uneventful ride there but I still enjoyed manning the GPMG from the commander's seat. On arrival at Shawqat Slim showed me all the relevant points of interest, then we had a quality brunch and I bought a crate of 7 Up for the lads before we headed back to Samsor. On my return I squared some admin before giving the boys their first set of patrol orders of the tour. As it was the first patrol they were pretty detailed (especially the 'Actions On'), but as the tour progresses they will inevitably become much briefer. After orders I found the time to reply to my first two e-blueys (from Amber and Ben Fowler), and then got kitted up for the patrol. Apprehension in the lads was evident, so I tried to act as laid back and relaxed as possible before stepping off – despite my own concerns about commanding a patrol on the ground for the first time. All was fine and a short 50-minute patrol in the immediate vicinity of the PB gave the lads a chance to make sure their kit fitted correctly and to get used to the weight we were carrying out here. All seemed fine, except one of the lads struggled with the GPMG and had to swap weapons with the ever-impressive LCpl Arran Twyford (fair one – the GPMG is a pain in the ass!). The patrol passed without a hitch and after coming back in I gave the lads a quick debrief before dinner. After dinner I managed to speak to Vic ... she seems to have acquired a cat – and used the word 'caught' to describe how. Only in Sierra Leone – TIA I suppose. After the evening brief I gave orders for the morning's patrol down to into Kushal Kalay, which was meant to be ANA led, but as they have been re-tasked as QRF for an Op by their Kandak (battalion), we will be on our own. I then spoke to Fergie – his PB sounds emotional. Minimal manpower, a massive PB and attempts to break through their perimeter at night means he has requested claymore mines. His call-sign will provide support to us on both patrols tomorrow. Anyway after unpacking fully and getting all set up in my little 'pod', I am off to sleep to awake at 0600. Rubbish.

24th September

Got up for a 0700 patrol in and around Kushal Kalay. The second patrol with the lads, and as such meant that over the 2 patrols I have now got all the lads out on the ground. Finch again did a sterling job as point man and we also altered our plan to meet the other half of my platoon (Sgt Ferguson's multiple) at an ANCOP checkpoint at West Gate. It was good to have a mini reunion with the boys. They're pretty threaders as at PB Silab, they are pretty undermanned and are thus being smashed with guard duty. They also had a couple of attempts at breaching their compound perimeter razor wire. Not cool. Anyway, on their way back, Fergie's boys picked up on some dodgy atmospherics and possible ground sign indicating an IED. This led to our 1700 patrol coming forward to 1500 so that we could provide flank protection as they head back to clear the route. This set off a pretty farcical chain of events, more of which later. I delivered orders, wrote a letter to mum and even managed to watch episode 9 of *The Pacific* – a happily productive interlude. As we were about to step off it emerged that Fergie's multiple were without an essential bit of kit for their route clearance and thus the patrol was then tasked to gauge atmospherics and observe vehicle movement to see if the route was safe. Which it was.

25th September

Another 0700–0900 patrol to start the day, this time with the ANA. The ANA decided to put in a VCP while we went firm [going static in your current location] (which lasted 25 minutes before they sorted it). The patrol we then went out on was pretty dull, except for being able to chat to the local Mirab (who controls the water supply), who was very pro-ISAF and thankful for our help providing security in Nad-e-Ali. On return I spoke to Mum to wish her a happy birthday. I think she was relieved to hear we are in a pretty quiet area. I suppose this is indicative of the success we are having out here, but it still makes me a little threaders as I am mega keen (probably naively so) for the opportunity to give the Taliban a kicking.

Back out on another ANA led patrol from Adam Khan at 1500. I, very annoyingly, stepped on a bank which gave way and sent me plunging into an irrigation ditch that was probably full of human shit. At least I've had my Hep B vaccination ... oh wait, I haven't. At least the boys found it highly amusing.

Back in for a shower, dinner, meeting, briefing to the lads about tomorrow, watching the final episode of *The Pacific*, cleaning my weapon, eating Doritos and getting my head down – in that order. Having my first patrol off tomorrow morning. Coops is more than capable of leading it, but I still feel I should be there. To be fair I am hanging out after being the only man in the PB to have been on every foot patrol, so will probably be of more use to my blokes rested. I certainly am looking forward to a few hours' sleep! Still ... will be gutted if they have their first contact without me on the ground.

26th September
A bit of a lie in until 0730 and then the boys went out on patrol at 0900. Hated not being on it, but I think the rest did me well. Thankfully it went swimmingly and they were back in by 1030. Had a letter from Nan and Grandad today which was nice. After lunch I briefed the lads on the afternoon's patrol and then pretty much chilled out while squaring my admin away. We left at 1500 – 5 minutes after being told that the patrol we had planned was to change and we were again to move north to Adam Khan for a joint patrol with the ANA. When we got to the ANA checkpoint they were far from being ready to roll. A good start! Eventually we patrolled through some fields and then towards some compounds which the ANA searched, finding nothing. We patrolled the ANA back to their CP [checkpoint] and then back into Samsor for dinner and then orders for a Company Op tomorrow. The Op is basically a patrol surge into an area where 2 PBs have recently been closed and thus an area where the TB could potentially re-emerge. 'Careful what you wish for' as the saying goes, but I think we could do with a contact or 2 to keep us on our toes, so we will see how it goes. We're out for 2 nights. So I will write again on Thursday (29th). Adios.

29th September
Well we're now back to Samsor after Op *Tora Bach 38*. A pretty grandiose term really for what was essentially 4 patrols in a slightly different area. Early on Tuesday (27th) morning we got a Mastiff move to CP [checkpoint] Azadi. I hate being cooped up in those things and was practically waiting for the IED blast that would send us crashing into the large (and deep) canal we were driving down towards Azadi. Thankfully that didn't happen and by 0830 we were out on patrol. The OC's TAC party tagged along with my multiple. Mega. Having your boss one place behind you in the order of march

whilst trying to command your blokes is not ideal! Anyway the patrol went well and the OC was given a lot of opportunity to engage with local elders, which is what he was after. Back in for lunch and then out again at 1430. This one was redders! Same stretch as before but slightly shorter in distance. The locals here seem massively 'on side', perhaps even more so than around Samsor. We got back to Azadi to hear that Lt Grant Reynold's multiple down at Dilawar had been involved in a contact. At 0800 (28th) we left Azadi to head east. 3 horrific hours later (we were carrying an emotional amount of kit, rations, water and ammunition for an overnight stay) we reached a compound, my multiple and Cpl Rain's multiple put in a cordon, and the ANA and Company HQ moved in to effectively evict the owner for the night for a fee of around $40 USD. We then moved in and I had my blokes filling sand bags and setting up sentry positions on the roof. It felt pretty weird to be moving into someone's home, and [I] couldn't help to feel a little bit guilty for such a massive disruption to someone just wanting to get on with their life in peace (truth is, the money probably went down extremely well!). At 1430 we went out with the quad bike to pick up a water re-supply from the Mastiff group and at the same time to drop the ANA off. After a fuck around with the vehicle call-sign we eventually saw the ANA off and returned to the compound with a trailer full of much needed water. A show of force by an F-18 at nightfall meant the TB didn't try it on for the night, and, after an outrageously uncomfortable sleep in a tiny little room that we crammed all 8 of my multiple into, we got up at 0300 (29th) and left for Azadi at 0400. Patrolling in the pitch black with a quad bike in tow meant using prominent tracks to avoid inadvertently stacking the thing in a surprise irrigation ditch. This obviously increased the IED risk, and with the dark meaning it was more difficult to look for ground sign everyone was pretty nervous. An uncool situation. On reaching Azadi we had a couple of hours sleep and then got taken back to Samsor in another hideous Mastiff move.

Back at Samsor we were effectively given the rest of the day off, which has been hoofing. Had letters from Cai, Scott, Dad, Lorraine (from A-Plan), Jimmy Gilbert and 2 parcels from Mum and Dad. Morale!! Replied to all of those, read my book for a while, washed some clothes and chewed the fat with Dickie Laybourne (a TA Officer who is a BA pilot in civvy street) and Billy Russell, the new ANA advisor. The lads seem happy too, so I'm happy. No patrol until 1600 tomorrow and a traditional Friday lie in with the morning meeting not taking place until 1100. I'll certainly sleep well tonight!

30th September

Correction – morning meeting not taking place until 1200, consequently I slept until 1110, which was epic (however I awoke freezing cold on several occasions – roll on the CLP which will bring with it our winter sleeping bags!). After waking I rolled straight into brunch, had a wash and collected an e-bluey from Graham, a book from Mum and a parcel from Cai. More excellent morale. Meeting at 1200 I was still half asleep for but picked up a few good points I can pass onto the lads. Gave orders at 1400 and then spent an hour or so replying to letters, pissing around doing nothing and listening to some pre-patrol music on the laptop. Out at 1600 and only got as far as Folad Se when we heard 34A had been unable to leave Silab. We consequently went firm in the ANCOP station and had a pretty successful discussion with the commander down there. Over some chai I managed to get him to agree to coming on some joint patrols with us, which will be very helpful as ANCOP are very popular with the locals. I then introduced him to all the boys and he offered them all some chai, which was really good of him and which the boys enjoyed. On the way back the atmospherics had changed and we began to feel pretty unwelcome. Very odd. The Mastiff group experienced this too on their travels today. I sense something afoot. Well they're entitled to try it on anytime they like, and it will certainly be the last mistake they ever make ('they' being the Taliban of course). Grabbed a shower when back at camp and then had a pretty gopping dinner that was advertised as 'pasta bake' but seemed to contain mashed potato instead of pasta. Bizarre. Tomorrow will be one longer patrol in conjunction with Fergie's half of my platoon, which should be good. We're heading down to an area that they use to transit from the USMC AO to ours. Hopefully we can entice them into a little scrap. Bombed up an extra couple of mags to put in my daysack just in case. Now to reply to a bluey or two (probably just one as it is now 2233), read a bit more of my book, and then get my fat schwad down.

1st October

A pretty dull day (can't believe it's October already though!) and certainly not a sniff of a contact – more of which later. Got up at 7 and shaved and then smashed down some brekkie – spam is really beginning to get to me and the sausages too are gopping. Morning meeting at 0830, again of which I can tell you little as I was half asleep (hopefully not noticeably!). Watched TV for a bit (*Celebrity Juice* – mega funny), got on the Internet which then swiftly crashed, and then hit the gym. The first weights session I've done in some time was pretty shocking by my old standards, but I will get back on it and back to where I was pre-Brecon (where there is zero time for Op *Massive*!). The aforementioned patrol at 1400 never happened. We then got tasked to conduct a 5 HOUR VCP outside the front gate. As local civilian traffic was for some reason minimal, I went to see the 2IC in the Ops room and luckily managed to get him to agree to cutting it short. Dinner tonight was pretty hideous (macaroni cheese with no cheese). Had the evening brief about the route security we're providing for the belated CLP, and for the company search/route clearance Op a few days after tomorrow. Then I briefed the blokes and spent some time chatting to Pte Ben Charles whilst waiting for the phone (which I sacked due to the obscenely long queue). Anyway I'm off to try the phone again and if all else fails get my head down as we step off at 0700 tomorrow.

2nd October

Up later than I intended and subsequently had to rush to be kitted up as QRF for the move from Silab of Fergie's multiple (for 0630). As it happens they ended up getting a vehicle move, so we weren't required (wish we'd have been told that last night!). Set off at 0700 with the ANA to patrol up to Adam Khan. There we stopped for half an hour or so and then headed back into Samsor for 0900. The rotation of patrolling call-signs worked in our favour, and by the time the CLP had arrived, unloaded and moved off, it was still prior to our next time out and so we stood down for the day. Sweet. I spoke to Mum and Dad which was awesome as it's been a while, wrote my orders for tomorrow's Op and then hit the gym for an enjoyable (if highly dehydrating) run of around 6.5km. Dinner was roast chicken which made a nice change and then I managed to deliver my orders to the boys in between evening meal and the 1900 meeting – which freed crucial time later to watch Spurs v Arsenal! I cut down a pretty complex concept of operations for the company to a pretty bare bones delivery, which I think left the lads pretty happy with what will be asked of them over the next few days. Essentially, a cordon and search Op tomorrow, followed by a route clearance the day after. Should be fairly straightforward. Will Terry Taliban show his face? Probably not, although if the target compound is indeed a weapons cache location he's likely to be pretty pissed. As we form the cordon, we may feel the brunt of his anger. Again, probably nothing will happen, but if it does I know we're ready for it. Anyway, will probably be operating out of Silab for the next two nights, so will write again most likely on Wednesday. Oh… Spurs won 2–1! Great goals from VDV and Kyle Walker. Great result and won a bet with Pte Charles of a crate of Mountain Dew from the little Afghan shop. Probably shouldn't be betting with my soldiers, but I like sugary carbonated soft drinks, so fuck it! Plus I shared it with the boys and so feel no shame. Laters.

3rd October

Didn't expect to be back at Samsor tonight, but thanks to a slice of luck we got the whole Op cracked in one day. Bonus. We got a vehicle move to Silab in the morning and got a bit of time to chat to Fergie and the boys over there which was cool. We patrolled down in the beating sun until reaching Compound 20, where I recommended we put in an Incident Control Point, put out security for this, and nominated an emergency HLS. The search team then pushed through us to clear and search 2 suspect compounds. Anyway we sat for a fair few hours in the sun providing an outer cordon as the search went on – finding nothing. Although the route clearance of Somerset was meant to take place tomorrow, by chance a US Linebacker call-sign had cleared their side of the canal this morning. This meant we could use a bridge to get over to their side, and get resupply vehicles to Dilawar that way, rather than risk the high assurance (+ high risk) search we had planned on our side. After overwatching the route for a number of hours the resupply was complete and we returned to Silab after 8 hours on the ground. Turbo dehydrated. Back to Samsor by vehicle, roast beef for dinner and then the evening meeting. Had 3 quality parcels today from Sue and Dave, Ed Rogers and Luke and Amber. My friends are awesome and I feel pretty humbled at the effort they are making to square my morale away. Do I deserve it? Probably not. I will make time to write to thank all of them. Anyway as you can see from my handwriting, I'm fucked. Sleep time awaits – cold weather sleeping bag is here now. Essence.

4th October

We went on a local area patrol in the morning with range of our Sangers. Pretty uneventful as we wove our way down to the centre of Kushal Kalay and back. I stopped to talk to a shopkeeper and found out that the local school is currently missing a large number of its teachers – probably due to intimidation. Back at Samsor for around 0945 and so hit the gym for a short weights session. Roast beef baguettes for lunch (the chef has certainly responded well to the complaints!). At the evening meeting the CSM had a moan about the blokes being dressed incorrectly and, as rules are rules, I will ensure they are enforced. Briefed the lads on tomorrow, went on the ridiculously slow Internet, and now getting my head down.

5th October

Cpl Cooper took the patrol out this morning. I did some weights in the gym, briefed the lads on the afternoon patrol at 1200 and then had lunch (cheeseburgers … good work chef). After lunch I got on the Internet to send some emails and then read some of my book, which I am absolutely loving. (*Gates of Fire* by Steven Pressfield.) Anyway a pretty dull day. Beginning to worry about not seeing any real action on this tour. Obviously the work we are doing is massively important, and it is still only early days, but I'm literally itching to test myself when our backs are up against the wall. 'Careful what you wish for' they say, and probably rightly so.

6th October

Up this morning at 0645 for a 0800 patrol. Out to the east of Kushal Kalay and then south down to Kokcha, where I spoke to the ANCOP commander – who then offered chai to me and the boys. We then patrolled back up through the centre of Kushal Kalay and back to Samsor. Gave the 1200 brief, had lunch and then hung around for a 1330 lunch served by the Terps and some Afghan local big shot. Lamb kebabs and flatbread – really tasty but I was convinced it would lend me a stay in 'Hotel D & V' – but thankfully not yet! Coops took the 1630 patrol out while I hit the gym – again feeling pretty guilty at not being on patrol, despite being in massive need of a rest. The patrol sounded like a good one which I was gutted to miss – a possible IED find and some interesting atmospherics. I'm going to patrol out that way in the morning to hopefully pick up on some of the same. Chatted to the OC today and he said joint Ops with the neighbouring USMC are on the cards. I made it obvious that I would be mega keen to be involved! Fingers crossed. Anyway a shit day all round as we earlier heard about an IED strike at Nahr-e-Saraj causing 4 x Cat A UK casualties. Gutting news and hopefully the docs are able to save their lives. An A Company multiple on their first day as their PB came under attack. A pretty bad day for British forces in Afghanistan. It makes you realise that every quiet day is in fact a lucky day in Helmand.

7th October

Morning patrol after a wholly inadequate bowl of sugar puffs to an area we'd not covered before, next to the wadi which delineates the border between us and the USMC. Atmospherics not great on this one and we hit Route Somerset feeling pretty exposed to some likely hostile compounds on the other side of the wadi. We cut through a tiny Kalay where we were very channelled. I kept on at the lads to maintain their spacing as a grenade over the wall could easily have taken several of us out if we were not careful. Anyway eventually we reached open ground and breathed a collective sigh of relief before heading back in to the news that Fergie's multiple had managed to detain a wanted insurgent. Great news. Found out at the weekly planning meeting that my multiple are scheduled to be moved across to the USMC for some joint patrols with our American cousins. This move is being conducted to 'blur' the boundary between our AO and the neighbouring USMC one, so as to deceive the Taliban as to where the boundary actually lies and to prevent them exploiting any gaps in between us and our neighbours. It will also help to provide mutual understanding between us and the Americans of the nature of the insurgency we are facing. Mega excited (and so were the majority of the boys when I let them know). In the afternoon we patrolled down to Haji Noor Mohammed Kalay, which is heavily influenced by the Taliban, and which hosted the firing point for a recent RPG and small arms attack on the ANCOP CP at Folad Aft. An ISAF call-sign had a grenade lobbed over a wall at them fairly recently too. Thankfully for us it was uneventful and before long we were back at Samsor. Nearly threw my toys out of the pram at the evening meeting as it turned out our 'day off' now involves a joint patrol with the ANA at 0800 (which had not been out onto the patrols matrix). I'm going to take only 6 out (me, Coops, LCpl Twyford, LCpl Millward plus 2 volunteers), and put a firm case across for a day off on Sunday instead. I don't think I'll brief the lads in advance of a day off in the future, as I can see many more being taken from us in similar circumstances. Anyway, stayed up to watch the England game at 2330 – a dismal 2–2 draw with Montenegro. I give up with watching the national side! It's now 0130 and I'm up at 0700. Night.

8th October

Up for an uneventful patrol with the ANA save for finding out about some pretty overt TB intimidation in Ismael Kalay. Only took 6 of us out to [give] the boys a rest, with Coops and me at the front. Not tactically sound but displaying good leadership I feel. After that we watched Wales beat Ireland and then England play badly and lose to France in the Rugby World Cup. A bit of a weights session, shower and an ORP paella meal with an added tin of crabmeat (lush) later, and the evening meeting was over and we were up until 0100 moving tents around massive piles of aggregate from the 57 trucks which arrived yesterday to help with the winterisation. Spoke to Cai earlier, it was good to hear about home and talk normality and not insurgency for at least a few minutes. No patrol tomorrow but a whole host of moving kit as we are moving out of our tent. And hopefully avoiding D&V! 3 of my blokes went down with it last night and the 2IC and JTAC have gone down tonight. PLEASE MISS ME OUT!

9th October

Thankfully the D&V has missed me – so far. No patrol today, but not really a day off as spent most of the day helping the lads lay the flooring in their tents and then ripping the flooring out of our tent and moving out so our area of camp can be winterised. It's now 2235 and I have moved in to the e-bluey ISO Container for the night until our tent is back in location tomorrow. Oh, I forgot, when we pulled up our flooring we found 2 dead mice which was pretty hideous. Anyway planned tomorrow's patrols (one a look at a potential IED location, the other looking into a compound linked to a high value target), and now off to bed. Actually looking forward to getting out on patrol, as today was pretty dull. Can't wait for the winterisation to be done, as it is a real pain. It's just started raining outside. Upsetting news.

10th October

Still no D&V. 0700 joint patrol with the ANA to investigate a potential IED. We led up to the site, showed the ANA where it was, and their commander then questioned a few of the locals. He was happy with their answers but I wasn't happy that the ground sign (crossed sticks next to a metal sheet covering an obvious hole) had not been checked. The ANA sergeant then confirmed it was not a device (after we had edged towards it) by ripping the metal sheet from the floor. Lunatic! Anyway no IED for this morning and we patrolled back in. I forgot to add that this patrol was conducted in the pissing rain. As John said – just as unpleasant here as on Dartmoor. Spent the rest of the day squaring our tent away, which turned into an epic and which I felt bad about for having to enlist the help of the lads. 1500 then came and we patrolled Cpl Collins (J2 cell) down to Ismael Kalay to do some human terrain mapping. He managed to get some interesting leads on the int he was looking for while we were entertained by a load of enthusiastic little kids (blatantly not used to seeing ISAF troops). A pretty surreal moment in what we thought was to be a pretty hostile place. Once back in, with our shoulders in turbo clip, we had an essence fillet steak and chips supper (certainly wasn't expecting that in Helmand!). Briefed the blokes on tomorrow's 2 day Op (another patrol surge out of Azadi), moved into and unpacked in the newly erected officers tent, and now bed. Stomach is feeling precarious … fingers crossed.

12th October

Back in from a 2-day patrol surge with lots to report! Yesterday we left early for Azadi and went out on the first of 2 patrols that day with the ANA. After lunch we went out and provided security while the Female Engagement Team (FET) chatted to some local women about issues affecting them. Whilst we were waiting for them to link up with us we were treated to a mega display of force by 2 A-10s over our position complete with chaff and barrel rolls. Mega. After picking up the FET and the OC's party we patrolled back. Fleming picked up on an individual on a bike dicking us and, soon after crossing the canal and heading north for Azadi, a 107mm Chinese rocket was fired at us from a distance. I initially thought it was a low flying jet, but with shouts of 'get down' and a rapidly intensifying scream coming towards us, I too hit the deck whilst looking helplessly to the sky to try to see if we were about to become brown bread. Fortunately it missed (although actually landed much closer than we originally thought). With my heart racing I got up on a knee and started to take control of the situation whilst the OC got on the net to report our near miss. We stayed firm to anticipate a follow up, and then belatedly headed off track to provide a harder target for them to have a second shot at. Although it felt like an eternity, I think I actually reacted pretty quickly, certainly quick enough to get the rear of a 17 strong patrol to draw their sights onto a motorbike racing away from a compound to our south – almost certainly an enemy spotter. Hopefully with my first 'heart in mouth' moment out of the way I will be able to react coolly to whatever they throw at us in the future. Cpl Cooper looked at me and said 'you said you wanted something to happen!', at which I had to laugh. A weird feeling having had someone trying to kill me for the first time. I'm sure too that it won't be the last. Anyway back at Azadi and int picked up the TB saying they 'want to fire some more' that night, which I kind of didn't buy into and which didn't prevent me getting a good night's sleep on the floor of a tent. The next morning we were up to go and find the rocket that was fired, but the local farmers were unwilling to lead us to it and we didn't want to smash through their cotton fields to find it, so we left it with them to report to us once they found it mid-harvest. After a further couple of FET engagements we were back in and before long back at Samsor in time for lunch. Squared my admin, had dinner, briefed the lads and spoke to Mum. Her and Dad were out in Cornwall – was good to hear them having a good time (obviously I didn't mention nearly getting blown up yesterday!).

13th October

Coops took the patrol out this morning so I did a bit of admin and tracked their progress for the Ops room. On the patrol they came across a compound owner who said that in the past week he'd been evicted from his home by the TB, who wished to use it as a base from which to attack an ISAF call-sign. I passed that up the chain and hopefully we will get the chance to 'investigate'. After doing some weights, having lunch and reading some of my book (still *Gates of Fire* – I really can't describe how good that book is!) we went out at 1530. We had the FET with us again. After they had finally finished we went to West Gate to pick up the Sgt Maj from Fergie's multiple who had been taking him around to pay the Terps in the AO. I get on pretty well with the ANCOP commander there, and he confirmed there was TB in the compound identified this morning – barely 200m from his front gate. He laughed and patted me on the back when I said we'd be back to smash them up. I wasn't joking. Anyway back in for an epic Chinese meal put on by LCpl Wan (Sigs Pl), firing off a few emails, watching *DodgeBall* with Coops and Ptes Lamb and Rickson and then opening two awesome parcels from Bruce, and Sean and Lucy – and a pillow sent by Dad. Looking forward to getting my head down on that in figures few!

14th October

A day off from patrolling today. Got up late-ish and spent most of the day chilling out and doing some admin. Went to the gym in the afternoon, briefed the lads on tomorrow and then went on watchkeeper at 2200. Opened my birthday presents a day early as, being conscious of Mum and Dad sending John a birthday parcel that was never opened, I thought that if anything happens tomorrow at least they will know that I opened my presents. What I received for my birthday was absolutely mega and considering where I am I am amazed by the effort people back home went to. My heart breaks though thinking of how Mum and Dad must have felt wrapping my presents, praying that this time they would be opened. Luke and Amber sent me a mini birthday cake, which I opened at midnight in the Ops room on a pretty dull watchkeeper shift. Watched *Tombstone* with Cpl Kusack (RMP – Royal Military Police) on his laptop as he was guard commander, finished at 0300 and got my head down on the start of my 30th year. It doesn't seem fair that John didn't even get 23.

15th October

Woke up at 0730, went for breakfast and then back to bed. At 0930 Coops woke me up, claiming I was needed in the Ops room! On coming outside I found all the boys plus Sgt Baines, the CQMS [company quartermaster sergeant] CSgt Iszard, Cpl Kusack plus a few others had lined up a gauntlet for me! I went for it and was immediately covered from head to toe in water, custard powder mixture and tomatoes! Pretty disgusting but I took it in good humour which I think went down well across the board. Got squared away, watched an episode of *Entourage* and then out for the 1530 patrol with the ANA. More apprehensive than usual about this one – I think the thought of anything happening today and my family and friends having to mark my passing on my birthday is particularly upsetting. Thought we might get a scrap in the Western Dashte, but the ANA sacked off going that far and so the patrol was short and uneventful. The medics gave me 3 cans of alcohol-free Becks and the chefs baked me a birthday cake so a pretty good day all round. Helicopter flight in tonight was cancelled as Pte Fleming saw a bloke with an RPG cutting around from one of the Sangers and fired some illum up to scare him off.

16th October

Randomly, it's getting hotter. Early morning patrol with the ANA of some distance, back in for 3 hours and then out again for a shorter patrol, but in pretty intense heat. Came back in dripping with sweat and pretty frustrated having achieved little. Found out this evening that our jaunt across to the USMC planned for tomorrow has been cancelled as a CLP is due in that we have to secure Route Devon for. THREADERS! We had a nice little plan in place including some vehicle-borne fire support for what was sure to be a dust-up, but now we will be staring at a road for hours. Anyway, got to speak to Vic which was nice, watched *Entourage*, then Spurs v Newcastle (2–2) and now bed.

17th October

Went out on a boring route security patrol and was back by 1200. The CO was here on a visit so I met him for the first time. Very easy to talk to and clearly knew a bit about me, which was nice. Went to the gym in the afternoon and then wrote mid-year appraisals for LCpls Twyford and Millward – actually quite difficult! Spoke to Mum and Dad and sat down finally to watch *300* with Coops. Pretty epic battle scenes, but not a patch on the book *Gates of Fire* which

I've just finished. Inspirational stuff. I think I'd like to go to Thermopylae some day in homage to the sacrifice paid there. Anyway, just heard what sounded like a miniflare fired from the nearest Sanger. Probably one of the lads flapping. Hopefully anyway – I'm grumpy if my sleep gets interrupted!

23rd October

Haven't written for a few days as have been epically (if that's a word) away from Samsor. On Tuesday (19th) we had a chilled out day of no patrols before moving to PB Shamal Storai for an Op the next day. Anyway got to Shamal, had a freezing night (19th) sleeping outside in a jungle sleeping bag, and got up for an Op to search some suspect compounds in Group e Shesh Kalay. After the op was finished we stopped at Samsor for lunch then headed to Silab for the first of 3 nights there as a platoon with Fergie and his lads. This was a great opportunity to spend some time chilling out with lads of my platoon that I don't know too well, and one which I greatly enjoyed. I have concluded that I genuinely haven't got one bad lad out of the whole bunch. Fergie is quality too, and we found out we would have been in the same year at school which is cool. Anyway we set off for that Op the following morning (20th) at 0900. All went well and I was pleased that my part in the plan went pretty perfectly. Professional pride! No fighting-age males at home for us to question, but productive nonetheless. Coops got a high Valon reading while clearing an EHLS so had to go down to fingertip search. Thankfully nothing there, but a nerve wracking moment nonetheless. That night a 'heroic' one round was fired at one of the Sangers! I heard it go overhead and immediately got on the Base ISTAR camera system, but couldn't find the firing point. The next day was a relaxed one (21st) until we set out on patrol at 1400. Pretty different in terms of atmospherics and ground, but nothing really to report. We went out on a night patrol at 1930 to the same area. Of all the patrols I expected this one to see us in a firefight, but the Taliban clearly didn't fancy it. A pitch black night that saw us crossing some pretty dodgy ground and I'm surprised we survived any ankle injuries. Despite that, patrolling at night is important to show the Taliban that they can never rest easy, and so we cracked on. In pretty difficult conditions, and helped by some strong work by Pte Fleming on point, I managed to navigate us to a disused compound where we met with Fergie's lads, pushed 2 sharpshooters up on the roof and lay in wait. After 45 minutes nothing had materialised and so we started leapfrogging each other back to Silab. On the way I thought we'd been contacted from 30m as 4 shots rang out from our right flank and we all hit the deck and I immediately sent up a contact report. I quickly had to 'cancel my last' as it emerged that one of Fergie's multiple had engaged a dog that had attacked him without warning. He was very lucky he didn't get shot at and we arrived back at Silab pretty stressed out at the fact we'd only narrowly avoided a blue-on-blue. Not cool. Up at 0600 the next morning (22nd) (after getting back at 2200 the night before) for a 0700 pick up, quick brekkie back at Samsor before an ANA led patrol to the ANCOP station at Kokcha and back. In the afternoon I gave all the lads who'd been out for the last 3 nights the afternoon off, and took all that had stayed behind out on another joint patrol to investigate a possible CW/CPIED [command wire/command pull improvised explosive device]. We conducted an isolation to look for command wires which saw us wading waist deep through a canal. Anyway no device was found and we headed back in soaked, but having had a good laugh and amused the locals with our river crossing. Was absolutely chin-strapped last night so got my head down asap. Was happy that Coops took this morning's patrol out and I so I hit the gym and did some washing. This afternoon we went out with the ANA to the Western Dashte. The ANA stayed on the east of the canal but we waded across and patrolled out into the Dashte. Probably getting dicked from the north, the desert out there is lunar-like in nature and the compounds are massively spaced out with some tentage of nomadic Afghans dotted here and there. The ground is quite high and from there you can see all across the flat, green zone of Nad e Ali to the south and east, desert and distant compounds to the west and the mountains (probably all the way up towards Musa Qala, Now Zad, Kajaki etc) to the north. Absolutely beautiful scenery and for the first time I really recognised the amazing landscape of Afghanistan. I really hope I can bring Mum and Dad on holiday here someday. A river crossing on the way back hugely amused the locals (and the ANA) and on return to Samsor all agreed it was possibly our best patrol to date. A strong roast beef dinner followed by watching Man Utd lose 6–1 at home to Man City (Cai will be pissed!) and now watching *Hall Pass*. Quality. The OC thinks we've got a chance of moving to the PB line north of Gereshk around the halfway point to replace the Danes, given that they are re-rolling. This will certainly result in many scraps and will see a massively increased risk of casualties. I am more than up for facing that challenge head-on, but will now make the most of the fairly quiet time we're having rather than spending every patrol wishing for a contact – as it sounds like many of those may be on the way...!

24th October

An easy day. Slept through the morning briefing (oops) and then went out on a 'route security' patrol down to CP Haji Alem as they are winterising there at the minute. Pretty dull really. Stopped to chat to the blokes at the motorcycle shop in Kushal Kalay but the intelligence gained was not exactly groundbreaking. All the talk today is of our possible move to Gereshk. From talking to the OC it seems like the clever money is on us to move over A Coy, 3 Scots, as they will, by December, be manning 3 PBs to our 2, and will also hold the Nad-e-Ali (South) HQ designate. It sounds like we could be in Gereshk by 15th December, if indeed we get the nod and if that is where they choose to send us. I've been checking what's going on up there, and it sounds pretty punchy. We'd be replacing the Danes, who are being re-deployed in theatre. Lots of small arms/UGL/RPG attacks and, hideously, some IEDs. Briefed the lads on this and some are quite keen for it, but others are less so being comfortable with the ground here and wanting us all to come home unscathed. Obviously I want this too but I have never tested myself in a scrap. Still, the fact that I'm certain we would take casualties up north, means that should we not get sent it may turn out a blessing in disguise as I'm not sure how I will deal with losing one of the lads whom I've become so close to and who's safety I care for so deeply. Furthermore, the increased risk to me only increases the risk of heartbreak for Mum and Dad, and

Vicky, which troubles me greatly. So, in summary: I really want to go north for a scrap, at the same time as being pretty apprehensive about doing so. Confusing, I know. Time will tell and for now I will enjoy the relative calm of Nad-e-Ali South Central.

25th October

Made the morning 0830 brief today – by the skin of my teeth and pre-shave and wash! (I had found time for breakfast however!). I always forget the morning ones! (Mainly because I'm never usually here for them.) Had some post in this morning – a letter from Tim at Bastion and Nan & Grandad, and parcels from Cai, Kelly and Fliss House. Genius. Went out about 1030 down to Folad Aft. Met the new ANCOP commander down there who is keen for some joint patrolling and seems a pretty good bloke. Came back in for lunch and then pretty much just chilled out and went to the gym. Had an evening curry at 2030 with the ANA commander to discuss future plans. He's crazy and loves to throw banter about the place. Despite the curry I still went to normal dinner at 1730 – and now feel pretty sick having had 2 evening meals. Get it in while you can is what I say. All the talk at the moment is of the possible move to Gereshk, I for one can't stop thinking about it, with both trepidation and excitement. Anyway a couple of fairly good patrols tomorrow – one back to the Western Dashte and one doing the rounds of the local ANCOP stations. A 1000 start means a bit of a lie in. I may even get up in time for the morning meeting.

26th October

Made the morning meeting, but getting out of my bag is becoming an epic (30 minute snooze … again). Went out at 1000 to meet the new ANCOP commanders at Folad Se and Kokcha. Both also good guys who are genuinely proud to be serving their country. Had chai with them and then returned for lunch. Went out again at 1500 to Western Dashte. Spoke to a few of the nomads up there. It emerges they are disenfranchised in Afghanistan and treated as squatters. We told them to elect a Wakil and a Village Elder to represent them in the

District Council and hopefully they can then tap into the wheat seed distribution programme. Gave a little girl a mini packet of Haribo, and she was literally jumping with excitement! Made my day! Crossed the river back holding the Terp's hand – who can't swim and was pretty worried about the waist deep fast flowing river! Back for dinner, a brief, a bit of TV and now bed. No patrol until 1430 tomorrow so a relaxing morning (hopefully).

27th October

A chilled out start to the day with some weights and letter writing. Out at 1430 for an epic 4½ hour patrol that was an absolute killer on the shoulders and back (obviously I didn't let this show!). Went west to speak to some locals to find out if there were any 'men behaving Jihadly' about, and then south to Folad Aft to get the new ANCOP commander's phone number. We then went out west to and did some uneventful meandering about before heading back to the east. Night came and we donned night sights and optics and I managed to navigate us back in across some pretty difficult terrain – probably more luck than judgement. Anyway, day off tomorrow which is ruined by me being watchkeeper from 0300. To that end, it is time to sleep.

28th October

A day off patrols. However, was on watchkeeper from 0300–1130 so am knackered. Went back to bed for a bit, went running on the treadmill for 40 minutes and that's about it. Found out that yesterday a DFC device (essentially a homemade claymore mine) was discovered 200m away and blatantly to target my call-sign as it was aimed at somewhere we recently used to cross a ditch back to the main route running north–south. It was command pull with the firing point being 40m to the east. We patrolled that way yesterday but thankfully crossed the ditch some 50m short of the device. With it being camouflaged at the side of the road the chances are we wouldn't have spotted it so would have been at the mercy of the firer (if he was in place) should we have walked further north. I don't expect we'd have received much mercy and it sounds like it would have taken 4 of us out. I was 3rd man in the patrol. Not a nice feeling and a reminder of how fragile our safety is out here. A useful wake-up call after being able to move freely about with impunity which is probably why the TB are pissed off enough to lay such a device. Cowards.

29th October

Up for an 0800 patrol with the ANA from Adam Khan to investigate a suspected IED. As I suspected (due to the location we were told to search being a stupid place to put a device), there was nothing there and the 'digging' being observed by Silab Base ISTAR was likely work being undertaken on an irrigation ditch. Back for lunch and a pretty lazy afternoon before going out on a 1 hour VCP at the front gate. Uneventful enough, and so back in for dinner, evening meeting and 3 episodes of *Entourage*. Went on TIGR [tactical ground reporting] today to look at Gereshk, but inevitably got drawn further north to Kajaki. Searched for past patrol reports and there, clear as day was 'IED Strike: 30 1649 Mar 08'. I zoomed in to see the ground, for the first time, where John and Dave were hit and played over in my head what happened that day. Weird to see the ground and imagine what the last things John saw were before the obvious happened. Probably the reason why I'm feeling pretty down today.

30th October

Another 'Equipment Care' (EC) day. Another classic wake up 9 minutes before the morning meeting. Enough time for a bacon sarnie, but not a shave. After that just smashed some admin: washed my clothes, cleaned my rifle and pistol, re-bombed my magazines (to rest the springs) and cleaned my boots. Went to the gym too and spoke to Vic – although only for 2 minutes as my credit ran out so will have to phone her for a proper chat tomorrow. After the brief tonight the lads were watching a film in the welfare room so I watched the Spurs v QPR game in the SNCO's tent with the CSM. Spurs won 3–1.

31st October

Apparently we're a quarter of the way into tour. Craziness. 0800 patrol with the ANA during which we tried giving the Terp a radio so we could satellite the ANA squad and keep in comms with them. It actually worked pretty well and the ANA were good with sending us locstats [location status] and SITREPs meaning we could work as 2 mutually supporting call-signs, rather than as one long snake. A lot more tactically sound. At 1500 we went out to Adam Khan to pick up their ANA and do a similar patrol with them culminating in us providing overwatch while they searched 4 compounds, finding nothing. Had my MPAR today [Mid Period Appraisal Report], which I was really pleased with. I feel like things have been going well, but to get the OC's seal of approval has been awesome. I couldn't help but think of John, who had a mega report whilst on tour, but then had his future so cruelly taken away from him. I really hope lightening doesn't strike twice. Chances are it won't, however should we move north then those chances certainly increase.

1st November

0700 patrol with the ANA which was pretty dull. Back in and feeling pretty rough from a cold so was glad that Coops took the afternoon patrol. Pretty quiet day really and can't really remember doing much! Had orders tonight for a helo insertion Op into the Western Dashte tomorrow. Should be pretty cool. Up hideously early for that so was about to go to sleep, but have just heard that the PWRR [Princess of Wales's Royal Regiment] had their first battle injury of the tour, and naive to think it will be the last. I don't know the lad but I hope he is doing ok.

2nd November

Up at 0445 for the helo insertion Op. Hideous. Breakfast at 0500 and at 0615 we set off in 2 Chinooks and had an enjoyable 30-minute joy ride around Helmand before landing in the Western Dashte and beginning a 5-hour company patrol south east and back towards Samsor. Uneventful and frustratingly slow, but good practice for future Ops. My daysack was probably at its heaviest so far and my shoulders and back are still in turbo now. Back in and broke the news to the lads about the PWRR injury. Apparently the injured soldier was in Bastion R3 within 34 minutes of wounding so the lads should take confidence from that at least. The pelvic protection we wear also undoubtedly saved his cock and balls too. Happy with that.

3rd November

Woken up at 0200 as had 'volunteered' to help unload mail from the Merlin that came in at 0245. Then up for a delayed (due to some HIIDE [Handheld Interagency Identity Detection Equipment] camera training bloke) patrol. Went to the ANCOP CP at Folad Aft and conducted a VCP with them. They were all over it and we were impressed with their skills and drills. Encouraging for the future indeed, especially given their popularity with the locals. Me and the boys received a load of parcels from the RBL [Royal British Legion] in Ferndown, which was incredible. The lads were really chuffed with the contents – 'on the ball' as they all agreed! They had 'we love and miss you all' on the back. They were accompanied by loads of Xmas cards from Ferndown First School. I actually got quite full up reading things like 'thank you for saving us,' 'thank you for protecting England', 'we will give you all that you need for all you do for us' and especially, from the little ones, things like 'good luck in the war' and 'I hope you save the village'! I will ensure that we thank them properly.

4th November

After brunch, we patrolled at 1145 over to Silab. Redders. Spent an hour with Fergie and the boys before patrolling into Ops *Box Cutlass*. Fergie's lads moved south to north as we pushed north to south with the Jocks from Takhta in their Jackals providing a mobile screen to the west. Anyhow, nothing significant to note other than part of an ISAF vehicle seen being used as a makeshift bridge. Not cool. Back in after 5 hours or so out (shoulders = fucked), and then the evening brief and watching *Fast and Furious 5* with the boys. Actually pretty entertaining. Spoke to Mum which was nice and was able to put her mind at rest for a day at least by saying I have a day off from patrolling tomorrow. The OC says the rumour still indicates we may get the nod to go north. Fingers crossed.

5th November

An EC day. Gym in the morning and ruined in the afternoon by having to cover Bobby on watchkeeper while he got his head down. The OC came back from a conference at FOB Shawqat and it sounds pretty much like we're getting the nod to go north to Gereshk. Briefed the lads accordingly and I could see the apprehension on their faces. I told them to get in the right frame of mind now and to use every patrol in the next 5/6 weeks as a rehearsal for what will be a very different few months. I think I got the message across and was happy with the words I chose to use. If we were staying in NDA I would have assessed my chances of surviving this tour at not far from 100%. In Gereshk? … I'm not sure, but reduced. I was always happy with these risks and keen to test myself in the thick of it – however, every time I speak to Mum, Dad and Vicky and sense the worry in their voices (even though they try to disguise it) I feel just guilt and fear – not of my own death but of what it would do to them.

6th November

CO 3 Scots was here this morning. After he met me and the lads we went out on a local area patrol to see ANCOP and wish them a happy Eid. Good blokes. After lunch a VCP got cut short as the ANA had the same idea and so we collapsed it. A pretty boring day to be honest. Just watched Spurs beat Fulham 3–1 and have to get up at 0120 as have been 'volunteered' to help unload a helicopter. Again. Cheers.

8th November

Yesterday Coops took the morning patrol out and in the afternoon we went down to see the ANCOP at Folad Se. Gave them some gifts to give out to the school kids for Eid, and arranged to return on Saturday to give them out with them. I gambled on leaving them in situ with the ANCOP as a display of trust so hopefully they will still be there! We then proceeded onto Silab and spent the evening there with the boys. We stood up as cover as 63B pushed out a VCP. We headed back to Samsor for around 11, had lunch and spent most of the afternoon on 15 minutes' notice to move (NTM). It sounds like we're definitely on for Gereshk and so I briefed the lads tonight on the information I've obtained on it so far. Not to scare but just to keep them in the loop. Essentially – IED threat: medium; small arms threat: high. Attacks against patrols and static locations. Pressure plate and command wire IEDs. Assessment: punchy.

9th November

Up for a patrol to the north-east of CP Adam Khan this morning. Some locals up there say their fields are sometimes used as an insurgent firing point onto Adam Khan so maybe somewhere to put a future ambush.

10th November

Had a robust lie-in and slept through the morning meeting. Treated myself to a morning shower and then did some contact drills and casualty extraction with the lads before lunch. At 1500 we patrolled to Silab and waited there on QRF as Cpl Dom Vineall took a patrol out into Cutlass. We then headed back to Samsor, had the evening brief and read the papers before chatting shit to Dickie and Billy in the tent. Truth be told, I couldn't be fucked today. Maybe due to Remembrance Day tomorrow? Not sure. Anyway spoke to Vic and Mum tonight. They were both pleased to hear I won't be patrolling again until I get a Hep B jab. I should get this tomorrow at Shawqat, but nothing wrong with them thinking it will be a couple of days until I'm out again. J Speaking of tomorrow I'm going to be interviewed at Shawqat about 11/11 and John. A difficult thing to do, but one I wanted to do to honour my bro. I shall let you know how it goes.

11th November

Remembrance Day. An emotional 0630 shower and then to Shawqat for a day of media. At 1100 we had the memorial service itself and I found myself in a position where I could be easily filmed. Not ideal as I thought of John and the sacrifice he made here. Following the service I did an interview live on BBC Breakfast – which was pretty difficult due to a turbo delay of about 5 seconds. Still, I think what I said was ok. After that I did radio interviews with BBC London and Solent, as well as Radio One's Newsbeat, and a pre-recorded interview that went to South Today and BBC News 24. And did a newspaper interview complete with horrifically chad photos. Needless to say I have already been 'crated'. Embarrassment aside, I just hope I did John justice.

12th November

Slept in until 1000 this morning, which was awesome. After lunch some medical training with the boys then gave them their mid-year reports. All seemed pretty happy. Spoke to Mum and Dad and had a nice long chat. Sounds like they had a good day with 40 Commando yesterday and they saw me on the news which is cool. Did a 2-hour joint patrol with the ANA. Nothing interesting but was good to get out after a day or so of no patrolling. Found out tonight that Gereshk is pretty much definitely on. Even if we have to leave force protection for the ANA advisors (Billy and Sheep) behind, it would be Coops plus half of my multiple with myself and the rest going north reinforced by Jocks. Would be pretty shit to be split up, but would mean I would be able to get amongst it and leave the lads behind who didn't fancy a change. This equates to about half of the boys and so means I wouldn't feel guilty about taking blokes who are quite happy not to be scrapping every day. So maybe not so bad after all. England beat Spain tonight. Surprising.

13th November

Remembrance Sunday. 0900 joint patrol with the ANA where we pretty much just followed them around in a big loop. Finished off giving my lads their reports before lunch, and after went on patrol at 1430 up to Adam Khan to drop the advisors off (plus Vicky the medic and a very threaders LCpl 'H' Millward) to do some training with the ANA. The rest of us, including LCpl Hendrickson (our female clerk) went 'wet balls or no balls' deep in the NEB [Nahr-e-Bughra] canal and crossed into the Dashte. An uneventful hour or so saw us back to collect the team from Adam Khan before heading back to Samsor. Apparently I was in the *Sunday Express* today – along with some horrifically chad photos. Nightmare. Spoke to Scott too which was cool. Now listening to some helicopter flying around and happily re-united with my sleeping bag.

14th November

The bag was so essence I slept through the morning brief and didn't wake up until 0900! Only had one patrol today so did some admin this morning and some weights in the gym. Went out at 1500 to Adam Khan. The ANA had already cracked on and headed west, so we went east and arrived back in for 1620. The lads are starting to get into a 'Gereshk Frame of Mind', which is good to see. Gave orders for tomorrow's helo insertion Op and now head down for a rubbish 0445 reveille.

15th November

On the helicopter by 0630 and lifted into Badullah Qualp. Established a block to the south-west while 63B and Company TAC pushed south through the compounds. It was probably too early for anything to happen and so it was job done pretty quickly. We then moved east, crossed the canal and pushed into Dilawar. Spent a couple of hours helping load the stores and then ended ISAF presence there by marching out of the closed checkpoint. It remains to be seen if the Taliban will use this opportunity to re-emerge from the west. We then had company HQ attached and so became a frustratingly massive call-sign as we moved back in via a stop at ANCOP CP Paraang. Back in by lunch and just chilled out for the rest of the day. Uneventful but a useful patrol – I'm now really confident in both myself and my blokes for pushing north. Pte Charles in particular has come on loads and really does the business as point man. New book, *Tommy* by Richard Holmes as a poignant reminder of the men who flew the flag that we now carry.

17th November

No entry last night as was a late finish so I will cover 2 days now. Yesterday (16th) morning. I was out on a short patrol with the ANA into Kushal Kalay just to show presence after the TB have been telling locals they intend to attack us down there. It will never happen and it's important the locals can see that. In the afternoon we did a joint patrol with Adam Khan's ANA – we're teaching them about depth and mutual support and so we satellited around each other. It worked well. At 2230 we got a vehicle move into the AO to our north and patrolled down to a layup position to try and catch some dudes who have been using the area as a 'shoot and scoot' firing point onto Adam Khan. No-one showed up for us which was disappointing as I'd briefed the lads that as soon as a weapon was pointed towards the checkpoint we could drop the firer due to there being an imminent threat to life (even though not to us). Still a worthwhile exercise as we split into 2 x 5 man teams and worked well covering the ground in the pitch black. Gave us all confidence in operating at night and the lads all enjoyed it. Got back in at 0115 so had a sleep in until 1000 this morning (17th). An EC day, so cleaned my rifle and filled a box of kit I don't really need to back load should we move forward to Gereshk. Put all the lads through the C-IED lane [Counter-IED]. We've started to smash the training seriously for our impending move to give ourselves the best possible chance of surviving and not taking casualties. Went over to the ANA Camp to plan the week's patrols with the ever-entertaining Najibullah. A funny bloke! Spoke to Vic tonight and thought how strange it was that we could speak as I stood in the middle of Helmand while she was at work in Freetown, Sierra Leone. Spoke to her about our possible move. Let her know it's a bit more punchy up there, but didn't tell her my genuine fear of not even making R&R if we do go north. Not that I think that will happen, but I'm just acutely aware of the increase in probability of me not making it home.

18th November

1000 patrol this morning into KHK. Stopped to see the ANCOP at Folad and then patrolled back through farmland to Samsor. Spent most of the patrol speaking to locals and reassuring them that security will endure in the wake of ISAF checkpoints closing down or transferring to ANSF. The consensus seems to be that as long as we maintain our larger PBs, and that ANCOP take the lead, then security should be maintained. After lunch I chilled out for a bit before going out to do a VCP from 1600–1700. My ankle is in a shit state at the moment. Not sure why but I get a massive pain when moving in boots. Have spent the last few days trying to suppress a limp whilst on patrol. Hopefully it will sort itself out. Filling in my aspirations on my mid-year report today, as follows: Next job – FSG 2I/C, then Recce Platoon Commander. Also do my Commando Course if an exchange job with the Corps arises (not just as a 'badge collector'), and to try to get on the exchange programme to NZ/Aus. The OC concurred with my plans so will hopefully square me away. To be honest, I'd be happy with any one of the above! Watchkeeper in 40 minutes until 0300. Thankfully Coops is taking out the 0800 patrol!

19th November

Coops took both patrols out today as wanted a lie-in tomorrow. Was happy with that so treated myself to a phone call to Mum and Dad, some phys (weights only as my ankle is still fucked) and some random admin. Grant (OC 8) had a contact nearby today. The first one of the tour on a dismounted call-sign by small arms. 5 x 3-5 round bursts from 200m away. The lads returned fire (heavily) and the firers fled like the cowards they are. Pretty jealous to be honest! Still 'careful what you wish for' springs to mind again! Pte Dan Clover's girlfriend had a baby last night, so I managed to get some fresh meat out on a Jackal for the boys at Silab to celebrate with a special meal.

20th November

2 non-eventful patrols at 0700 and 1600. Then some shit news. Lt Rob Coates' 4 Platoon lost a lad in Nahr-e-Saraj (South). An IED killed Pte

Tom Lake, seriously injured both legs on another and fragged up one more of Rob's lads quite badly. Rob himself, after squaring the casevac, returned to his PB to find he'd been fragged in the leg, and was subsequently casevac'd to Bastion. The OC broke the news and a few of my lads are in bits as were quite close to Pte Lake. I got the lads together and had a chat with them and said I'd talk through anything with them if they needed to – mentioning John and that I know what the family will be going through. Pretty upset myself over Rob, so hopefully that didn't show. Thankfully he sounds like he'll be fine, but I know just how devastated he'll be to lose one of his own. Absolute gutter. Had a cigarette (my first of tour). Once again, I'm faced with confirmation of my own mortality, and the fact that had the decision to send Rob to B Coy and me to C been opposite then I would be lying in hospital with one of my blokes dead. I'm not sure I'm ready for that even now, as can't imagine losing one of the lads I've grown so close to. But then, who is ready for something like that?

21st November

Coops took the morning patrol out. We then did some compound clearance training before I took out a 1600 patrol to Adam Khan. When we got there the ANA had gone on a route security task without telling us, so patrolled back in under the most beautiful sunset I've ever seen. I even stopped the patrol to let the lads take photos! Had a remembrance service for Tom Lake on the helipad when we got back, which was very moving. The lads have made a memorial to him and after my evening orders we lit candles on it and just stood in silent contemplation. I've been nominated to be the colour party, with Grant, at Bastion for the repatriation on Thursday and fly back to Bastion tomorrow. What an honour.

22nd November

Flew back to Bastion in the morning. Dropped my kit off and then headed straight to the hospital to see Rob. Bought him some bits from the shop and woke him up as he was sleeping after an SIB [Special Investigation Branch] interview. He's got a massive hole in his leg with a machine attached that's sucking the crap out of it. Managed to have a bit of a laugh with him but can tell that he's absolutely gutted about what happened. As would I be. I think he appreciated the visit. Saw his lads too – LCpl Jones is hurt the worst. He's got quite bad nerve damage to the legs and will probably take about a year to make a full recovery. Cpl Kennedy is doing pretty well and should be fine in a couple of days after being fragged down the left side. It sounds like they got hit with a hastily-laid DFC, put in their path while they stopped to talk to some locals. Tom Lake took the brunt of the blast and was killed instantly. Really upsetting to see them all, hurt and so upset.

23rd November

Up early for a rehearsal for the vigil. Saw Rob in the morning and then did some flag drill with the RSM at 1200, then a rehearsal at 1400 and were set for the Vigil at 1615. With all 3500 people in place we marched on to lead the Battalion's representatives on to the Vigil site, and then stood rigidly to attention throughout (actually quite hard work). The service was obviously very moving and we then marched off having thankfully done the colours proud. Went to see Rob straight after. I was literally heartbroken to learn that Tom Lake lived by himself with his Mum. This has upset me so much more than I would have expected. Left Rob to get some sleep and then sat on the Internet all day waiting for the repatriation, which began at 0245. So moving and as we saluted the coffin was carried past and we then stood to attention in silence as the ramp was closed and the C-17's lights extinguished. I couldn't help to not think of how I was in the unique position of having been on both ends of a military repatriation. I just thought of Tom's poor Mum in a hotel waiting to see her boy's coffin being carried off the back of a plane at RAF Brize Norton.

24th November

Went to see Rob before he flew home. He had to go in for an op to clear up some of the infection in his wound and was then flying to Selly Oak, via Kandahar. Was good to see him off and he will be in my thoughts very much. After that drank some coffees and then waited to fly back to FOB Shawqat in the evening. The Chinook wasn't delayed and, so landed back in Nad-e-Ali and got some much needed sleep.

25th November

Chilled out all morning and then got a lift back to Samsor by Sgt Baines and the Mastiff Group at 1400. Was good to see everyone back here again. Heard that Pte Finch found a possible IED relatively close to the PB. Told the lads about what exactly happened to Tom Lake and the others. On reflection from the past few days, my sadness has been replaced largely with anger – especially after spending time in the hospital and having seen what these pricks are doing to our people.

26th November

A 0800 local patrol with the ANA. Spoke to Mum and Dad which was good – needed to talk about the last few days. Hopefully it didn't upset them. A pretty pointless afternoon patrol – also with the ANA – but all good practice for the move north. LCpl 'Gok' Wan made a mega Chinese dinner tonight. Enjoyed a nice 'Black and Mild' (pipe tobacco cigars) smoke with the boys too that was a good social. Bedtime. Night.

27th November

No patrol today. Did some training this morning on casualty reporting, treatment at the point of wounding, and after lunch a full scenario. We patrolled around camp and then simulated me losing a leg in an IED blast and Arran being shot simultaneously thus leaving the patrol with no commanders. The lads responded really well. I had a tourniquet on within 4 minutes and they had us both at an EHLS within 22 minutes meaning we'd have been back at Bastion within 40. Happy with that. The Doc filmed it too which was really useful. Found out today we're definitely going to the PB Line north-east of Gereshk. CAN. NOT. WAIT.

28th November

Joint patrol with the ANA in the morning. They did A VCP at the centre of KHK while we patrolled to their south around the ANCOP CP Paraang, which has just been collapsed. The locals seem unconcerned by this. Picked up the ANA and then headed back in. Can't really remember much about the time before the next patrol, other than watching *How to Make it in America* and nailing some essence duck pate with crostini as provided by Luke and Amber. Went out again with the ANA from Adam Khan and essentially just gave them some security while they searched a compound. That's pretty much it. A pretty dull day. I'm up for watchkeeper from 0300–0800 tomorrow too. And it's freezing. Mega!

30th November

A patrol from 0900–1030 in support of an ANA patrol. Uneventful but we're starting to operate as we would in Gereshk (ie in a high IED threat area) and the lads are really getting it. Good practice for me too. At 1400 we went out to try to deter a bit of interest from compound roofs which has been happening recently when helicopters fly in. Probably just kids in all honesty but a worthwhile exercise. Found out tonight that the bloke whose IED killed Tom Lake was probably killed by an Apache strike yesterday. Serves him right. The Jocks of the 3 Scots FSG are here now. Their Fijians cooked us an essence curry tonight. Good lads. We've now collapsed our officers' tent and are living in the plans room as the PB prepares to pack up and move out. Pretty cosy in here but a bit warmer than the tent. Anyway up at 0630 for a patrol so now off to bed.

1st December

Can't believe it's December already. Pretty Baltic as I got up at 0630 and left on patrol at 0730 heading over towards the NEB canal and back. Chilled out for the rest of the day, wrote some letters and spoke to Mum on the phone. Some of the boys came back from R&R today so it was good to see them again. Sounds like we're now going to spend about a month working out of MOB Price before moving up to PB Clifton. Less unpleasant living pay, as is a pretty mega camp by all accounts. Suits me fine!

2nd December

At 0915 left to do an investigation on a track junction where some suspicious digging was taking place last night. Predictably, no IED to be found but worthwhile practice in this procedure. It made me realise too just how vulnerable we are to small arms fire whilst carrying it out. Our afternoon patrol was cancelled because the lads were busy moving tents as we start to collapse some down here and so I wrote some letters and generally got bored. Went over to see the ANA commander to plan the week's patrols with him and managed to get him to deviate slightly from his usual patrol pattern. Managed to jack up a lunch next week hosted by the ANA to which all the local ANCOP, ALP [Afghan Local Police] and AUP [Afghan Uniformed Police] commanders will attend. It could really square away security in Nad-e-Ali once we go so fingers crossed.

3rd December

A small patrol with the ANA this morning. Met a local who was celebrating his return from the Hajj Pilgrimage to Saudi Arabia. He invited us to sit and drink chai with him and so we did. I genuinely enjoyed the company of him and his family and took the chance to forget the insurgency for once and have a pleasant, normal conversation. I gave his grandchildren some sweets which seemed to go down well. Came back in and chilled out for the rest of the day. Went to the gym before dinner and then watched Spurs beat Bolton 3–0, having a good laugh with some mindless and pretty childish banter with Luke (Malpass – JTAC) and Dickie in the process. Found out tonight, from the OC and CQMS' recce, that 300m is as far as you can go without getting contacted from PB Clifton, and that the point man really needs to be switched on at all times and be alert to any dangers for the good of the whole patrol. Lots of contacts = happy with that. Lots of IEDs = not so cool.

4th December

At 0830 we got a lift to Takhta and then patrolled through Haji Kalay to get picked up from where CP Azadi used to be. Anyway on the way to the pickup point I jumped an irrigation ditch and twisted my left knee pretty badly on landing. It made a horrible cracking noise and was mega painful, and my initial thought was that 'this is me' and that I'd be on a plane home. Eventually however I managed to put some weight on it and slowly hobbled to be picked up. Got the Doc to check it out and thankfully it's my hamstring and not my knee, and thus am off patrolling for a couple of days, which should square it away (hopefully!). As a result Coops took the evening patrol out, where one round was fired at them from a distance. Under usual circumstances I would have been threaders at missing out, but given the baptism of fire that is to come, I'm not quite so fussed.

5th December

A boring day due to my injury. The boys went out at 0730 and reported no local national activity – probably due to the bitter cold today (for the first time, it just didn't warm up. Hideous). They went out again at 1400 on an uneventful patrol with the ANA. I spent the day packing for the move out and generally drinking tea with various people. We had a man test with some of Sheep's hot sauce, 'Insanity'. A lot of men were in a lot of oral pain – me included. Anyway today dragged. I want to be able to patrol again.

6th December

It's 2100 and I'm now in bed as will be up for watchkeeper at 0300. No patrols out today as it was an EC Day. Did some admin, went to the gym and had an emotionally cold shower. The ANA hosted the key local ANSF players for lunch and I went along with the head shed from our side. Some nice chips (cold) and chicken and veg all cooked up in a pretty tasty sauce. Washed down with a can of Pepsi and no ill effects so far! Touch wood. A pretty meaningful discussion afterwards was the first time the ANA, ANCOP and ALP have sat down together and as such will be pretty important to the forthcoming transition. Spent the rest of the day pretty bored and so ended up having lots of quality banter with Luke. Anyway going to get my head down for a bit now before my hideous wake up time.

7th December

Watchkeeper 0300–0800 then got my head down while Coops took the morning patrol out. Woke up for lunch around 1220 and then briefed the lads on the afternoon patrol. We went out at 1500 and soon thought the ANA (who had left 10 minutes before us) were in contact but it turns out they had fired 4 warning shots at a local national who wouldn't slow down on a motorbike. My knee just about held up despite giving me some grief when I overstretched it. Anyway back in and again bored and cold so am going to bed. My last patrol in Nad-e-Ali tomorrow as am flying back to Bastion on Friday to do a 5-day Mastiff commander cadre before the rest of the boys arrive on the 14th. Will be pretty boring but at least another few days for the folks and Vicky to not worry about me.

8th December

Took a 1 hour patrol out this morning into Kushal Kalay. A short patrol that was long enough to give my knee some dramas. I shall have to get some physio at Bastion. I shall miss this place and its people, and truly hope that the security which they have currently will endure once we are gone. Particularly for the elderly, tired of generations of fighting and the young, so that they may continue to go to school and play outside in safety. For me now though, the focus switches to Nahr-e-Saraj (North) and the PB Line. Coops took the afternoon patrol while I packed. We gave him a surprise, advanced birthday party on his return. This evening a request came for a platoon to be ready to move as early as this weekend, but sadly Grant's 8 Platoon got the nod over us – primarily as my platoon features the search team – an asset that the OC wouldn't want to lose. Anyway, all packed now and ready for a few days of hot showers, good food, and undoubtedly boredom at the home of the 'Task Force Helmand Support Group'.

9th–27th December

Haven't written during this period as it was pretty dull. Moved back to Bastion, completed my Mastiff Commander Cadre, and also spent lots of time avoiding the physio after stupidly going to see him after my knee injury. After being threatened with a flight home for surgery (!), he eventually caught up with me (via the Battalion Adjutant) and is happy for me to patrol. He thinks I have a small cruciate ligament tear, but fortunately it should heal as long as I am careful with it. To be honest, I thought for a while my tour could be over and so am pretty happy to get the green light. My platoon is moving into CP Malvern East tomorrow to begin protection of the bridge build being done by the engineers. I went to recce the site recently and flew into Camp Price to then drive up through Gereshk and along the Band e Barq Road. 4 IED strikes in 11 days with 800m of the CP meant I was a little apprehensive, but it all went fine and a worthwhile recce was conducted. An absolute dream as a new Platoon Commander to be given an opportunity for my own little domain, and one I will sink my teeth into. The threat up there is significant however, and I think all of us are pretty nervous about getting up there. Gave the boys a fairly upbeat confidence boosting brief about how we're going to operate up there tonight, and hopefully they will be able to sleep well and not be up all night worrying (like some have secretly told me they've been doing). Off in the morning so we'll see how we go. Phoned home tonight, conscious that it could be my last call home – as they all could be from now on. Granny is really ill and it sounds like her time may nearly be up. Obviously gutted that she will probably go before I get home, and that I can't be there for the family. The next few weeks could be pretty straining with that on my mind too. It reinforces too, that as much as I don't fear death, for my family's sake I cannot afford to die out here. Got hold of a little wooden crucifix from the Danish coffee shop in Price today in the faint hope that it may somehow help to keep me safe.

29th December

No entry yesterday as, after the journey to PB Clifton turned into a 6 hour epic, time was pushed and so we spent a night up there with the

Danes. Moved into PB Malvern East this morning and have spent the whole day setting up the place. A big challenge and responsibility for me, but I am relishing the prospect of truly independent command. I spent the day on our STAP [Surveillance & Target Acquisition Plan] while Fergie squared all the admin and we are now good to go, with the engineers having moved in to begin their work on the bridge tomorrow. Lots of int suggesting the Taliban are up for a scrap, so the coming days and weeks could be interesting! Set up my poncho next to Fergie's (the boys are in 2-man tents but there wasn't enough for all) and we spent a while smoking and listening to Eminem, which was cool and took me back a few years! On watchkeeper at 0400 so in bed now (2100) and out on our first patrol here at 0730. Can't wait.

30th December

Absolutely freezing on waking for Ops room stag at 0400, and remained so until going out on patrol at 0730 with Dom's lads. Just put in security on the southern bank of the NEB canal for the engineers to do some survey work, and also questioned some locals in order to provide some answers to the J2 cell at PB Clifton about who lives where etc. Were heavily scouted but not engaged and so came back in. Went out again at 1400 and spent an hour clearing only 150m to the east so as to clear a prominent BUND [built-up natural defence] line as a base line location for fire support in the future. Thought we'd been contacted on the way out but it turned out to be the ANA firing their .50cal in to the River Helmand. Obviously. As we approached the tree line we could actually see blokes moving into position in and around the 2 compounds that are known firing points. Contact was imminent but just as we expected it to come an Apache (en route to another task) flew overhead thus causing them all to jump on their motorbikes and bale and within minutes the women and children were back and all was normal again. Bizarre and frustrating. It turns out the air cover was up as the MERT was inbound to a nearby IED strike. Back in and debriefed the boys and then just chilled in the Ops room. Reporting suggests an IED belt laid just a couple of hundred metres away to our west so we'll have to be careful tomorrow. I think this will be a busy little AO, and I pray we all come home in one piece.

31st December

In the Ops room from 0300 and remained so as Coops took a short patrol out over the sluice gate to clear an area there. I then went over to speak to the ANA at 1000 while Dom took a satelliting patrol out around their patrol base (Malvern West). Got some useful information off the ANA commander about the Taliban. After that Coops cleared a small area east of our PB on which we can now move a Jackal down to if needs be. Finally Dom went out to the north-west and we now have a small secure area that is permanently overwatched by our Sangers and ISTAR. The other side again very interested in what we're up to, but as yet have not decided to take us on. Tonight a local came to the PB offering to be a source for us and pointed out a number of IED locations. I set the ball rolling with our intelligence people and so will see how that develops. Fingers crossed we could be onto something pretty useful. Spoke to Vic briefly earlier and Mum and Dad tonight. Granny is still very poorly but also still hanging on in there. Mum and Dad obviously concerned about where I am now so tried to play down the threat level, so hopefully they won't worry too much. I just hope I make R&R.

2nd January 2012

On New Year's Day we just sent out a couple of VCPs and some very local patrols, which activated the dicking screen quite significantly. I then went to PB Clifton to plan a joint patrol with the Danes this morning – which resulted in me unexpectedly giving a set of orders to a Danish platoon! Spoke to Luke O while I was up there on the phone too, which was good for morale. This morning I finished Ops room stag at 0300 and then woke up for the patrol at 0530, which was pretty hideous. We pushed out at first light with me in the lead with Dom, and Fergie and Coops providing some depth to the west. We covered a lot of ground to the north-west and were dicked from practically everywhere. I thought at one point we would be engaged as women and children started fleeing the area, and ISTAR picked up 2 blokes around a murder hole in a compound wall, but they decided against it for whatever reason. On the way back in we found a command wire IED in an irrigation ditch, just 200m from our PB. It wasn't until loads of us had crossed directly over it and it was actually the bloke in front of me who saw it. A blatant command wire running into the far bank as we jumped across. By chance, it was either not connected to a battery pack, or wasn't working. Thank God. Smoked a lot of cigarettes on my return to Malvern pondering how close we were to taking our first casualty on our first proper patrol on the PB Line. Back in and I had to go back to Clifton to receive orders.

3rd January

Slept until 0800 by which time Dom's section had been out on an uneventful patrol to the south-west limit of our Ops Box. Spent some time tracking suspicious looking blokes on the Base ISTAR and then pushed out east at 1345. Massively expected a contact on this one, but bizarrely there was no obvious build-up of insurgents. Although quiet, it went really well and we were able to cover the ground really effectively and pushed our boundaries out even further. Back in, briefed the blokes and had the classic rat-pack paella plus tin of crab meat and sweet chilli sauce for dinner. Essence. Now going to bed as running with an emotional midnight–0600 Ops room stag so 3 hours of sleep again. Great. However, with the Icebreaker top that Mum and Dad sent out combining with a hot water bottle created by leaving a bottle of Bastion drinking water in the 'Puffing Billy' for a few hours, I am now warm in my sleeping bag at last. Night.

4th January

On watchkeeper from 0000–0600 and then back to bed for a couple of hours. Up again at 0830 to get ready for a 1000 patrol east. We pushed out further than ever before and pretty soon the atmospherics changed and a steady stream of women and children began rapidly leaving the compounds to our east while a number of fighting age males on motorbikes sped towards the compounds we were headed for. As 63B spoke to the locals at compound 42, we put in some security to their east. As they gained all they could we began to move back west, thinking that the A10s and Apache buzzing around had put the Taliban off. As we reached and began moving through a treeline, Fergie's lads were still in position covering our move back when – bang! My heart hit the ground as I thought we'd had an IED strike. However, with more explosions and a contact report from Fergie it soon became clear we were under UGL attack – with one landing only a few metres away from Fergie's lads (they were saved by the dampness of the ground absorbing the blast). My call-sign then formed a baseline having pinged the firing points and began heavily suppressing as more UGLs and now small arms fire winged their way towards us. (I even treated myself to a few rounds in between SITREPs on the radio) Fergie's call-sign then pulled back to our location after both them and us had put down a massive weight of fire causing the enemy to extract. An awesome display of force by an F-18 then covered our move back to Malvern as the int suggested an imminent suicide IED threat – which fortunately amounted to nothing. I was very pleased with both how the lads reacted and my own performance in keeping a cool head while co-ordinating things on the net. I hope JT would be proud. The whole firefight was probably over in about 20 minutes or so, but what an adrenalin rush. I think we all had a big smile on our faces on our return knowing we had given Terry a good kicking with 200+ LMG rounds, 50 GPMG rounds, 25 UGLs, 360 rifle rounds and also a few sniper rounds fired for good measure. After a debrief I had to go to Clifton for orders for our part in the Deh Adam Khan clearance starting tomorrow – which sounds pretty boring as we have to commit blokes to a desert OP [Observation Post] (*Golden Eye*) while the rest of us remain fairly static here to prevent escape/reinforcement for the insurgents to our east. Back to brief the blokes and it starts royally pissing it while we hear an ANA CP a short distance away getting fairly heavily smashed. An exciting day. I love my job (despite the Brecon-style rain!). I smoked far too much today but then it's not every day that someone tries to kill you and your friends!

5th January
After the excitement of yesterday, a fairly dull day. With the ANA beginning their big Op to clear the DAK to our west, we are tasked with blocking the PB line and so just maintaining a constant checkpoint to prevent escape or reinforcement of the Taliban across the line. The ANA are taking the lead on maintaining a constant presence outside our PB, and so we are just sat inside with little to do. Had a little snooze in the afternoon and was woken by a Danish Leopard tank on the high ground to the north engaging a lone insurgent nearby with rounds from its main armament. Unlucky, fella. Dom's section has gone up to the desert to take over the *Golden Eye* OP task, and so we couldn't patrol effectively, even if we wanted to. Thankfully this clearance should be done in 3 days or so, which will free us up to go back to smashing up the Taliban in the east. Today dragged.

6th January
Watchkeeper from midnight–0600. Watched *Happy Gilmore*, *Bad Boys II* and *Black Hawk Down* with Arran and then went back to bed until 1000. Met the RE Sqn OC who'd come for a visit and then absolutely no change to yesterday. Very dull. No watchkeeper for me tonight as Coops and Fergie are covering, so should achieve a 10 hour kip. Sweet.

7th January
Again, no real change. Had a visit from the Danish OC, Danish CO and our OC. Fortunately the boys (me included) were all shaved so we looked pretty squared. Put my case across for keeping us here, saying that the routine is sustainable and that it makes tactical sense, which I think he bought. Other than that, sent blokes out to do some HIIDE enrolments while the ANA were on task. Heard the ANA in contact as well as a couple of IED strikes, so hopefully no one is hurt too badly. I'll head to Clifton tomorrow to hopefully convince the Danish OC to let us off the chain again.

8th January

Spent most of the day at Clifton trying to jack up some good combat patrols to take me up to R&R. Unfortunately however, the Danish OC seems unwilling to let us off the leash without fully consulting with our OC. Fair one, but the prospect of only 2 patrols in between now and me flying out to Bastion on the 17th isn't exactly great. And not to mention doesn't exactly dominate the ground in the manner we should be. I am consequently going to hijack the OC before his 'OC Meeting' tomorrow to try to get us some leeway. Had a hot meal brought down to us tonight, just finished watching *Generation Kill* on watchkeeper and now bed. Frost on my poncho already. Mega.

9th January

Woke up and headed to Clifton. Met the OC and outlined my concerns about our lack of patrols whilst under Danish command – primarily that we are failing to dominate ground, and that we are almost inviting the Taliban onto the bridge build rather than pushing them back. He agreed and we went to see the Danish OC. He however did not agree and said he thought the IED risk was too high to keep pushing us out on non-deliberate patrols. 18 casualties in 5 months probably speak for the reasons behind this view, but if we restrict our own movements due to these little pricks and the IEDs then they've won haven't they? To maintain relations our OC let him have his way, but assured me we'd be back to pushing out twice a day once our Company had taken command of the AO. I left thoroughly pissed off with the prospect of only 2 more (deliberately planned) patrols until my R&R.

10th January

Went to Clifton about 1200 to plan a patrol for 12th Jan with Janick, one of the Danish platoon commanders. A very good bloke. Then had a CIMIC brief. Very interesting but a lot went over my head as was full of local names etc. The lad is doing me a handout to refer to so should get to grips with the local elders etc after a read or two. Then had the traditionally boring 1600 O Group before heading back to Malvern having secured a donated box of cake, crisps, donuts etc off the Danish lads. This went down well with the boys. Just been 'chair dancing' with Fergie and Coops to some of LBdr Lewis' shit music in the Ops room, and now bed – for a whole 3 hours.

11th January

Watchkeeper 0000–0600 and then back to bed until 1030 (Coops and Fergie had already gone up to Clifton and told the lads not to wake me – heroes). Washed some clothes and did some pull ups (the engineers have now built a small gym) and then had a shower. Our patrol for tomorrow has been postponed by 24hrs due to an opsec [operational security] breach (someone saying patrol timings on an insecure net – pretty basic error). Watchkeeper again 1800–2359. Another day closer to R&R.

12th January

Went up to Clifton for the every other day O Group and then came back to brief the boys. Tomorrow we move up to Clifton at 0730 to patrol out at 0930 with a complete platoon, plus some Danes and a section of ANA. I'm giving orders to all at 0830. Have a feeling it will be a quiet one but we can hope.

13th January

Up at Clifton for 0730 to deliver orders to the Platoon complete (Dom's lads were back from *Golden Eye*) and the attached Danes. A section of ANA were meant to be there too but were a no-show. The full Danish company HQ came along to listen, so it felt a bit like an assessed Brecon O Group! Fortunately I was prepared for that, out at 0930 and we patrolled west through a high IED threat area to the new ANA CP 1. Spent some time there looking down into Markhenzai as a reference for the next patrol. Left the ANA and headed east past Clifton and to a position of overwatch on some high ground in a possible legacy Russian minefield. Once in position the int cell picked up on some insurgents trying and failing to organise an attack on us. Intended to push further east, but on realising we would have to cross a massive killing area I decided to hold us back as even a section in overwatch would not be able to effect the likely firing points with their effective weapons ranges. We collapsed back in for lunch, an 'assessed' debrief, and then gave the boys a couple of hours to get on the Internet before heading back down to Malvern. Spoke to Mum and Granny is still holding in there. An incredibly tough lady. Now have the whole platoon back together which is really cool. I've got an awesome bunch. Janick is coming to London in August so I will probably try to catch up with him then as he is one of a number of really good blokes I've met so far on tour. Friday 13th survived after a patrol with 2 x 13 man call-signs. Happy days.

14th January

Up to Clifton to plan the patrol for the 16th with Janick. Spent most of the day up there and then came back for 2200–0200 watchkeeper shift. Played FIFA Manager 2012 the whole time. That's pretty much it.

15th January

Up and awake to find the PB has been destroyed by a storm last night. Heaving rain meant that some of the lads were living in puddles and the wind had blown shit everywhere. Upsetting. Lt Jamie Frampton came down in the morning to have look at the place for when his lads take over from us, and then we went across for lunch with the ANA. Some good rice and bread, along with some dodgy looking 'beef'. No ill effects yet. Stayed with them until about 1400 and then came back and just sat in the Ops room all day. The OC came down so I gave him a quick brief from the Sanger and then I've just been squaring my kit and writing orders for my last patrol before R&R. I hope it's a good one.

16th January

My last patrol before R&R. Up to Clifton for breakfast and to give orders. We went out and covered the north of Markhenzai slowly and carefully due to the mammoth IED threat. A lot of scouting but no real combat indicators and after climbing an epic hill on the way back in, we got back to Clifton pretty worn out after 5 hours on the ground. We all came back in one piece, so as far as I see it, it was a job well done. Spoke to Vic tonight and finally allowed myself to get excited about going home. However, pretty gutted to be leaving the boys for what will undoubtedly be a punchy couple of weeks.

4th February

After an awesome R&R that was a much needed respite and where I spent some really good quality time with friends and family, it was nearly time to head back. Sadly Granny had passed away as I was flying home from theatre, and her funeral was just 2 days before I headed back out. On the day of her funeral, Fergie called with the devastating news that Cpl Jay Baldwin had trodden on a PPIED and had lost both legs. Absolutely gutted for him as well as feeling that I should have been there with the boys. Hopefully he will be the first, and last, C Company casualty but, in reality, that is probably wishful thinking. After arriving back in Bastion at 0200 yesterday morning, we retrieved our ammunition, morphine etc and spent the day pretty bored and in low spirits. At 1025 this morning we flew back to Clifton. It was great to see the boys again. Obviously morale is not great with some dealing with Jay's injuries better than others. We are straight out on a patrol tomorrow, so with that now planned, I go to sleep with the slightly bizarre feeling that, having been at home only a few days ago, I will quite possibly be being shot at etc in the morning. I'm looking forward to finally getting out again, but with the IED threat now all too real, am slightly apprehensive.

5th February

Up for breakfast, gave orders and then out on patrol at 1100. Moved down to Bridzar and then intended to push east but the fields were far too boggy and if we took a casualty we'd have been fucked. Ruled out another route as it was massively channelled and so pushed round north to the high ground and around some compounds to the east to try to get down into the green zone. Got to a good position from where we could see right down into it and gain some good appreciation for a forthcoming Op to Fakharan. Decided against pushing into the green zone – mainly due to wanting to get back in on the first patrol with no dramas to give everyone a bit of a confidence boost. I was a little nervous about that one – not because of the risk to myself as that is a constant – but due to the fact that a casualty today would have rendered us ineffective in terms of morale. After that, a visit from the CO before planning the operation for 2 days' time. It should be a good one as we sound pretty likely to get the chance for a little payback after what happened to Jay. A day of battle prep tomorrow.

6th February

Vicky's birthday. Gave her a call this morning to wish her a good day. Was then into orders and battle prep for tomorrow's Op. The plan is to move towards a Taliban hotspot with me leading a multiple in, basically as bait, in order to draw a contact and fix the insurgents in place enabling an Apache to smash up the firing points. It should be a good one, although I'm slightly concerned that the ground we have been detailed to move into leaves us exposed to a possible ambush from 3 sides. We will have another multiple in reserve, an FSG on the high ground and air support on call so the odds are definitely with us – however if in the initial engagement we take a casualty we will be in a world of hurt. The boys are pretty up for it which is good. After we were all prepped to go I had a brew with the other lads in the officers' tent (I am, happily, living with Fergie, Dom, Coops etc in a Platoon HQ tent) and then chatted to Sandy, a mate from Brecon who is out on a recce for *Herrick 17*. Found a quiet little space to have a cigarette by myself and, overlooking the darkened green zone under a full moon, I said a little prayer to ask that we all come home safely tomorrow. Just watched an episode of *How to Make it in America* in bed and will now try to get some sleep.

7th February

A good day. Out after an early lunch at 1200, headed east and then pushed south into the green zone, crossing a canal with epically steep sides in the process. We then moved through a pretty dodgy treeline next to a compound and took up position facing south. At this stage the Apache support was offline due to sensory failure. As if they knew, we were then engaged by 2 compounds, with one firing at each multiple, only 80m or so away. The rounds were pretty accurate and whizzed straight over our heads and even landed in and around a couple of the boys. We returned a massive weight of fire while I sent a contact report before it all went quiet. Unfortunately a compound wall obscured my view of both firing points and so I couldn't engage (threaders!). After the contact we spotted an insurgent in between the two firing points, apparently dead. Int heard a Taliban commander trying to raise his fighter on the radio and getting no response, which probably confirms it. After that we continued to move towards our objective, with Pte Kemp doing a great job in a turbo high threat area at the front, with the aim of drawing a bigger contact for the Apaches to get involved. En route we got 2 really high readings which led us to mark and avoid these probable devices in treelines, which just goes to show the threat we are facing. For whatever reason the enemy chose not to take us on again. We could have probably drawn their fire by moving further south, but I decided against it as to do so would have been to invite a pretty emotional 360° ambush. We collapsed back in, happy to have got some retribution for the injury to Jay. A chilled out evening now watching DVDs before going out again tomorrow. I love my job!

8th February

A patrol down to the western edge of Kakaran. Managed to chat to some locals and really just show that no matter how often we get contacted, we will always be back and that we will always win. Int picked up the Taliban watching us and saying they were preparing an ambush. Knowing that they know that we listen to them, we called their bluff and just waited for it. It never came and so we moved back in after a couple of hours out. Up early for a joint patrol with the ANA to Sangchal so time for sleep.

10th February

Yesterday our planned patrol with the ANA got canned. Instead we patrolled west across the high ground to see the ANA at CP Sakala 3 in the afternoon. I was watchkeeper until 0300 this morning and so had a lie in until 1000 before doing orders and then heading out in vehicles to ANA CP Sakala HQ to plan a patrol into Deh Adam Khan tomorrow. We were there an hour or so before driving back and then I managed to have a nice chat with both Vic and Mum before spending the rest of the day doing very little. Our last patrol before a week of boredom on guard is tomorrow.

11th February

Got a vehicle move to the ANA CP Shahala HQ. The ANA then pushed into the compounds of Deh Adam Khan Pay and Markhenzai while we covered their northern and western flanks with the FSG and snipers in overwatch. We were expecting a scrap but as we moved towards the village there was no significant movement of women and children away from the compounds and the farmers in the fields just cracked on. Very odd. We managed to speak to a few locals to gauge their thoughts on an ALP being raised locally ... they are not too keen. After heading back in we got sorted and then took over guard for a week. Obviously this means no patrols, which is slightly boring for me as I love getting out. Still, spirits were high as we celebrated the fact that, for a week at least, we would all be alive and in one piece. Me and Fergie had to laugh at the ridiculous nature of our job – where an extra guaranteed week of life is genuinely cause for celebration!

12th February

Now on guard so not much to do for me! Did a patrol report for yesterday, spoke to Mum and Dad, read some of my book (still *Tommy*) and watched a couple of episodes of *Entourage*. Bored already! Found out however that we have a fighting patrol to the east planned for when we are back on patrols next week. Happy days.

13th February

Got up to see Fergie and Coops off for their R&R. Going to miss them both, both professionally and personally. After that did some weights in the gym and then some general admin. Wanted to go on the treadmill but can't find my trainers. Threaders. Only me, Arran and Cpl Matty Atkinson now left in our tent and it is just a bit quieter as a result!

14th February

Gave Vicky a call to wish her a Happy Valentines' Day, and also to thank her for a mega parcel which arrived this morning when the FSG returned from a trip to Bastion. Did some work on my adventure training proposal for the Battalion 2IC (very sketchy on detail), and also wrote the beginnings of a handover pack for the incoming Grenadier Guards platoon commander. Smashed some weights in the gym and then smashed down some BBQ food put on as a treat from the chef (who also did 9 hours in the Sangers last night to give our boys a bit of a break – top bloke). The tent is now quiet with only me, Arran and Matty remaining. (Fergie and Coops on R&R, LCpl Dave McCracken and Dom on *Golden Eye* OP tasking). Watchkeeper now, and it's 0330 on the 15th. R-S (the signaller on duty) woke me up 25 minutes before I was due to start. Threaders. Still pretty bored and can't wait to get back on patrol. With home coming soon I realise just how much I'm going to miss this place. Weird. Still, will certainly be good to get back and get on leave!

15th February

On watchkeeper until 0800 so went back to bed until lunch. After that I managed to get to speak to Jay Baldwin in hospital. He's doing really well and seems in good spirits. He even said to me, 'I know my legs have gone, there's no point crying about it', which is inspirational really. Matt Tubbs (Jay is a massive Crawley Town fan) has sent him a little get well soon message too which is cool. After that went to the gym with LCpl Bobby Walsh, had dinner and then watched *4 Lions* in our tent with a few of the lads which was cool. Cpl Atkinson made a projector screen out of wood and white spray paint that worked pretty well.

16th February

Didn't do a lot today. Read some of my book, smoked with some of the boys. Another gym session. That's about it.

17th February

Pissed it down all day. Had a pretty boring 'effects planning meeting' and smoked a lot. 2 CPs in the Kar Nikah AO go smashed simultaneously tonight. Taliban amazingly braving the rain to exploit the lack of visibility, fair one. Back on patrol soon. Oh, had a 'Gentleman's Lunch' too with the other officers as it was a rations day due to a kitchen deep clean. Lots of nice pate and some olives. The lads would rag me if they knew!

18th February

Rubbish sleep last night due to torrential rain and the 105mm artillery guns from MOB Price firing overhead all night. Another boring day really. Back on patrol tomorrow and now in bed. The rain is torrential once again.

19th February

Patrolled the ANA advisors down to Bridzar in the morning. After an early lunch drove up to the *Golden Eye* OP and then patrolled north into the desert and spoke to some locals (a nomad community). No sign of any Taliban here. Spoke to Vicky tonight. Still it rains.

20th February

Took the advisor down to the ANA at Bridzar this morning before giving orders for a Markhenzai patrol to go out after lunch. Got down there without a hitch, and managed to speak to a large group of around 40 locals who all seem very keen to engage with us, ANSF and GIRoA [Government of the Islamic Republic of Afghanistan]. Very positive for an area which until only recently saw lots of fighting. On the way back we stopped at the ANA CP Sakala 1 and said hello to a few of their Warriors who passed us on the way out. Within an hour, 3 of these lads would be dead as, soon after we left them, they detonated a massive IED (probably a legacy device planned to target a Danish tank). A fourth lad was casevac'd to us at Clifton where I had got myself to the front gate to help out with the medics and stretcher bearers. The lad had really serious facial injuries and had almost definitely lost at least one of his eyes. The medics treated him really impressively and he was on a MERT on the way back to Bastion soon after. At one point we thought the ANA dead were coming to us, and so we got stretcher parties ready. I asked the lads from my platoon if they were really up for helping, as it was sure to be a gruesome sight. As it stands, the ANA chose to take the bodies to Bridzar to be dealt with by their own chain. I felt for the FSG lads who got mobilised to help them transport them, leaving camp with body bags at the ready. Not our blokes, but soldiers with families nonetheless, and ones who fight for the same cause as we do. A sad day.

21st February

Patrolled Sangchal in the morning. Went firm to provide support to an ANA section who pushed into the village. Locals a lot happier to come and chat openly to us than the last time we were there, which is encouraging. Our afternoon patrol was meant to be with the [ANA] lads who took the casualties yesterday and so, predictably, was cancelled. I still had to take 4 blokes and a search dog out to do a check for IEDs in a location right under our noses after some bloke was spotted acting suspiciously. It came to nothing. Rest of the day spent planning, being briefed, and then briefing my lads for tomorrow's Op. Essentially an advance to contact, with my multiple as the bait. Obviously a risky game plan, but one I'm excited by. Hope it doesn't go on too long as I'm knackered!

22nd February

Left at 0800, breached the wire on Route Sephton, and then began pushing east through some pretty hideously IED'd treelines. Eventually reached the likely contact point, but nothing happened. Int suggested it would go off, so we re-set and continued probing. All of a sudden we found ourselves engaged by 4 UGL bombs from a compound to the south. Pte Josh Drane pinged the firing point and returned fire, but as quickly as it had begun it was over. Again, the incoming fire was very accurate and we were only spared casualties by the fields being damp. After that, the Taliban thought we were withdrawing but we spun around and moved towards the likely firing points. As we were in the open, heavy and sustained PKM fire rained down towards us from a treeline behind a mosque to our east. In the confusion over where the rounds were coming from some of the boys went static. Dom was stood up at the front literally grabbing the lads there, whilst under fire, and putting them in position. I then had to run forwards to try to get the lads at the rear to follow. Eventually we were all in a baseline, and smashing the enemy positions. An Apache was 'cleared hot' but had a 30mm gun stoppage which meant we had to up our rate of fire to 'rapid' to pin the enemy down while the Apache spun round for another attack run – this time with flechette rockets. I was able to point out the enemy positions clearly, and very soon witnessed 8 x rockets, each releasing 80 x tungsten darts (hideous) being fired to 'saturate' the treeline. The pilots BDA confirmed 3 x enemy KIA. We headed back, finally arriving in after an emotional 8½ hours on the ground. The OC was very happy with our work, calling it a 'textbook' operation, and I even got a handshake in congratulations from the mega high standards-enforcing, soon-to-be-recce platoon 2IC, CSgt Martin. The boys were in really high spirits, although some who had a close shave with a UGL were understandably shaken up. I'm just a) pleased we had no casualties, b) proud to have led such a successful op, and c) fucking knackered so now going to sleep. Happy days.

23rd February

Was meant to patrol Markhenzai today, but 'Patrol Minimise' is on everywhere due to some American soldier inadvertently burning a load of religious material, including Korans, in Bagram. Predictably, the Afghans are pretty pissed about it, as are we, and demonstrations in Kabul and Lashkar Gar meant that TFH [Task Force Helmand] didn't want us going out and potentially stirring things up. So, went to the gym and had another 'gentleman's lunch' as it is a ration day. Got crashed out in vehicles as the ANA were going to try to snatch some Taliban commanders, but we weren't allowed to dismount so just sat in our Mastiffs while they did their Op and then drove back. They didn't get their targets. Out within 15 minutes of being given the nod though, which was pretty pleasing. After that just smoked a bit and watched some DVDs.

24th February
All is kicking off it seems due to the Koran burning incident. Got the lads doing some first aid training in the afternoon. Spent this evening having a good old chat with the JNCOs about our recent contacts.

25th February
Mostly a day of nothing. Wrote one of my LCpl's annual reports and generally did not a lot. Anyway, a fast ball this evening means I now have to take a multiple and 2 x Mastiffs to Camp Price tomorrow to be a QRF for a big ANA Op, which starts the day after tomorrow. Took a while, but thanks to LCpls Twyford and McCracken being all over it we are now all squared for a morning move across the desert for 5 days away...

27th February–5th March
A longer than expected trip to Price. After getting bogged in on several occasions through the desert, we arrived and I bumped into Jack Hancock, who was on the Op we were supporting. We moved into the welfare tent (initially sleeping on the floor) as there were no free bed spaces. At 0600 the next morning we left on the Prelim Move which involved dropping the advisors and their force protection at the start line. We then returned to be told that 8 Platoon had got a

vehicle stuck back on Route Sephton and so another epic journey through the desert ensued to escort the recovery truck all the way back. Once done we got dicked around a bit and by the time we left to return the sun had set and we found ourselves getting bogged in again in the pitch black on the way back. Not good. The day after that we took MSST [Military Stabilisation Support Team] bods all the way through Gereshk and down to Yakchaal and back, which I actually quite enjoyed as it was good to see Gereshk and the landscape to the south. A day of nothing followed, where I went to the gym and spent some time on the Internet, and after that we were back out with MSST visiting some ANA CPs and also helping the BGE [Battle Group Engineer] to conduct a recce of the bridges in the centre of Gereshk, where we got swarmed by locals and traffic, and where I was genuinely concerned about a snatch attempt or a suicide IED. Our only other tasking included taking the CO and Brigadier to the OCC(D) [Operational Coordination Centre (District)] on a couple of occasions (on one of which we hit the front wall and smashed part of it down – oops) and being part of the vehicle move to the Malvern bridge opening ceremony. Being the first vehicle to cross the bridge was pretty cool, and we then waited while the ceremony finished. As we were about to leave, the Danish vehicles who were coming down to give us protection for the way back hit an IED on a spot we'd just driven over, meaning the Band-e-Barq road was blocked and so we had to go back through the desert – with the inevitable 5-vehicle bogging in session turning it into another late night.

On the morning of the 5th we returned to Clifton after a week away. Mostly boring, with some interesting stuff thrown in, but which also gave me a good opportunity to spend some time with the lads away from the rest of our command structure.

6th March

Last night an 8Pl vehicle was just about to cross the 'Golden Egg' bridge, when the bridge itself was destroyed by a huge command wire IED. The vehicle commander, LCpl Reid, was just about to dismount to 'ground command' over the bridge, and so had a very lucky escape. We drove over the bridge only a few hours before, and so amazingly have driven over/past 2 IEDs in 2 days which have subsequently detonated against others. Outrageous. I think the device was a big 'fuck you' after the bridge opening. At 2200 last night I got tasked to take a vehicle down to overwatch the site until Brimstone could get down to clear/exploit the scene. Was eventually relieved at 1030 this morning after 12 hideous hours sat in the wagon looking at the now fucked bridge. After our relief arrived I had lunch, slept till dinner, showered, briefed the blokes and then went to bed, knackered.

7th March

Brimstone arrived in the morning, and they will begin their clearance of the site whenever a replacement bridge arrives. Spent the rest of the day in orders and then battle prep for an Op tomorrow, and likely our last big offensive Op of the tour due to the platoon rotation. Fingers crossed. Today we are also hit by the news that an IED strike had hit a Warrior containing blokes from 3 Yorks and 1 Lancs, killing 6 of them. The largest single loss of life to enemy action out here. A shitty day. May God comfort the families of the fallen.

8th March

After moving east from Route Sephton we moved into position where we thought we might draw a contact. We waited as Cpl Johnston's section, who were with the Tiger Team (ANA SF) [Afghan National Army Special Forces] to our south were engaged by a couple of bursts of automatic fire. When they'd extracted we began to push slightly further east. Just as we did a pretty accurate single round came towards us. We stopped to assess where the fire was coming from. Very quickly we were engaged again with a succession of single rounds and some UGL. We PID'd both firing points, returning fire with a massive amount of fire power, with literally the whole platoon engaging. Pretty quickly, having confirmed the firing points, Luke Malpass (JTAC) cleared the Apache 'hot' and I shouted to the boys that a Hellfire strike was going in 'danger close'. We got down and a nervous few seconds expired before the missile screamed in and destroyed the compound, leaving one enemy KIA. We then extracted without incident, despite int suggesting we would be ambushed from 3 sides on the way back in. After the debrief I got a 'well done' from the OC, which was good. Another long (7½ hour) patrol and I'm now in bed shattered and watching Season 7 of *Entourage*, which arrived today. Int reports suggest an IDF attack on the camp tonight, and so helmets and body armour are to hand. Frankly though I'm too tired to be that fussed!

9th March

No patrols today so a dull day of writing reports, and also my adventure training proposal for after tour. After the excitement of yesterday, the rubbish side of platoon commanding! I did however manage to convince all the blokes I think deserve it to do the Fire Team Commanders Cadre after tour so that they can promote to Lance Corporal. Pleasing and rewarding.

10th March

A quiet 2-hour local area patrol with the Tiger Team, who gained some good information from the locals. The rest of the day spent writing handover/takeover notes for the incoming Grenadier Guards platoon commanders and finding time to speak to Vic. Up at 0530 tomorrow … threaders.

11th March

Got up to patrol the engineers down to the bridge site so they could put a new one in, following the IED. Headed back up for breakfast and then a morning of writing press releases for 'home town stories' on 3 of my blokes. PB Sponden got contacted around lunchtime, and so the FSG crashed out to get involved and hammered the firing points in support of the ANA. A big dust storm today, and once again the Taliban take advantage by giving it a go. Another quiet day otherwise. Roast beef for dinner and, finally, proper roast potatoes.

12th March

Patrolled down to Bridzar this morning to check the arcs of my section which have been placed down there to overwatch the new bridge. Decided they didn't need any extra defences. Back to Clifton for lunch, a read, a snooze and then the gym. The non-patrol boring work continues as I have to prepare a brief for the CO who is visiting in 2 days.

13th March

Out at 0930 with a multiple worth of my lads and the Tiger Team. We intended to conduct a shura in Malim Kalay, but as soon as we crossed into the green zone, all the locals began leaving the area, suggesting imminent attack. As we approached the compounds, a UGL attack on us began, followed by small arms fire. Pretty soon we were under fire from 3 firing points, suggesting a pre-planned and well-coordinated assault. We smashed the firing points, as did FSG who were positioned on the high ground in overwatch. I got Gunner Richards, our MFC lad, to bring smoke in from the mortars to screen the firing point, to allow us to extract. Once the smoke had been dropped we began to peel out of the killing zone only to get hit again. This time we called for HE rounds to get the enemy's head down, and again us and the FSG opened up with a massive weight of fire. This finally caused the TB to break contact, and we patrolled back in, stopping to talk to locals on the way back. A pretty exciting contact, that was completely unexpected – I think the fighting season is on its way. Later it emerges there was an allegation that our mortar rounds had killed a 12 year old boy. I actually felt sick at the thought of that, and spent a large portion of the evening going through in detail what had happened. This included speaking to the Battle Group Commander on the phone – on speaker phone so all his staff could listen in too. Not ideal. In the end he was happy with the calls I had made on the ground, and from how I described the fighting would be surprised if indeed any civilians had been hurt. To be fair the only reporting of this death was from an ALP guy who tipped up at Clifton. The CO said my response was correct in escalation and proportionality. I just hope it turns out to be false reporting as, although I know I did nothing wrong, [I] wouldn't want that on my conscience.

14th March

Didn't sleep well last night. The CO visited today (our CO – not the Grenadier Guards CO discussed above). Visit was pretty standard, then went to the gym. Nothing further reported reference possible civilian casualties, so fingers crossed it's not true.

15th March

Patrolled Paul Seligman, the ANA Advisor, down to Bridzar in the morning and spoke to Mum in the afternoon. Apparently John's diary is to be published, and they want to include mine also in comparison. Chuffed to bits about seeing John's diary in print, but unsure as yet as to how I feel about mine being done to be honest. Watchkeeper 2100–0300. It is sounding increasingly like we didn't cause a civilian casualty the other day, which is a massive relief.

16th March

Horrendously hot day. Took Paul down to Bridzar, and then pretty much hid from the sun all day. Probably my last time on the ground. Although the OC is talking about commanders going out on a HO/TO Op with the Gren Gds platoons when they arrive – 2 days before we leave. So, if anything is to happen to me, it will be then... after thinking I could relax. Already told Mum she could 'stand down' worrying as I was unsure of the potential plans. I hope I was right.

17th March

Did literally nothing all day but play Champ Man, speak to Vicky, and speak to Scott. And watched a Danish vehicle get blown up by a legacy mine as it drove towards the camp through the desert. Thankfully no casualties. We're on guard now, so a boring final week in store.

18th March

Another day on guard. Did some paperwork, went to the gym and then spent ages trying to sort out manpower dramas as there are currently only 26 blokes from 3 platoons in Clifton due to the ongoing Op that some lads have been detached to Price for. A bit of a nightmare, but sorted in the end (I think).

19th March

The worst sand storm I have seen in Afghanistan. A hideous day. Wrote another (!) press release about our time in Malvern East and then just chilled out in the tent with the lads all day. Fergie and the Bravo multiple leave for Bastion tomorrow, which is crazy, and means the remainder of us will only have 4 days left. Dave has just finished our tour video – an awesome effort, but one which makes me realise how much I will actually miss the job out here!

20th March

Fergie and 15 of the lads left this morning. The beginning of the end! Spent the rest of the day chilling out and hitting the gym. Then found out I'm going out on an Op the day after tomorrow – without my platoon, but as an attachment to 8 Pl and the Gren Guards due to my experience. 2 days before flying home. I have a bad feeling about it to be honest (mainly due to telling Mum and Dad that I was all done out on the ground). I can't tell them I'm going out again so as not to worry them, but am conscious that if something does happen they'll think I was lying to protect them. Can't wait to get it over and done with.

21st March

All change and it turns out I wasn't going on the Op. I love getting out and getting amongst it, but with 2 days to go I certainly won't lose any sleep over missing out. The main body of the Gren Gds arrived today, which was good for morale. Hamish Hardy and Freddy Simpson, who I was at Brecon with, are among their platoon commanders, so it was good to see them. The remaining 8 of us from my platoon are now all packed up and living in the corridor outside the welfare room. Not ideal, but as we're out of here in 2 days I don't really care!

22nd March

The Op went off without contact, but an insurgent spotted with a weapon led to a Hellfire strike and gun run by an Apache. For a while it looked like I would be doing one last patrol to help out Lt Alex Stonor on his patrol tomorrow, but that quickly changed as it emerged there are enough seats on a flight due in tomorrow to get the remnants of my platoon back to Bastion, so Ollie is going out and I am flying out of here a day early. Result!

23rd March

After saying good luck to Hamish and Freddy, and goodbye to Luke (JTAC), Tom (Doc) and Jim (FST [Fires Support Team] Comd), who don't end their tour for a couple of weeks yet, we were set at the HLS for a 1245 flight. The Chinooks came in and before long we were lifted out of PB Clifton, with the boys cheering and high-fiving each other, for one last time. Eventually we landed at Bastion, and the realisation we were bringing everyone home dawned. I went up to Coops and said 'we did it Coops', and he just nodded and replied 'we did it Boss'. We handed in our body armour plates, weapons and morphine and then moved to our tent. The feeling of exhaustion after the worries of 6 months were lifted from my shoulders was immense. Went out for a pizza meal at the 'Blue PX' with the lads, and then just monged it in front of the TV. Heaven.

24th March

The remainder of the Company flew in this morning. Loads of time subsequently spent on the Internet, in the NAAFI and phoning the folks and Vic to say I was safe and coming home. I think they were as relieved as me. Now trying to make sense of how I have made it through, but how John didn't. To be honest I don't think I ever will. Watched Spurs draw with Chelsea after that, and that's pretty much it.

25th March

CO Gren Gds came to give us a 'well done' speech this morning, which made me really realise what we've achieved these past months. Then watched a bit of F1, smoked too many cigarettes and drank too much coffee, and pretty much just got bored, waiting to fly to Cyprus. Tomorrow night we will leave Afghanistan behind.

GLOSSARY

.5	type of heavy machine gun
2IC	second in command
accom	accommodation
Adj	adjutant
AE	Assault Engineer
AH	attack helicopter (AH-64 Apache)
ALP	Afghan Local Police
ANA	Afghan National Army
ANCOP	Afghan National Civil Order Police
ANP	Afghan National Police
ANSF	Afghan National Security Forces
AO	Area of Operations
arcs	arc of fire
ASSESSREP	assessment report
AT	anti-tank
AT4	anti-tank weapon
ATMP	all-terrain mobility platform
ATO	Ammunition Technical Officer (bomb disposal)
ATV	all terrain vehicle
AVM	armoured vehicle mechanic
BCR	battlefield casualty replacements
BDA	Battle Damage Assessment
Bergan	type of backpack
BG	battle group
Big Top	Taliban stronghold
bite	a trick

bluey	slang for the free blue aerogrammes that British forces are entitled to when deployed on operations
Bootneck	British Army slang for Royal Marines
BPT	Brigade Patrol Troop
BSN	Bastion
CAS	close air support
casevac	casualty evacuation
CCL	combat configured load
CCT	close combat troops
Cdo	Commando
chad	slang for cheesy
CIMIC	civil-military cooperation
CIVPOP	civilian population
CLP	Combat Logistic Patrol
CLU	command launcher unit
CO	commanding officer
COB	contingency operating base
comms	communications
coord	coordinate/coordination
Coy	Company
CP	checkpoint
cpd	compound
CQMS	company quartermaster sergeant
Crypo	secure codes which enable secure communication
C/S	call-sign
CSM	company sergeant major
CW/CPIED	command wire/command pull improvised explosive device
CWS	Common Weapons Sight
DC	district commissioner
dems	demolitions
det	detachment
dhobi	slang for washing
dit	Royal Marine slang for story
Doc	doctor
DZ	parachute drop zone
EC	equipment care
EF	enemy forces

EHLS	emergency helicopter landing site
Engs	Engineers
EOD	Explosive Ordnance Disposal
essence	slang for beautiful
fabloned	covered in clear plastic
famil	familiarisation
FET	female engagement team
FF	friendly forces
FFP	final firing point
fizz	exercise
FLET	forward line of enemy troops
FOB	forward operating base
FP	firing points
frag	fragmentation
FS	fire support
FSG	Fire Support Group
FUP	forming up point
galley	slang for kitchen
ganners	slang for Afghanistan
Gen	slang for the truth (genuine)
GIROA	Government of the Islamic Republic of Afghanistan
GMG	grenade machine gun
GMLRS	Guided Multiple Launch Rocket System
GPMG	general purpose machine gun
GPMG(SF)	general purpose machine gun (sustained fire)
gravs	slang for rifleman, 'gravel bellies' – the dismounted close combat troops (used by the vehicle mounted FSG troops)
HE	high explosive
helo	helicopter
HIIDE	Handheld Interagency Identity Detection Equipment
HLS	helicopter landing site
HMG	heavy machine gun
HOD	heads of department
HO/TO	handover/takeover
hoofing	slang for brilliant
HPW	High Performance Wave
icers	slang for cold weather

ID'd	identified
IDF	indirect fire
IED	improvised explosive device
IEDD	improvised explosive device disposal
intel	intelligence
IR	Illum infra-red illumination
IRT	Immediate Response Team (for casualty evacuation) (in the British Army this is commonly known as Incident Response Team)
ISAF	International Security Assistance Force (NATO troops)
ISTAR	Intelligence, Surveillance, Target Acquisition and Reconnaissance
JDAM	Joint Direct Attack Munitions
JOC	Joint Operations Centre
JT	John Thornton
JTAC	Joint Tactical Air Controller
KAF	Kandahar Airfield
KIA	killed in action
LCpl	Lance Corporal
LD	Line of Departure (a theoretical line from which troops commence an action)
LN	local national
locstats	location status
LOE	Limit of Exploitation
LS	landing site
Lt	Lieutenant
MAOT	Maritime Air Operations Team
Mastiff	an armoured fighting vehicle used for protected patrols
MERT	Medical Emergency Response Team
MFC	mortar fire controller
Mne	Marine
MOB	main operating base
MOG	Mobile Operations Group
Mors	mortars
MP	military police
MSST	Military Stabilisation Support Team
nause	nuisance

net	radio
NTM	notice to move
OC	officer commanding (a company)
OJAR	officers' joint appraisal report
OMLT	Operational Mentoring and Liaison Team
OP	observation post
oppos	friends, as in 'opposite number'
Ops	operations
ORBAT	order of battle
ORP	operational ration pack
pax	person
PB	patrol base
PID	positively identify
Pinz	Pinzgauer, a large Land Rover-type vehicle
pit	slang for bed or bunk
PKM	Soviet-made light machine gun
POTL	post operation tour leave
PPIED	pressure-plate improvised explosive device
ptl	patrol
PVCP	permanent vehicle checkpoint
QRF	quick-reaction force
R&R	rest and recuperation
REs	Royal Engineers
recce	reconnaissance
REST	Royal Engineer Search Team
RIP	relief in place
RL	report line
RM	Royal Marine
RMYO	Royal Marine Young Officer
RO	radio operator
ROE	rules of engagement
RPG	rocket propelled grenade
RSM	Regimental Sergeant Major
RSOI	Reception, Staging, Onward Movement and Integration
SA	situational awareness
SAF	small arms fire
scran	slang for food

SF	sustained fire / Special Forces
Sgt	Sergeant
Sgt	**Maj** Sergeant Major
SH	support helicopter
Shura	Arabic for consultation
SIR	serious incident report
SITREP	situation report
SofM	Scheme of Manoeuvre
T1	Triage Category 1 – very seriously injured/needs immediate treatment
T3	Triage Category 3 – walking wounded
TAC	Tactical Headquarters
TB	Taliban
Terp	interpreter
threaders	slang for fed up or annoyed
TIC	troops in contact
Tp	troop
TQ	Troop Quartermaster
Two way	**range** on the battlefield, with the enemy firing back
UAV	unmanned aerial vehicle
UBACS	Under Body Armour Combat Shirt
UGL	under-slung grenade launcher
Unknown Left	ANP/ANA base
VCP	vehicle checkpoint
VM	vehicle mechanic
went firm	static on the ground
wets	slang for hot drink
WMIK	Weapons Mount Installation Kit (a variant of a Land Rover Wolf armoured utility vehicle)
WO	warrant officer
yomp	slang for moving by foot with heavy packs and weapons across country
zero	slang for zeroing rifle sights

INDEX